Decolonial Metal Music in Latin America

Advances in Metal Music and Culture

Series editors: Keith Kahn-Harris and Rosemary Lucy Hill

Advances in Metal Music and Culture publishes monographs, edited collections and short books on metal and its associated sub-genres.

Metal music studies is a fast-expanding interdisciplinary field that spans across subject area fields in the social sciences, performing arts and humanities. Intellect's Advances in Metal Music and Culture book series builds on and continues the series Emerald Studies in Metal Music and Culture, with the same series editors. It continues to provide a home for the growing number of scholars – from a wide variety of backgrounds – who wish to critically reflect on metal music around the world as a cultural product.

Decolonial Metal Music
in Latin America

Nelson Varas-Díaz

Bristol, UK / Chicago, USA

First published in the UK in 2021 by
Intellect, The Mill, Parnall Road, Fishponds, Bristol, BS16 3JG, UK

First published in the USA in 2021 by
Intellect, The University of Chicago Press, 1427 E. 60th Street,
Chicago, IL 60637, USA

A catalogue record for this book is available from the British Library.

Copy editor: Newgen KnowledgeWorks
Cover designer: Aleksandra Szumlas
Cover photo: Kadriel Betsen and Daniel López, Cuneiform Creative Agency.
Production manager: Laura Christopher
Typesetter: Newgen KnowledgeWorks

Hardback ISBN 978-1-78938-393-5
ePDF ISBN 978-1-78938-394-2
ePUB ISBN 978-1-78938-395-9

Series: Advances in Metal Music and Culture
ISSN 2752-4426 / Online ISSN 2752-4434

Printed and bound by CPI

To find out about all our publications, please visit our website.
There you can subscribe to our e-newsletter, browse or download our current
catalogue, and buy any titles that are in print.

www.intellectbooks.com

This is a peer-reviewed publication.

She danced in the university courtyard
as if no one was watching.
The faculty called her crazy. She kept on dancing.
This book is for her.

Contents

Illustrations

Table

Boxes

Preface

As a child growing up in Puerto Rico, I was keenly aware of coloniality, even though I could not name it as such at the time. As many family members explained, without the *Americanos* (referring to the United States), we would be lost. "If the *Americanos* leave, they will take the paved roads with them," I remember someone saying in one of the many conversations that still resonate with me today. If we were nothing without them, then what exactly were we as a people? Although the answer to this question was never outright discussed, and might seem elusive even today, one thing was clear then: we were not Latin Americans. We were not a third world country enmeshed in dictatorships and coups. We were not *that* poor, or at least so they said. We were citizens of the United States! We were different. We were *anything but* Latin Americans; that much was clear. This is how one grows up in an ongoing colonial setting: learning to negate what and who you are. Music would be my only connection to the region. In this sense, music has been a revolutionary revelation in my life.

During my early childhood and adolescence, my mother would play albums by Tony Croatto, an Italian-born singer who self-identified as a Puerto Rican, and who sometimes sung about Latin American figures. Further explorations led me to the salsa of Panamanian Rubén Blades, whose rhythms and song lyrics were clearly Latin American and, more importantly at the time, political. Dominican merengue and bachata singer Juan Luis Guerra would speak to me about the Caribbean region's poverty. The same happened with Silvio Rodríguez, the Cuban songwriter whose lyrics were marked by the 1959 revolution. Just as these musicians made their way into my everyday life, rock and metal music equally consumed me. Although to some these musical genres seemed contradictory, and metal was deeply embedded in the moral anxieties of the time, they coexisted in my life in a majestically seamless manner. It was not long before tapes from bands like Rata Blanca (Argentina) and Sepultura (Brazil) made their way to the Island and served as another window into the Latin American experience. This music, all of it, spoke to me. They made me feel like I was part of a larger story, a wider geography, and a deeper historical experience. These musicians connected me to a region from which coloniality had separated me. They spoke to me as a Latin American.

Later in my life I would be given the chance to integrate this experience into my academic career. Thus, for the past decade I have explored through documentary films and academic publications the ways in which metal music has manifested in Latin America and, consequently, how it has found a place in a cultural and sociopolitical scenario that is distant from its places of origin, specifically the United Kingdom and the United States. My documentary films in particular have allowed me to travel extensively throughout the region and to interact with metal fans and musicians who have been generous in sharing their stories. This book is the product of those interactions, through which it became evidently clear that a large sector of the metal scene has engaged in a decolonial project by "pulling back the curtain" on the history of colonization in the region, its consequences, and ever-present manifestations.

Throughout this process I have traveled, on multiple occasions, to nine countries in Latin America: Puerto Rico, Cuba, the Dominican Republic, Chile, Argentina, México, Perú, Colombia, and Guatemala. There, I engaged in extensive ethnographic observation in concerts, rehearsal rooms, music stores, and people's homes, among many other places where metal music was present. I engaged in formal and informal interviews with more than 80 individuals, including metal musicians, fans, researchers, scholars, and community organizers. All of them were involved in metal music in one way or another. Many of them participated in video-recorded interviews for my films, which are freely available online. I engaged in this research process fully influenced by research approaches from the fields of community psychology (participatory methods), anthropology (ethnographic observation), and filmmaking. I implemented these strategies guided mostly by theoretical contributions from Latin American scholars. I made this choice as a decolonial strategy aimed at highlighting regional knowledges capable of bringing us closer to an understanding of metal music in Latin America.

I would not dare tell you, the reader, how to go about navigating this book – other than recommending that you read the first chapter as a starting point, in order to outline the characteristics of decolonial metal music. The rest of the chapters can be read in any order of your choice. Of course, I have organized them in a manner that makes sense to me, and part of that decision is purely emotional and, admittedly, somewhat political. For example, I begin with Puerto Rico because it represents home and end with Argentina because it is the farthest I traveled from that home. My hope is that, taken together, these nine reflections on metal in the region serve to evidence the many ways in which metal music has become decolonial by reflecting on its context and working to transform it. Of course, this book is an initial window into decolonial metal in Latin America, as there are other countries and axes of decoloniality that I continue to explore. But that is a matter for subsequent publications and films.

The field of metal studies has grown exponentially in the last two decades. Still, Latin America, and many other sectors of the Global South, remain a virtual blind spot in metal-related academic research. I have written elsewhere about the reasons for these blind spots; these include, but are not limited to, close links to the precarious economic situations faced by scholars in the region that inhibit the dissemination of their important work, the lack of attention placed on this research by academic outlets (i.e., journals, conferences) traditionally located (both physically and ideologically) in the Global North, the supremacy of English as the language of "universally shared" knowledge, and outright academic imperialism, which has deemed much of this research as unworthy of the "real" academia. While this happens, metal music in Latin America continues to transform lives and to help develop critical subjects that can understand and challenge their context.

My hope is that this book contributes to the ever-growing scholarship on metal music emerging in Latin America and the rest of the Global South. More importantly, I hope that it serves to echo the complex reflections and actions taken to challenge coloniality in the region through metal music. If metal music represents a decolonial school of thought for artists, fans, and scholars in the region, including myself, I am sure it serves the same purpose for many others.

1

Metal Music's Decolonial Role in Latin America

Tendrás que saber, mi hijo,
te reclaman por ahí,
que hay gritos por todos lados,
para aquel que sabe oír.

(You should know, my son,
they call for you out there,
there are screams everywhere,
for those who know how to listen.)

(Arraigo 2012: n.pag.)

One hour into our interview he uttered a phrase that would completely change the direction of my research. "We are not here to entertain you." He said it with such conviction and strength that it shook me to the core. The interviewee was Gustavo Zavala, the bass player for the Argentinian metal band Tren Loco. I asked him what he meant by it, and he went on to describe how metal was a way to "feel and see the world." I asked him to elaborate. He took a deep breath, looked at the floor, and, with the reluctance of someone who had explained this before on many occasions, began to speak about the region's colonial history. He described the colonial exploitation historically faced by the Latin American region, how that experience was later manifested through foreign support for local dictatorships, and how those practices were still present today. "For us metal is not entertainment. It is not." A long silence filled the room.

This book is the product of almost a decade of travel throughout Latin America, researching heavy metal culture in nine countries: Puerto Rico, Dominican Republic, Cuba, Chile, Argentina, Perú, México, Colombia, and Guatemala. During that period, I was heavily engaged in ethnographic research throughout the region, which yielded, alongside multiple academic publications, three documentary films examining the intersection of heavy metal music, history, and culture in Latin America.

The three films were released sequentially as my travels continued throughout these countries: *The Distorted Island: Heavy Metal and Community in Puerto Rico* (González-Sepúlveda et al. 2015), *The Metal Islands: Culture, History and Politics in Caribbean Heavy Metal Music* (Varas-Díaz et al. 2016), and *Songs of Injustice: Heavy Metal in Latin America* (Varas-Díaz et al. 2018).

As a heavy metal music fan, and a social scientist who has lived in a colonial setting for most of my life (i.e., Puerto Rico), I felt there were many reflections, based on my research endeavors in these settings, that needed further attention as they were limited by the restricted running times of the films and the constrained space afforded by short-format publications. I aim to extend these ongoing perusals by providing readers with a conceptual framework to understand the relation between metal music and the colonial experience, which I hope, alongside very specific examples from each country, can shed light on the role of heavy metal music in Latin America.

My travels through the region and conversations with musicians, fans, and researchers have led me to a conclusion that stands above all others: a significant number of metal artists in Latin America have become decolonial[1] in their respective artistry, philosophies, and lives. Thus, in this book I aim to define *decolonial metal*, describe its main characteristics in Latin America, and explain how it invites individuals to engage in critical reflections about the region's history, politics, and everyday actions in each of their contexts. I posit that metal in Latin America fosters what I define as *extreme decolonial dialogues*, that is, a way to cope and transform oppressive contexts in light of the profound and ever-present consequences of colonialism. In this initial chapter, I will address the colonial experience in Latin America, explore its relation to metal music, and define the characteristics of decolonial metal in the region. Furthermore, I will address some of the tensions faced by decolonial music in Latin America with its musical counterparts in the Global North. The subsequent chapters will provide readers with specific examples of how decolonial metal is created, consumed, and used for social transformation by artists and fans throughout the region. Before defining decolonial metal, it is useful to examine a general idea of how colonialism, and more importantly coloniality, are experienced in the region.

Coloniality and the Latin American experience

To examine the manifestations of colonialism in Latin America, we must take an inclusive approach that is not constrained to a specific historical moment in the region's development. Some analyses on the effects of colonialism tend to examine it solely as a phenomenon of the past and, therefore, relegate these efforts to the realm of historical studies. In many cases, particularly for outsiders, a discussion of Latin America's colonial experience might seem limited to the European colonization process that began in the fifteenth century and was later challenged by the emergence of independent nations in the nineteenth and twentieth centuries at the hands of local liberation movements. This is an important piece of the colonial puzzle for Latin America, as it marked the imposition of foreign cultures and worldviews on these lands and populations. This initial colonial experience was characterized by the subjugation of local indigenous peoples, the pillaging of natural resources for the development of the colonial metropoles, and the imposition of Western worldviews (i.e., notions on religion, morality, progress, knowledge production, and social order) on local people. Said colonial process, along with its plethora of consequences, was firmly established on the devaluation of local people through racial categorization; more specifically, the colonial process was, and remains, inherently racist. The colonial experience would have been hard enough for the region if it were limited to these axes of action and had culminated with the constitution of new nations as a challenge to the imperial powers of Europe, but it did not end there. Even after independence (for those who achieved it) and the symbolic end of political colonialism, many countries in Latin America faced the seemingly everlasting consequences of this experience.

Peruvian sociologist Aníbal Quijano has described the ever-present legacy of colonialism in Latin America, long after the fifteenth-century period of colonization in the region (Quijano 2010). He has used the term "coloniality" (e.g., *colonialidad del poder* ["coloniality of power"]; Quijano 2000: 24) to describe a "form of domination in the world today, once colonialism as an explicit political order was destroyed." Coloniality, therefore, encompasses a structure of oppression, linked to the colonial experience of the fifteenth-century, but one that simultaneously surpasses the end of that very period. This structure of oppression was based on the "superiority of the dominant, and the inferiority of the dominated" and was justified via racial categorization (2010: 25). But this strategy would not be limited to the control of racialized bodies, as it would also aim to colonize the locals' imagination, knowledge, culture, history, and memory, rendering them all as inferior in the eyes of the colonizers.[2] This oppressive strategy may have been created, implemented, and/or exploited during the colonization process, but it became pervasive, as it served to sustain the project of modernity in Europe. Arturo Escobar has described Quijano's coloniality as "a global hegemonic model of power in place since the conquest that articulates race and labor, space and peoples, according to the needs of capital and to the benefit of white European peoples" (Escobar 2010: 39). In this sense, the tactic of categorizing the local as inferior, used in colonial times to justify oppression, is still present today.

Furthermore, it is used to explain and justify the project of modernity, which has relied, and still depends heavily, on the systematic exploitation of the local. Thus, coloniality remains an ongoing project.

The pervasive implications of the devaluation of the local generated through coloniality are best understood through particular examples. Two of them are exceptionally important: the devalued identity of indigenous peoples and the conceptualizations of local geographies, including nature itself, as an unending exploitable resource. The conception of local indigenous people as less than human enabled their extermination during colonial times. Their placement into a devalued social position (i.e., indigenous as nonhuman) was later used during the twentieth-century dictatorships and regional armed conflicts to justify their continued eradication. Finally, this devalued category is used today to justify the hostile takeover of their lands as part of the neoliberal exploitation of communities and geographies in the region. This continued exploitation of devalued local peoples is also present in conceptualizations of local geographies and nature. Under fifteenth-century colonialism, natural resources found in local geographies were conceived as settler property, exploited, and exported to the colonial metropoles. This notion was also present in the neoliberal policies that characterized many of the dictatorships in Latin America, which fueled the unbridled use of natural resources (e.g., deforestation in the case of Chile), and continue unchecked in the region today (see Chapter 4). Coloniality frames these examples, among many others, as reflections of the devalued categories of colonial domination that are still used and exploited in the present for the benefit of others – specifically, the modern project that fostered European expansion. Since this modern project was understood as unending, coloniality is, therefore, perpetual. As explained by Walter Mignolo (2010: ix), "There is no modernity without coloniality and that coloniality is constitutive, and not derivative, of modernity." That Western modern project was, and continues to be, anchored in the exploitation and devaluation (geographical, physical, and psychological) of the colonial settings (Mignolo 2011).

As previously mentioned, the hierarchical categorizations that fostered oppressive experiences during the early stages of European colonialism remain in place to this day. The devaluation of indigenous people, local cultures, and regional knowledge/experiences continues in many of the countries that comprise the region. This devaluation of the local has been an intrinsically important component in the establishment of other mechanisms of oppression in Latin America. Some clear examples have been the imposed political dictatorships that have plagued the region in countries like Chile and Argentina, to name a few. These regimes were established mostly in collaboration with local and international powers, to the detriment of local peoples, particularly dissenters (Pizarro and Wittebroodt 2002; Díaz Vergara 2006; Soto 2008; Robaina 2015). Even today, when these dictatorships have been mostly vanquished throughout Latin America, the neo-liberal practices implemented by local governments and international private companies (i.e., illegal use and privatization of essential natural resources) per-petuate the effects of said dictatorships, as the new model continues the exploit-ation of local peoples (Mojica 2010; Campos Medina and Campos Medina 2012; Barandiaran 2016).

Furthermore, the devaluation of individual lives and groups that character-ized the initial colonial experience remains alive and well in more current forms of oppression. This process of devaluation is not limited to individuals and com-munities. In fact, it extends to cultural practices, including the development of local knowledge, memories, and histories. These are seen as less valuable and sometimes dangerous, as they can challenge the long-lasting effects of coloniality. For example, the value placed on Western ideas and ideals, which are promoted as universal and all-encompassing by the Global North, has, on many occasions, sought to devalue locally produced knowledge. The same can be said of local his-tories and memories, which have been subsumed under the universalistic approach toward history promoted by Western universities, among other spaces of know-ledge production. While facing this devaluation of the local through coloniality, an important question arises in the face of said coloniality: What shall local people do about it? The answer to this question is multifaceted and never simple, yet strides have been made throughout Latin America to engage with this very question.

Walter Mignolo has championed the need to engage in "border thinking," that is, a way to generate knowledge outside of the Western colonial view, which continues to hold its ideas as universal. The knowledge generated from other geographies and populations was deemed and continues to be seen as less valu-able. Border thinking, then, becomes essential in order to "decolonize know-ledge" and "build decolonial local histories" that focus on the narratives of those who have been traditionally oppressed within the project of modernity (Mignolo 2000: x). It is a way to develop knowledge from "a subaltern perspec-tive" (2000: 11) that highlights the experiences of local people in the region as a way of "displacing hegemonic forms of knowledge into the perspective of the subaltern" (2000: 12). This type of border thinking, which can take place through a variety of actions (i.e., activism, research, art) can serve as a liberating prac-tice in the face of coloniality; consequently, these acts become decolonial acts. As Mignolo has argued, decoloniality, or the project of being decolonial, entails "both the analytic task of unveiling the logic of coloniality and the prospective task of contributing to build a world in which many worlds will coexist" (Mignolo 2011: 54). Becoming decolonial is, as a result, the active nurturing of an awareness of the historical force of colonialism, a recognition of its ongoing effects through coloniality, and the engagement of individuals and communities in critical acts that challenge it. One way to achieve this is through the recognition and promotion of the very plurality that characterizes the Latin American region, particularly in terms of race, ethnicity, language, gender, and historical processes/experiences, among other axes of analysis.

This decolonial endeavor entails the production of knowledge and experiences that challenge coloniality. Boaventura de Sousa Santos has championed the need to respect and value local knowledge and histories based on the experiences of oppressed groups, including those that have suffered through colonialism. He has termed this type of knowledge production "epistemologies of the south," and their objective is to "allow the oppressed social groups to represent the world as their own and in their own terms" (Santos 2018: 1). Of course, this includes knowledges that challenge coloniality. Since these epistemologies of the south emerge from social struggles against oppression, they are frequently produced and disseminated far from traditional academic settings and methodologies (i.e., through rigid scientific methods and written texts). Thus, other forms of knowledge production that are oral, visual, and aural become vitally important. In this scenario, music can play a vital role in generating and sharing knowledge that emanates from the perspective of oppressed communities that have experienced, and continue to live through, coloniality. This perspective poses what is perhaps the most important question for the purpose of this book: Can metal music in Latin America be decolonial?

Extreme decolonial dialogues: How is metal music decolonial in Latin America?

The arts have been identified as an important strategy in fostering decolonial answers to social oppression (Santos 2020; Mignolo and Walsh 2018). In the case of Latin America, they have been very effective in their engagement with a reflection on the colonial experience in the region and its consequences (Neustadat 2004). For example, plastic artists like Carlos Raquel Rivera in Puerto Rico, musicians like Silvio Rodríguez in Cuba, and novelists like Gabriel García Márquez in Colombia have all fostered in one way or another reflections on coloniality. They represent examples of how artists (e.g., painters, musicians, novelists) have recognized the legacy of colonialism in Latin America, while simultaneously looking to develop a critical approach toward its persistent legacy. The decolonial agenda these artists foster through their work brings to mind a key question that has yet to be developed in detail in the context of metal studies: What role does metal music have in this decolonial process? This question is simultaneously complex and currently urgent in light of the increasingly oppressive colonial practices present in the region.

Metal music is, and always has been, a reflection of its context (Weinstein 1991, 2011). Therefore, the social and political context in which metal music emerges throughout various regions of the world is inarguably pertinent to any analysis of the genre's musical practices. Latin American scholars have addressed this issue in their work (Avelar 2003, 2011; Azevedo 2012; Sánchez 2014; Belén Calvo 2016; Calvo 2016, 2017, 2018; Domínguez Prieto 2017; Scaricaciottoli 2016, 2018; Dos Santos Silva 2018; Nuñez and Rivas 2018; Varas-Díaz and Mendoza 2018; Varas-Díaz and Rivera 2014). This does not mean that discussions on the link between metal music and its sociopolitical contexts are easy or even considered so by sectors of the larger international metal community. Scholars have documented how political discussions within some sectors of the international metal scene are seen with disapproval as these have the potential to open rifts into the long-established sense of community that metal tries to foster within its borders (Kahn-Harris 2007; Scott 2012). Other scholars have opened the door into the examination of the interrelation between politics and metal music, positioning its output as an effective critical vehicle of popular culture (Scott 2016). These positions coexist within metal music and its fans. The discussion over the integration of politics into metal music seems to have no end in sight and continues to push people into uncomfortable terrain.

Latin American metal music has also faced discussions related to this integrative tension. Still, an examination of its output reflects how the integration of politics into its music has been present since its very origins (Sánchez 2014; Scaricaciottoli 2016; Calvo 2018). More specifically, the incursion via its lyrics and imagery into the region's colonial past has positioned the subject of coloniality front and center, making it almost unavoidable in Latin American metal music. It has done so by using subject matter familiar to the musical genre (i.e., violence, war, injustice) and applying these to local colonial experiences (Mendoza et al. 2018; Pack 2018; Varas-Díaz et al. 2016; Varas-Díaz 2018; Varas-Díaz et al. 2018; Varas-Díaz et al. 2016; Varas-Díaz and Mendoza 2018, 2015). Although the subject of coloniality has begun to emerge in metal-related studies, it has been mostly associated with indigenous populations in North America (Thibodeau 2014) and has only recently been explored in the Latin American region (Varas-Díaz and Morales 2018; Varas-Díaz et al. 2019).

I posit that a significant sector of heavy metal music in Latin America is engaged in a process of social transgression that is decolonial. That sector explores the historical process of oppression through colonization linked to fifteenth-century European expansionism, the devalued categories created in that historical process (e.g., race, ethnicity, geography, local history, local knowledge), and its ongoing manifestations today. Of course, this endeavor is not limited to heavy metal music as many other decolonial efforts take place throughout Latin America, and the rest of the Global South, which aim to challenge the history of oppression in the region. What is, however, of utmost importance for the reflection presented in this book are two particular questions: First, why has metal music been largely ignored and isolated from this decolonial agenda? Second, how does metal become decolonial in response to its context?

There have been two main reasons why the decolonial agenda contained within metal music in Latin America has been largely ignored. The first has to do with the international attention placed on metal music originating from the Global North. Most academic ventures still focus on metal music created and consumed in the United States and Europe. Although some scholars have called attention to this deficit (Wallach et al. 2012; Clinton and Wallach 2015, 2019; Turner 2018), Latin America remains a blind spot in academic literature published in the Global North. The same can be said for media outlets like international metal magazines, where Latin American artists rarely, if ever, grace their covers. Rarer still is to find any of these outlets focusing on Latin American musicians as a main story. This blind spot on the analysis of Latin American metal music in the Global North impedes the framing of a more important and in-depth question about the music and its implications for the region: What does this music do socially and politically in Latin America? Needless to say, this is a difficult question to even consider for the international metal scene given the North's lack of attention and interest in the region's musical output.

The second reason is more closely linked to how people in Latin America, including scholars and activists, have neglected to examine metal music's decolonial agenda. These groups have seen metal music as mere entertainment with few linkages to its social context. While some scholars in the region directly engaged in metal-centered research have begun to challenge this notion (Scaricaciottoli 2016), major academic settings have not integrated the subject matter into their classrooms. The same has happened with scholars who, while writing about social movements and activism in the region, have neglected to examine the decolonial role of music in these processes (Flórez Flórez 2015; Almeida and Cordero Ulate 2016; Caouette and Kapoor 2016). Examinations of the role of music in social movements have rarely addressed decolonial agendas in the Latin American region (Eyerman and Jamison 1998), with the notable exception of the "Nueva Canción" movement, which will be considered later (Morris 2014; McSherry 2015). Finally, decolonial scholars who have begun to consider music as a tool of resistance against colonial oppression have done so by focusing on varying musical genres (Cervantes and Saldaña 2015; Williams 2017; McFarland 2018). Metal music, however, rarely enters these conversations (Thibodeau 2014; Banchs 2016), as it continues to be deemed unworthy of academic attention in some Latin American settings. Fortunately, it must be noted that this reticence has diminished over the past decade. When these two factors converge, the blind spots are simultaneously northern and southern in their origin; thus, decolonial metal music is relegated to the less-frequented obscure corners of academic, activist, and entertainment considerations.

Nevertheless, decolonial metal exists and can be recognized by those who pay close attention to what is happening in the Latin American metal scene (Varas-Díaz et al. 2017; Varas-Díaz and Morales 2018; Varas-Díaz et al. 2019). It is present, and it is actively interacting with its context in a constant move to describe and, more importantly, transform it. Heavy metal music achieves this by engaging in what I call *extreme decolonial dialogues*. These are invitations made through metal music to engage in critical reflections about oppressive practices faced by Latin American communities in light of coloniality. Let us examine each component of the term *extreme decolonial dialogues* individually.

I label the interactions carried out under decolonial metal as *dialogues*, given that they reflect an interaction between those who are informed about coloniality and those who are yet to understand it. Still, this dialogue is an exchange of information between equals, and not one defined by a hierarchical organization of knowledge, where one party alleges to possess unequivocally correct information at all times. Practitioners of decolonial metal do not see themselves as participants in a formal educational system where people go to learn about one predominant viewpoint. They see themselves as co-constructing a space for discussion and reflection between equals who might have differing points of view on how to overcome a specific social or political problem, but who can share the notion that oppressive practices are at play in the generation of that problem. This echoes Paulo Freire's call to share information by means that are not aligned with what he calls the banking model of education (Freire 2000), that is, the mere accumulation of facts about which one population (i.e., the educated) informs the other (i.e., the uneducated) through a power-laden form of pedagogy. In a critique to traditional education systems, he proposed active dialogue as a learning strategy in which all parties bring something to the table. This is vitally important to understand how decolonial metal can navigate sociopolitical waters. It does not propose a set of analytical or practical rules, like a political party would, in order to grant membership into a group. Rather, it proposes the development of critical skills that identify oppression and aim to dismantle it. On many occasions during my investigations, metal artists in the region would tell me outright, "We are not trying to teach or preach;" rather, they were interested in fostering a way of thinking through these oppressive situations together.

The nature of these dialogues should be apparent to the reader by now; they are markedly *decolonial*. This means that some metal bands engage in dialogues (through lyrics, artwork, t-shirts, and activities) that are concerned with the historical process of oppression faced by the region, stemming from fifteenth-century colonialism and its ripple effects into the present day. That is why the subject matter contained within decolonial metal can range from the extermination of indigenous peoples in the Americas (see Chapter 3) to a critique of neoliberal practices imposed today by the Global North. Their dialogues do not take place in a social vacuum, and their critiques are not general in nature. On the contrary, they are specific, contextual, and focused on these oppressive practices. The subject matter being performed or narratively reflected upon through other metal-related practices (i.e., conversations, film screenings, activism) is the effect of coloniality, a subject that is approached with great nuance and attention.

Finally, these dialogues are *extreme* in several ways. First, they are perceived as extreme for those unfamiliar with metal aesthetics and sounds. The use of metal-related lyrical content closely related to topics like death, violence, and oppression worries unfamiliar listeners in the region; this includes politicians and the media. They are also extreme, in comparison to other regional styles of music, in their use of sounds unavoidably linked to metal in the Global North, particularly the usual heavily distorted guitars and coarse singing styles. These extremities are usually not understood by those outside the metal scene in the region, including other local musicians. The integration of traditional local instrumentation into metal music is still misunderstood and mostly celebrated only when done within more familiar musical genres, like rock music (e.g., Los Jaivas and El Polen). As if this were not problematic enough, metal integrates subject matters that are deemed too highly politicized in many Latin American countries, doing so through its visually disturbing choices and inflections (e.g., armed conflicts, mass killings, dictatorships, forced disappearances). These are frequently met with resistance from people who would rather forget that these events ever happened or are otherwise politically motivated to erase them. Thus, decolonial metal artists tend to be frequently ignored and highly stigmatized for their sound and content, which are considered extreme in many Latin American settings.

Despite these challenges, decolonial metal makes its presence felt throughout Latin America. In order to engage in these *extreme decolonial dialogues*, this type of metal music has adopted a very specific set of characteristics. Below I outline them individually.

Decolonial metal defined

In studying decolonial metal, I have used ethnographic observations, interviews, image/lyric analyses, and my personal history to develop what I see as the six main salient characteristics, which I outline in detail below. First, it is concerned with a historically anchored reflection on oppression. Second, it is regional in its content, sounds, and imagery. Third, it serves as a transformative intervention in its context. Fourth, it is informed by other Latin American music. Fifth, it is strategically communal and celebratory. And lastly, it is in constant tension with other sectors of the metal scene, including the Global North. Let us look at these in greater detail.

Decolonial metal is concerned with a historically anchored reflection on oppression

This first characteristic of Latin American decolonial metal might seem like an obvious one, but it is nevertheless the most important and salient. All of the other features I subsequently describe are contingent on this one and rely on it to provide meaning to what metal aims to do in the region. People who engage in decolonial metal are aware of the plight of oppressed populations throughout Latin America. This includes the oppressive realities faced by indigenous populations, workers, farmers, and women, among other marginalized sectors of the population.[3] In light of this awareness, decolonial metal makes a choice, sometimes symbolic and occasionally practical, to side with those who have been impacted by coloniality – those who Frantz Fanon (1965) called "the wretched of the earth." Although some might argue that these are the populations that have "fallen by the wayside" of universalist and modern ideas of progress proposed by the Global North, it would be more accurate to state that they have been systematically "expelled" as a consequence of the oppressive practices put in place to benefit a select few. Decolonial metal makes these communities, and their context, the principal subjects of its endeavor.

The decision to engage in reflections about the oppressive practices faced by these populations in the region is historically anchored and critically specific. It is not made in a contextual vacuum, but rather through a very detailed approach that aims to explain how these oppressive tactics came to be, how they are maintained today, and how people experience them. Thus, the events linked to fifteenth-century colonialism become an important stepping stone to explain present-day oppression in the region. In this sense, decolonial metal is keenly aware of coloniality and its ever-present manifestation in the region. This historical anchoring is vitally important to understand decolonial metal, as it provides it with a level of specificity that distinguishes it from many of the bands that

11

local musicians and fans usually describe as initially influential for them – most emanating from the Global North.

For example, the British band Black Sabbath (1970) sung about the perils of war in the song entitled "War Pigs." However, their reflexive intervention is general in nature and it would be difficult for the listener (now decades away from the context in which the song was released) to immediately determine which specific war, geography, or oppressed community is being described. In contrast, decolonial metal in Latin America takes that critique of war a step further, placing it in direct historical context by referencing specific battles between indigenous groups and colonizers as a way to discuss war from a more personal and specific vantage point. It also does this with more recent conflicts that have taken place between colonial powers and Latin American countries (i.e., the Falkland Wars). Furthermore, it explains how certain wars are still being fought by oppressed groups in specific towns and geographies (i.e., the Zapatistas; see Chapter 5). The same historical anchoring can be seen in reflections on environmental exploitation. While the United States-based band Metallica might have sung about the perils of global warming in a song like "Blackened" (Metallica 1988), Latin American bands discuss this event in a more localized manner through reflections about the mistreatment of *Pachamama* and the exploitation of local resources in the Amazon forest by foreign companies (e.g., songs by the band Curare in Ecuador).[4] Other historically anchored reflections about local matters and events address issues like colonization (both fifteenth-century and ongoing experiences), regional wars, local massacres, indigenous perspectives, and social justice movements.[5] These decolonial reflections are carried out from the perspective of and in solidarity[6] with oppressed communities in the region, and thus, musicians take social and political positions that can be dangerous for them in contexts that have historically suppressed these critiques. Furthermore, the critical specificity of decolonial reflections through metal music brings local narratives to the forefront, challenging notions of universal knowledge and simplified essentialist (mostly Eurocentric) accounts of history that tend to erase those at the margins as a strategy of coloniality (Grosfogel and Cervantez-Rodríguez 2002). Thus, it reminds listeners that the colonial experience is alive and well in Latin America.

There is another dimension of importance for the historical anchoring in decolonial metal music. It is one related to memory. In many colonial contexts, and therefore throughout the entirety of Latin America, there are concrete efforts geared toward fostering forgetfulness or erasure of past events (Schwarzstein 1995; Iglesias Saldaña 2005; Drinot 2009). There is a push, from local governments for example, to avoid reflections about past actions through which systemic oppression has been manifested. The displacement of traditional knowledge away from indigenous communities, the atrocities committed against them, and their long-lasting effects still present today are seen as things to forgive and forget, in order to "move forward" under the banner of "we are all the same people." This is a strategic technique whose purpose is to wipe out the historical past of oppressed communities and foster uncritical interpretations of the future. As such, the poor are perceived to live in detrimental conditions, not because of the historical oppression they have faced, but because of personality traits such as laziness, to name just one example.

Similar logics of forgetfulness and erasure are used to avoid discussions of the effects of dictatorships in the region, the role of foreign governments from the Global North in that process, and the current neoliberal exploitation faced in these settings. To face this push toward forgetfulness, bottom-up historical memory becomes an important strategy of resistance. Decolonial metal music proves to be a vessel of this type of memory for many of its listeners, who would never be exposed to these histories of oppression through official channels like the government or the educational system. Listening to metal music becomes a learning experience in the historical manifestations of oppression in the region. In this sense, metal music allows listeners to engage in what Enrique Dussel (1985: 59) has termed "ethical conscience," or the "capacity one has to listen to the other's voice," in order to understand the injustices they face. Through fostering historical memory, metal music engages in an ethical positioning on the side of the oppressed. Still, this positioning comes with a cost.

One such cost is the lack of international reach; given that decolonial metal is grounded in historical specificity, a band's efforts to find a wider audience become inevitably hindered. Although Latin American bands have had a presence in international metal festivals, their participation has been very limited and sometimes subjected to a fetishizing European gaze that regards these bands as a window into the "exotic" (more on this later). Also, some of the decolonial techniques used by bands, like singing in indigenous languages, can hinder sales when it comes to wider audiences. Moreover, the historical specificity of decolonial metal and its siding with the oppressed are interpreted by many as ventures into the realm of traditional politics; consequently, these efforts are shunned by some members of the broader metal scene who wish to keep their music as far away from politics as possible. These are just some examples of how decolonial metal can frequently pay a high price within the metal scene for its historical positioning and focus on oppressive experiences.

The reluctance shown toward this historical anchoring in systems of oppression is not limited to the broader metal scene; it can also be seen in academic conceptualizations that are distrustful of music that highlights its local and regional character. Some scholars have interpreted the linking of music to the local as an idealization of place. In this view, the exaltation of the regional experience potentially "results in a romanticization of the local as inherently 'subversive', 'oppositional', and 'authentic'" (Biddle and Knights 2007: 3). Although there is always the risk of romanticizing local histories or figures through decolonial metal music, one must recognize that many of these histories have been erased and devalued by the colonial experience, and therefore, their inclusion in metal music is more an act of resistance toward the suppression of memory through coloniality than a mere romantic gesture toward the past. Furthermore, as metal artists use decolonial music to actively intervene and effect change in their colonial context, their music transcends mere romantic, idealized, or nostalgic functions. One could argue, as Boaventura de Sousa Santos has posed when writing about decolonial options, that this is a form of nostalgia for a past experience approached from "an antinostalgic mode" or as "guidance for the future" (Santos 2018: 30). It is looking at the past in order to move toward the future with a decolonial vision. In such a context, remembrance becomes a sociopolitical and cultural act. Although scholars have examined the role that local settings and histories have in the development of metal music (Karjalainen 2018), these efforts have rarely included Latin America as a place of interest or examined such regions from a decolonial perspective.

Decolonial metal is regional in its sounds, imagery, and language

Another important characteristic of decolonial metal music is its regionalization through sounds, imagery, and language. This is key to understanding the role of this musical genre in Latin America, as metal music in general emanates from the Global North at a historical moment when globalization is rapidly aided by technology and mass communication (Wallach et al. 2012; Weinstein 2011). Its initial manifestations in the region would inevitably originate as imitations of the foreign sounds and aesthetics young kids were exposed to, either through tape trading or via the limited number of magazines and albums circulating locally, in many cases brought by those who had the resources to travel. Although there is a large strand of metal music in the region that to this day imitates those initial metal molds, decolonial metal distinguishes itself from this practice through regionalization.

There are many ways in which metal music in the region has been adapted and modified in order to engage in decolonial reflections. One of the most salient is through the integration of regional instruments into its sound. It is not uncommon to find local wind instruments like *quenas, zampoñas*, and the *bandoneón* accompanying lead guitarists as protagonists in the sounds of a metal song. The same can be said of the integration of a regional string instrument like the *charango*.[7] It is also evident in the rhythm sections, where one finds the use of the *bombo legüero* and the *batá*. Finally, there is also the integration of indigenous instrumentation into the music with the use of shells and rain sticks. Some of these instruments were banned during the dictatorships that spread throughout many of these regions as they were deemed markers of left-wing ideologies. The metal musicians that use them today described them as symbols of a region, metaphors of a feeling (i.e., melancholia), and purveyors of social meaning. This integrative process sets apart the sound of these metal bands, while also transforming their on-stage aesthetics. The sight of indigenous instruments sticks out in the context of a traditional metal concert.

The role of imagery is not limited to the use of regional instruments, but also encompasses the use of artwork for decolonial purposes.[8] Bands in the region frequently opt to use artwork that places them dead center in their place of origin through the use of indigenous imagery, for example. The artwork is also used to reflect on traumatic social and political events in their respective countries. Bands have used the cover artwork from their CDs to depict massacres carried out by local governments upon farmers, the perils of deforestation, and their admiration for armed rebel groups who have tackled these issues head-on in light of the seemingly hopeless role of traditional politics in addressing these problems. The artwork is also used in a more positive light to teach others about local legends and myths that have been repressed by colonial imposition and to familiarize the metal scene with work from local philosophers, poets, and artists. In this manner, the artwork is regionalized to promote a critical awareness of the region's history and its plights, while allowing for a more positive reflection about the future.

A third important strategy in the regionalization of metal music in Latin America has to do with the use of language. Although metal music is seen by many, from a universalist standpoint, as a genre mostly sung in English, this has never been a uniform phenomenon in the region. Important metal bands in Latin America, which released their first albums during the 1980s, sang completely in Spanish as a way to appropriate the genre from the Global North. Although Spanish is in and of itself a remnant of the colonial experience, it nevertheless allowed locals to differentiate themselves from bands based in the United States and the United Kingdom. More recently, there has been an increasing number of metal bands singing in indigenous languages, such as Quechua and Nahuatl. This strategy, although considered commercially problematic for their internationalization, has served to make metal even more regional and allowed it to further reflect the challenges faced by indigenous communities today. These are not dead languages, but rather those of living communities that to this day continue to be ignored by governments and, worse yet, become the massacred casualties of armed conflicts.

The regionalization of metal music through instrumentation, imagery, and language needs to be understood through a decolonial framework. This transformative dialogic and reflective process is intended to bring attention to the oppressive history experienced in the region, which has consequences that are still felt today. To a metal fan from the Global North, these regionalization strategies might seem like commercial ploys, but they are more than that. They are rarely intended to commercially promote a geography/destination or to increase the exotic credence of a band or metal scene.

Recent scholarly contributions to the idea of sovereignty in colonial settings can shed light on regionalization and localization in Latin American metal music. Although the word "sovereignty" has been mostly linked to the formation of nation-states, more recently authors have argued for an interpretation of the term that defines an individual's and community's capacity to exert power over situations in which they have been historically powerless (Frances Negrón-Muntaner 2017). One such area is the way communities represent themselves visually. Frances Negrón-Muntaner has called this act of visualization the "look of sovereignty," which she describes as "a way to style, display, and move the body to denote that a political actor is willing and able to exercise self-governance and full citizenship rights at any time he or she determines" (Frances Negrón-Muntaner 2017: 256). From this perspective, the transformation of one's visual representation toward the world is an exercise of power to overcome oppression. Although her specific reflection is related to the Young Lords (a Puerto Rican grassroots organization in New York and Chicago founded during the 1960s), it can be effectively applied to the use of decolonial aesthetics by other groups and in diverse settings. For Muntaner, "sovereignty is also a performative and aesthetic act" (2017: 256).

The focus on notions of sovereignty to challenge social oppression has also been addressed by scholars working with Native American communities in the United States, particularly as it pertains to their representation on film. Michelle Raheja (2010) has used the term "visual sovereignty" to explain how these historically oppressed communities have used their representation on film to challenge the negative depictions made of them by the nonindigenous gaze. It is another example of how the visual is used to challenge oppression. Decolonial metal music does not stray far from this endeavor, as it changes its original content and aesthetics (based on the Global North) to highlight the history of colonial oppression, and its everlasting presence in the *here and now*. Therefore, when decolonial metal transforms its sounds, imagery, and language to challenge coloniality, it also engages in sovereign acts to question and subvert power.

Decolonial metal is an intervention in its context

Another characteristic of decolonial metal music is its need for clear positioning or action outside of the usual entertainment-focused expectations of music. Metal bands throughout Latin America have called for direct actions that transcend the mere critique of social problems experienced in their settings through lyrics and songs. For these bands it is not enough to sing and raise awareness about the effects of coloniality in their daily lives; rather, they argue, there is a need for acts that represent direct interventions within the social sphere. This call echoes those made by decolonial scholars regarding the need to understand how practical acts of decoloniality happen in everyday life (Mignolo 2010). Although conversations about decolonial efforts are warranted, and can be quite complex in and of themselves, many are left wondering: What do these interventions actually look like? Metal musicians have answered this question through a lens of plurality and a diverse set of actions.

For example, decolonial bands have integrated visual components into their live shows to highlight a plight presently being faced in their country. Members of the Colombian band Tears of Misery wear a red thread on their knees to remind the audience about those who have lost limbs as part of the country's civil war. Colombia remains one of the countries most heavily impacted by hidden land mines. Other metal bands have openly become part of decolonial protest movements, too. The Puerto Rican band Puya released a song and participated in concerts to remove the US Navy from Vieques, a small municipal island where the population was displaced in order to use its fields as a military test range (see Chapter 2). These bands aim to foster a decolonial reflection in their music and live sets, and help their audiences become aware and more informed about a particular problem.

Fostering awareness of a particular problem linked to coloniality is closely related to reflections on the role of education in decolonial efforts. Scholars have argued for a decolonial approach toward education as a strategy to challenge the effects of coloniality in the region. This entails an education process that fosters a critical awareness of historical events, highlights local Latin American history told from the perspective of the oppressed, and promotes an understanding of the categories through which power is exerted (e.g., race, ethnicity, gender, control of knowledge, control of culture, exploitation of natural resources) (James Díaz 2010; Ocaña et al. 2018). In this sense, decolonial metal music can act as an educational resource to its listeners in the region. To some, this particular manifestation of metal music might still feel like entertainment and a strategic ploy on the part of musicians to differentiate themselves amid an ever-growing number of bands in the region. This may be true in some instances, but a closer look reveals that the lessons learned through decolonial metal extend beyond the stage.

Metal fans throughout Latin America have used the music to engage in decolonial acts beyond the metal scene. For example, fan groups have organized in Guatemala under the banner of metal music to rescue rural schools from government abandonment as a way to support Mayan populations impacted by war (see Chapter 9). The same can be said for metal fans in Colombia who, inspired by the critical messages in metal music, have joined armed struggles against the government (see Chapter 8). These are just two examples of decolonial acts that transcend the stage and find ways to intervene in the streets and countryside, where social problems stemming from coloniality actually take place. On many occasions, these are subject matters completely ignored by local governments or problems caused by government oppression of marginalized communities, and metal musicians/fans have used their music to confront them.

Although some of these examples might seem overtly political to some readers, as they certainly are to other members of these local metal scenes, it is important to highlight the ways they demonstrate an often-neglected shift away from metal in the Global North. Whereas research in the Global North has documented how members of the metal scene disengage from political reflections, this is somewhat different in the decolonial metal music found in the Global South. This position in the Global North has been well documented by Keith Kahn-Harris through his coining of the term "reflexive anti-reflexivity," which denotes a tendency by many to be aware of the political dimensions at play in society, but which is accompanied by an avoidance of active reflection in metal music in order to deflect the tensions carried by these types of political discussions (Kahn-Harris 2007). Decolonial metal in Latin America could not be any more different in this regard. Whereas some still express a need to disconnect metal music from politics, decolonial metal has found a way to become political, without losing itself in this pitfall.

For those engaged in decolonial metal, these musical acts are related to social justice. They transcend party politics, which is what people usually refer to as "politics" during everyday interactions. Addressing a social issue with political nuance through the lens of social justice, and more specifically through a decolonial approach, allows metal musicians and fans to engage in acts and reflections that have political connotations, without feeling like the discussion is happening within the boundaries of traditional political party establishments and logics. Metal in Latin America has found a way to be political without feeling the need to adhere to formal structures and rules, which are very prevalent in party politics and even in informal social or political movements.

This shift in the integration of politics into metal music in the region also represents a challenge to scholarly work on music that has neglected to see this musical genre as political. Michelle Phillipov (2012) has argued that academic research on music has tended to focus on genres such as punk and hip hop, as these were perceived as giving voice to groups that were socially oppressed. Working-class youth and racial/ethnic minorities could voice their critique of society via these genres. On the other hand, heavy metal music was somewhat abandoned in light of the perception that it was unable to voice the concerns of any oppressed group. It was perceived as lacking any political agenda on behalf of those who consumed it. Metal scholarship outside the Global North has challenged this idea, with research in the Middle East (LeVine 2008), Asia (Wallach 2003, 2005), and Africa (Banchs 2016) shedding light on the political dimensions of metal music. Similarly, decolonial metal in Latin America challenges this perspective while focusing on the political dimensions of social injustice and, simultaneously, steering clear of the pitfalls of party politics in the region. There is a sense of suspicion toward the entities (i.e., political parties) that continue to support coloniality via neoliberal policies, the oppressive use of force, and their abandonment of communities. Decolonial metal becomes a political intervention in its context outside of that arena.

Decolonial metal is influenced by other Latin American music: An extreme *Nueva Canción*

Metal music has found inspiration to engage in decolonial reflections and practices in the music created in its Latin American context. The musical genre has looked beyond its origins in Europe and the United States to incorporate local influences into its sounds and lyrics. For an outsider unfamiliar with Latin America's musical history, the integration of these local sounds and themes might seem fortuitous, but this would be far from accurate. When metal music integrates local influences into its practices, it does so with a purpose, one inflected by a decolonial resolve. One way in which metal wears these influences on its sleeve is by revisiting regional artists who have themselves engaged in decolonial reflections and acts. One clear-cut example is the reinterpretation of music from artists who are precursors to, are members of, or were subsequently influenced by the *Nueva Canción* ("New Song") movement in Latin America.

Commonly referred to as the "Latin American New Song," this group of artists and their musical productions can be understood both as a musical genre unto itself and, simultaneously, as a social movement (Morris 2014). Its sounds were inspired by local folk music, reminiscent of life in the countryside, which mostly focused on the use of the acoustic guitar and the singular voice of the performer. The *Nueva Canción* movement aimed to extend and transform this traditional folk sound and infuse it with socially committed and politically charged lyrics (Marsh 2017). This integration stemmed from the social cues of the 1960s and 1970s. The Cuban Revolution in 1959 and the election of President Salvador Allende in Chile in 1970 are two of the most important events that have been described as influential for this musical shift (Vila 2014). Both events infused the Latin American region with hope that antidemocratic governments could be toppled by different means – armed revolution in the case of Cuba and democratic elections in Chile. Allende's death in 1973 as part of a coup d'état would plunge the country into a dictatorship and simultaneously foster the *Nueva Canción* movement in Chile. It would spread throughout Latin America, have a major impact on social movements for decades to come, and be constantly persecuted by political establishments (Marrero 2018).

Research on the *Nueva Canción* movement has pointed out that the songs generated by these artists have transcended their initial geographical locations and spread throughout the Latin American region. Just as important as this geographical proliferation, the songs generated by the movement have been described as artifacts whose meanings morph with time. Eileen Karmy Bolton (2014) has explained how songs from the *Nueva Canción* have been reinterpreted and transformed after their initial release in order to address different political problems in varied social contexts. She uses the song "Cantata Popular Santa María de Iquique" as an example. The song, originally used to describe a 1907 massacre linked to a workers' strike in Chile that emerged from a struggle for better wages, was later used to denounce the 1973 Chilean dictatorship and has been more recently used to denounce neoliberal practices in the country. Therefore, these songs denounce both injustices of the past and those that are currently happening, while calling for unity in the face of these struggles. Although she stresses how other musical genres, like rock, have contributed to these transformations of the *Nueva Canción*, metal music is absent from her analysis.

A close examination of metal music in Latin America shows a very different scenario. Metal has systematically looked to the *Nueva Canción* as a source of inspiration. This is evidenced by the plethora of reinterpretations of these songs developed by metal artists in the region. Table 1.1 provides multiple examples of metal reinterpretations of songs initially developed by artists who were precursors of the *Nueva Canción* movement (Atahualpa Yupanqui), others who were important members of the movement itself (Violeta Parra, Víctor Jara), and subsequent artists who were later inspired by them (Hugo Giménez Agüero).

Some examples stand out as vitally important and capture the breadth and impact of the *Nueva Canción* movement on metal artists in Latin America. Argentinian band Tren Loco covered the song "Preguntitas sobre Dios" ("Small Questions about God") by folk singer Atahualpa Yupanqui, an important precursor of the movement who was tortured and subsequently exiled from Argentina due to his music's content (Molinero and Vila 2014). Bands like Aztra in Ecuador have covered songs by Victor Jara, a key figure for the movement who was also tortured and eventually assassinated during the 1973 coup d'état in Chile. Bands like

Song	Original Artist	Metal Artist
"El Condor Pasa"	Daniel Alomía Robles – 1913 (Perú)	Flor de Loto – 2019 (Perú)
"Guajira Guantanamera"	Julián Orbón – Lyrics 1929 José Fernández Díez – Music (Cuba)	Tendencia – 2009 (Cuba)
"Anticueca 2"	Violeta Parra – 1957 (Chile)	Pentagram – 2018 (Chile)
"Qué he Sacado con Quererte"	Violeta Parra – 1965 (Chile)	Egregor – 2018 (Chile)
"Qué Diría el Santo Padre"	Violeta Parra – 1965 (Chile)	Dracma – 2001 (Brazil)
"El Canto de la Cuculí"	Quilapayun – 1966 (Chile)	Aztra – 2012 (Ecuador)
"La Muralla"	Quilapayun – 1969 (Chile)	Puya – 2010 (Puerto Rico)
"Preguntitas sobre Dios"	Atahualpa Yupanqui – 1969 (Argentina)	Tren Loco – 2008 (Argentina)
"Flor de Retama"	Ricardo Dolorier – 1969 (Perú)	Indoraza – 2012 (Perú)
"De los Pagos del Tiempo"	José Larralde – 1970 (Argentina)	Almafuerte – 1995 (Argentina)
"La Partida"	Víctor Jara – 1971 (Chile)	Aztra – 2012 (Ecuador)
"Todos Juntos"	Los Jaivas – 1972 (Chile)	Massacre – 1989 (Chile)
"Techos de Cartón"	Alí Primera – 1972 (Venezuela)	Paul Gillman – 2004 (Venezuela)
"Alturas"	Inti-Illimani – 1973 (Chile)	Aztra – 2008 (Ecuador)
"Manifiesto"	Víctor Jara – 1974 (Chile)	Aztra – 2010 (Ecuador)
"Si se Calla el Cantor"	Horacio Guarany – 1975 (Argentina)	Malón – 1996 (Argentina)
"Canción Mansa para un Pueblo Bravo"	Alí Primera – 1976 (Venezuela)	Paul Gillman – 2004 (Venezuela)
"Mambo de Machaguay"	Los Jaivas – 1982 (Chile)	Recrucide – 2018 (Chile)

(*continued*)

TABLE 1.1 Continued

Song	Original Artist	Metal Artist
"Cinco Siglos Igual"	León Gieco – 1992 (Argentina)	A.N.I.M.A.L. – 1998 (Argentina)
"Amutuy, Soledad"	Marcelo Berbel – 1993 (Argentina)	Yanaconas – 2016 (Argentina)
"Ayer Bajé al Poblao"	José Larralde – 1995 (Argentina)	Azor – 1998 (Argentina)
"Cacique Yatel"	Hugo Giménez Agüero – 1997 (Argentina)	Ricardo Iorio, Flavio Cianciarulo – 1997 (Argentina)
"Cacique Yatel"	Hugo Giménez Agüero – 1997 (Argentina)	Aonikenk – 2014 (Argentina)
"El Témpano"	Adrián Abonizio – 1997 (Argentina)	Arraigo – 2014 (Argentina)
"500 años, ¿de qué?"	Hugo Giménez Agüero* (Argentina)	Tren Loco – 2006 (Argentina)

TABLE 1.1: Metal covers of regional Latin American songs.

*Note: I was unable to find the original release date for the song "500 años, ¿de qué?" by Hugo Giménez Agüero. Even members of the band Tren Loco were unable to remember the first time they had heard the song or when it was initially released. It is usually best known for its release in 2008, as part of one of the artist's later albums.

Pentagram (Chile), Egregor (Chile), and Dracma (Brazil) have covered songs by Violeta Parra, who is considered by many to be the mother of the *Nueva Canción* movement. Metal bands would also cover artists from subsequent generations who were inspired by the *Nueva Canción* movement. Paul Gillman's metal renditions of Alí Primera's songs in Venezuela stand out, as the latter's songs were used to inspire the Bolivarian Revolution during the 1990s (Marsh 2017). These examples demonstrate that metal music has looked to the *Nueva Canción* as a source of inspiration for decades, although music scholarship has neglected to examine this link. This brings up an important question: What does metal achieve in this process?

Through this process, metal music engages in the multifaceted conversations that are integral to *extreme decolonial dialogues*. The first dialogue is between musical genres, specifically metal and the *Nueva Canción*. This conversation aims to show that metal is aware of, and present in, the discussion of social injustices in the region and does so being fully conscious of the political leanings of its sources of inspiration. It is no coincidence that metal artists decide to cover politically charged songs that address coloniality outright. This is an agenda that is being displayed intentionally.

The second dialogue is intergenerational. The adaptation of politically inflected songs serves to connect young metal fans and artists to events of the past in their respective settings. This is why phrases like "never again" are so prevalent in the promotional material of metal shows throughout the region. There is a clear understanding that the events of the past experienced by previous generations (e.g., dictatorship, murder, political repression, international interventionism) must not be repeated. In a context that sometimes aims to make these events invisible, metal seems to be stating to the previous generation that these events did in fact happen and they are here to bear witness. "I believe the previous generation" seems to be an underlying motif.

The third dialogue stemming from this process is between historical events. Metal has contributed to the ever-changing meanings ascribed to the songs from the *Nueva Canción* by applying them to more recent events. For example, Tren Loco's (2006) cover of the song "500 años ¿de qué?" ("500 years of what?") by Hugo Giménez Agüero is not only about denouncing fifteenth-century colonialism but is, rather, used by the band to denounce current colonial exploitation via neoliberal practices in the region. The band has described this connection during its concerts, particularly when introducing the song to the audience.

Finally, there is an emotional dialogue taking place. Whereas the folk-sounding songs of the *Nueva Canción* movement feel completely steeped in melancholia (e.g., a single guitar, one singer), metal transforms them into anthems full of power and, therefore, full of hope for the future. The use of electric guitars, driving percussive rhythms, and layered voices in their melodic choruses inject these songs with a sonic sense of power they did not possess in their original versions and turn them into anthems for a new generation of people who need to feel full of hope for the future. Thus, metal's extreme sounds and transgressive attitude inform these songs with new energy, a sense of optimism, and hope.[9] It is always interesting to watch metal audiences mosh and scream to a metal version of a *Nueva Canción* song.

Decolonial metal is strategically communal and celebratory

Another important characteristic of decolonial metal music is its focus on the communal aspects of the genre and its invitation to joint celebration. It uses multiple strategies that foster collective identities in order to challenge the effects of coloniality and exert change in its social context. The communal experience has been widely documented as important for the international metal community and local metal scenes (Hill 2013; Snaza and Netherton 2016; Varas-Díaz and Scott 2016; Varas-Díaz et al. 2016). That sense of belonging and togetherness is mostly fostered via collective experiences tied to music, and both its benefits (i.e., social support, sense of belonging) and challenges (i.e., racism, sexism, ageism, homophobia) have been documented in metal-related scholarship (Kahn-Harris 2012; Dawes 2013; Clifford-Napoleone 2015; Clinton and Wallach 2015; Hill 2016). I posit that the communal experience in decolonial metal goes a step beyond traditional conceptualizations of social support to encompass a larger decolonial and political agenda.

Decolonial metal uses the communal experience to show social support among its members, but it also uses collective experiences strategically to both foster dialogues about the manifestations of social oppression in the context and, even more importantly, engage in collective actions to challenge it. Throughout my ethnographic work I witnessed this process in five specific examples of collective action: (1) highlighting the power of oppressed communities through song (see Chapter 5), (2) using collective and coordinated action to fight racism (see Chapter 7), (3) using group mobilization to actively change political structures (see Chapter 6), (4) collectively showing support for metal fans engaged in armed conflicts (see Chapter 8), and (5) using celebratory terms to foster solidarity in everyday interactions (see Chapter 10). Allow me to elaborate on each of these examples.

Many of the themes encompassed in decolonial metal songs position members of oppressed groups in a positive light. This may happen by describing them as war heroes (in the case of indigenous populations) or relentless fighters (against colonial invasion) or by highlighting the importance of the ideas they expressed in their writings (in the case of Latin American poets and philosophers). In this manner the content of the songs proposes an inverse examination of coloniality, by positioning those affected as a resilient and powerful collective. This is not an imaginary act concerned solely with fostering a romantic ideal of the local people. On the contrary, it frequently references actual communities (i.e., Zapatistas in México, students in Guatemala) who engage in decolonial resistance effectively in their current settings. Those communities are celebrated and vindicated through the lyrical content of decolonial metal.

The communal component of decolonial metal is not limited to lyrics and albums. It takes a hands-on approach to challenge social oppression and its effects on the lives of the scenes' members. For example, metal fans have joined together and used radio shows in the Caribbean setting to challenge issues of social class and racism within their scenes. Such is the case of the Dominican Republic, where a mostly upper class and racially White scene emerged during the 1980s. Metal fans used a radio show to reach poor *barrios* and foster the inclusion of Black youths in the scene. They effectively changed the racial composition of metal bands and the local scene itself, in a country that has historically manifested high levels of racism. The same can be argued of metal fans in Cuba, who gained government support for metal music under the argument that their output was art and, therefore, warranted safe spaces, much like those held by other musicians. Finally, metal fans in Colombia have held concerts to raise funds for scene members imprisoned due to their engagement in armed struggles against corrupt governments. These are all concrete and practical examples of how decolonial metal uses the communal experience to transform its setting.

Decolonial metal has also impacted the manner in which metal fans "talk" about their solidarity. One clear example is the use of the word *aguante* in Argentinian metal music to express support between individuals and bands, but also as a politically charged term of resistance toward oppressive practices. All of this is done through a celebratory and hopeful approach toward life, which seems to tell metal fans that oppression must be understood and fought against, without forgetting that, simultaneously, one must enjoy and celebrate life collectively. This celebratory approach toward decolonial reflections and actions is best exemplified by the live concert experience. In these settings, the critical approaches toward decolonial reflections and actions are seamlessly intertwined with the usual celebration of a musical event or encounter. It is in this coming together at a concert that the spaces for celebration and critical action become one. These collective and communal experiences challenge more individualistic perspectives promoted through neoliberal approaches throughout society, which tend to value personal success over communal welfare (Cheshire and Lawrence 2005).

Although this might seem alien to individuals engaged in more traditional social or political groups, such as those characterized by a more rigid and institutionalized approach toward social action, decolonial metal sees no contradiction in this joint venture. It echoes, even if inadvertently, the position of Argentinian philosopher Enrique Dussel when writing about a philosophy of liberation for the region and the role of proximity, celebration, and happiness in the process of liberty (Dussel 1985). In writing about the celebratory interaction with others, Dussel expressed that "proximity is a festival." This focus on a simple act like the celebration is key, as those burdened by oppression also need to celebrate their experience and the possibility of liberation. For him, this proximity "is a feast – of liberation, not of exploitation, injustice, and desecration. It is a feast of those who are equal, free, and just, of those who yearn for an order of proximity without counterrevolution or relapse" (1985: 21). This potential for liberation generates happiness and hope, which in turn "makes it possible for us to continue living" (1985: 105).

The positive feelings generated by a sense of community and celebration are important, particularly in the Latin American setting, where concerns over *fatalismo* ("fatalism") have been discussed in the academic literature for decades (Camisassa and Moreno 2004; de la Corte Ibáñez 2000; Ratner 2015; Sánchez 2005). Borrowing from Ignacio Martín-Baró's work with liberation psychology in El Salvador, fatalism has been described as the manifestation (through ideas, feelings, and behaviors) of a worldview that conceptualizes life as predetermined, with an inescapable adverse destiny, regardless of how much one tries to fight against it (Martín-Baró 1994). For him this was not a personality trait attached to the people in the region, but rather a worldview imposed by the harsh sociopolitical conditions experienced in the region and a strategy used to keep marginalized populations under control. Therefore, when decolonial metal music engages in activities that foster communal actions to face this context, and does so in a celebratory manner, it directly challenges fatalism and imbues listeners in the region with a sense of hope moving forward.

Decolonial metal is in constant tension with its context

In providing detailed characterizations of what constitutes decolonial metal and what it does for scene members, one runs the risk of understanding this process as an unproblematic endeavor. It might seem to some that when this musical genre engages in decolonial dialogues and acts, there is little pushback from the metal community. This could not be farther from the truth. In fact, decolonial metal is a dialogue in constant tension. Some of these tensions come from practices within the metal scene and others from external forces that diminish the decolonial approach. I would like to highlight two of these tensions with examples from interactions between the metal scene and its contexts in Latin America. I will later describe how tensions are manifested in interactions with metal scenes in the Global North.

As I have already highlighted in this chapter, decolonial metal is characterized by a strong sense of regionalization, and this, in turn, is manifested through areas like a band's imagery. Bands use their artwork to reflect their place of origin and, in some cases, to offer some sort of critical reflection about oppressive practices related to coloniality in their context. On many occasions they face criticism from their context, which discourages them from engaging in these reflections. For example, in 2015 the Puerto Rican band Calamity released their album *Imminent Disaster* (2015), with cover art developed by a local artist. The album cover showed the Island's military fortifications dating from Spanish colonial times (i.e., *garitas*) under attack by a *Vejigante,* a local representation of a demon (see Figure 1.1; for more information on metal and *Vejigantes*, see Varas-Díaz and Mendoza 2018). A year after the release of the album, the band was signed to a

FIGURE 1.1: Original artwork for the album *Imminent Disaster* (2015) by the Puerto Rican band Calamity. Artwork by Kadriel Betsen.

German label who decided to re-release the album, but not without first changing the cover artwork (see Figure 1.2). The decision was taken in order to make the album fall "more in line with the new label."[10] Some local fans saw this as a way to "de-regionalize" the album and make it appeal to a larger audience. The revised artwork exchanged the local *Vejigante* figure with an unspecified entity, which, although demon-like in appearance, seemed more akin to Central American indigenous-built structures than the Caribbean ones found in the initial art. Decisions like this one fostered by members of the metal scene, and based on market

FIGURE 1.2: Revised artwork for the album *Imminent Disaster* (2017) by the Puerto Rican band Calamity. Image provided by Berny Santos.

forces and sales expectations, limit the manifestations of decolonial dialogues through metal music in the region.[11]

Some of the limitations to these decolonial dialogues are not forced upon bands by the market, but rather willingly adopted by the musicians and seen as signs of commercial success. One key example can be seen in Mexican metal with the band Miquian. The band describes itself as pre-Hispanic metal in reference to their visual aesthetic and their lyrical use of Nahuatl, a local indigenous language. This language and its accompanying imagery are heavily used throughout their entire 2015 album *Tlaltecuhtli* (Miquian 2015). The band, upon initial analysis, embodies almost all of the decolonial characteristics I have described in this chapter. On the other hand, their chosen decolonial dialogue angle distances them from anti-oppressive practices. In 2018, the band's music was used in a commercial for the local beer Victoria. The commercial shows several individuals with body paint intended to represent native body art, while simultaneously displaying indigenous concepts, now translated into Spanish, defined for the benefit of the viewer. The commercial ends with a cross-promotion of the local beer and the metal band's name and music. This is an instance in which a decolonial metal band uses its characteristics to engage in the marketplace, and the messages that once focused on issues of social oppression are used purely as an entertainment strategy to sell products. There is no reflection in such a commercial about the plights of indigenous communities, the systematic use of their land by commercial companies, and the neoliberal practices that affect them. Here, the *extreme decolonial dialogue* is devalued in the service of mere product placement, in order to promote a local beer and a metal band.

Both of these examples point toward the challenges faced by bands engaged in a decolonial agenda through metal music. Some of these challenges are imposed by external forces fixed upon them to conform to the expectation of a music market, and others are self-imposed under the expectation of breaking out of their setting and accessing a larger international audience. The complexities do not end here; rather, they become even more challenging when decolonial metal bands engage with the international metal scene in the Global North.

Decolonizing metal: Tensions with the Global North

The tensions faced by decolonial metal are not limited to reactions from within Latin America, as described earlier. Some of the most salient tensions emanate from its relation to the metal scenes in the Global North, more specifically, to the ways in which metal from the Global South, including Latin America, is perceived, interpreted, and represented by individuals in Europe or the United States. This tension is important since, in order for metal music to become decolonial, it has to be aware of the potential pitfalls of this process when the northern gaze is placed upon it. In this sense, it is not enough to describe the decolonial efforts of Latin American metal music; we must also decolonize the manner in which the Global North describes it. In other words, metal music itself needs to be decolonized. I argue that metal-related output from the Global North tends to devalue the role of metal in the Global South, and decolonial metal in particular, through three strategies: (1) the silencing of southern voices, (2) the fetishization of the visual aspects of decolonial metal, and (3) the appropriation of its features for promotional purposes. In elaborating this argument, I will use three examples that illustrate the need to decolonize metal music's northern gaze toward the south.

The first example of the colonizing manner in which the Global North examines metal in the Global South can be seen in film. In 2008 Sam Dunn released the documentary film entitled "Global Metal" (Dunn and McFadyen 2009) in which he, after self-identifying as an anthropologist, sets out to explore metal in the Global South (e.g., Asia, South America, Middle East, etc.). The film is a useful tool for individuals who are unaware of metal music in these regions, and many immediately recognized its value for the international metal scene. Even today, it is heralded as an important documentary for metal music studies. Unfortunately, the filmmaker engages in practices that inadvertently silence the voices and experiences of metal fans and musicians in the regions he wants to highlight. For example, the film begins with music from a famous North American band (Metallica) and with visuals of arguably the most important festival in the Global North (Wacken Festival in Germany). Although metal music in the Global South abounds and festivals of similar magnitude take place in these geographies, those from the Global North are set immediately as a comparison. It is as if the histories of metal in the Global South could not be told without reference to metal in the Global North. In this sense, Dunn limits the possibility of fostering the visual sovereignty of metal artists in the Global South throughout his film.

This limited exploration of metal in the Global South continues throughout the film via the integration of metal artists from countries like the United Kingdom and the United States. The descriptions of metal in the Global South are overlapped by their presence, as if the history of metal in the region could not have been told without their interjections. Very frequently during the film, after local metal musicians speak, a counterpart from the Global North is presented in dialogue as if to ratify the arguments. Finally, and most symbolically, the film closes with an Iron Maiden concert in India, amid the frenzy generated by the band's presence in the country. It is telling that the film ends with this event, and not a concert showcasing famous bands in the Global South. Even more telling is the fact that the historical relation between the United Kingdom (the home of this important band) and India is not explored in depth; coloniality is absent in the film. Added to this problematic approach, the history of metal in the Global South is addressed without a critical examination of its relation to metal in the Global North. It is as if their story could not be told comprehensively unless voices from the Global North intervened.

The tensions of decolonial metal with the scenes in the Global North do not end with their representation in film. They extend to very practical dimensions in the everyday lives of bands, specifically those touring abroad, as is evidenced in the second example. Mexican band Cemican have become very successful at touring Europe. They participated in the 2018 Wacken Festival in Germany and were also part of the 2019 installment of the Hellfest Festival in France. Although these might seem like important steppingstones for Latin American metal, they raise a flag of concern about the tensions of decolonial metal with the northern scenes.

Cemican describes itself as pre-Hispanic metal (see Figure 1.3). Their attire and instrumentation reference the indigenous communities of their region of origin. The band embodies most, if not all, of the characteristics I have described as particular to decolonial metal in Latin America. Still, their continued invitation to these festivals raises many questions. Are they invited only because of their indigenous aesthetic? Why are other Latin American bands, which do not share these visual and sonic characteristics, not invited as frequently to these festivals? Is it possible that European promoters focus on these factors to make their

FIGURE 1.3: Mexican band Cemican at the French festival Hellfest. Photo provided by Raul Lucido.

decisions and participate, either knowingly or unknowingly, in the fetishization of the indigenous populations of Latin America? In a case like this one, an act that is interpreted as transgressive and decolonial in the Global South is used by the Global North as pure entertainment. It echoes Italian artist Luigi Gregori's painting of Christopher Columbus presenting indigenous peoples of the Americas at the Spanish court. There is a colonial undertone in the frequent presentations of a band like Cemican in Europe that is problematically ignored. Not all Latin American metal looks and sounds like Cemican, and thus, certain subgenres risk being completely ignored by the Global North.

Unfortunately, ignoring the complexities and contributions of metal music in Latin America is not the end of the problem. Another more important manifestation of the need to decolonize metal music's gaze exists in the Global North; here I am referring to decolonial appropriation. This happens when bands from the Global North emulate the decolonial characteristics of bands in the Global South, including Latin America, for commercial gain. This is the case of the third example mentioned here, the French/Spanish band Impureza, which self-describes as Hispanic extreme metal. The band uses imagery of indigenous peoples of the Americas in their album artwork and writes lyrics related to this content. An initial look at their visual and musical output would signal their alignment with the features I have outlined earlier to denote the decolonial approach of metal in Latin America. A closer look at the band, however, reveals problematic interpretations that distance them from this endeavor. For example, their Facebook description states that "Impureza's conquistadors will make you discover their Hispanic universe and you will drive in a full Spanish conquest through their unprecedented musical concept!" A similar problem arises from their promotional materials in which they are described as "Death Metal Conquistadors." The tension between the use of indigenous imagery and their self-identification as oppressive conquistadors is not explored. In this example, the aesthetics of decolonial metal are used and appropriated by metal in the Global North uncritically. Their production seems to be on the side of the oppressed, but upon closer examination, their output simply reproduces the perspective of the oppressor.

These three examples – from documentary film, international music festivals, and bands from the Global North – point to a problematic tension with metal in Latin America in general and with decolonial metal in particular. For the Global North, these manifestations of metal music, which are visually and sonically different, tend to become fetishized and are deprived of their critical positioning in the decolonial agenda. They become the "new thing" in the Global North scene, another subgenre to consume. It is not surprising, then, that these bands are easily categorized as folk metal or pre-Hispanic metal, among other labels, without a reflection of the critical positioning that underlies their artistic output. The Global North sees their difference as something to consume, and not as a source of critical reflection, even less a source of decolonial dialogue.

Decolonial metal music in Latin America – moving forward

Having defined the main characteristics of decolonial metal in Latin America and having discussed its tensions with its immediate context and the Global North, an important question remains: What does this approach mean for metal music and the study of this genre moving forward? The answer is simultaneously motivating as it is complex. I would argue that even though the moral panics experienced in North America surrounding metal music (Weinstein 1991; Walser 1993) persist in the region (Actualidad 2018; Campos Garza 2018; Charner 2019; Pavón 2019), the ever-growing studies on metal music demonstrate that these are misplaced.[12] In fact, metal in Latin America has served and continues to serve a different purpose by aligning itself in solidarity with the plight of the oppressed. It has done so by helping build a body of knowledge about the region's histories and experiences from the perspective of the oppressed. More importantly, it has fostered concrete actions to address those experiences. This does not mean that all metal music in Latin America is decolonial; far from it. Yet, the body of decolonial metal is vast enough to merit detailed attention. If there is any panic that should be experienced by those that do not understand decolonial metal's agenda, it should be the one felt when oppressive practices are brought to light, critically questioned, and acted upon in order to change them.

When telling decolonial stories and actions, metal music has not forgotten that the plights of modernity, which are so frequently addressed in this musical genre throughout the world, are different for the Latin American region, and I would argue for the Global South in general. In line with decolonial theorists, metal recognizes that the European ideal of modernity is built upon the exploitation of colonial subjects throughout the Global South. Therefore, its critique of modernity and its subsequent effects are not universalistic in scope, but focuses on the colonial experience faced in the region. Metal in Latin America has become a decolonial project that looks at the past, the present, and the future; it is so much more than the sum of its musical entertainment parts.

The future study of metal music practices from within academic epicenters in the Global South and the Global North needs to take this decolonial shift into account. It has become impossible to tell the histories of metal music, and engage in academic research on the matter, without examining the plurality of its manifestations in the Global South. These research efforts should not be mere descriptions of how metal music in the Global South is different from that of the Global North; considerations such as these are no longer enough. It should use a decolonial perspective to understand how it aims to reflect, and potentially change, the plight of the oppressed in those regions. In the following chapters I discuss how metal manifests this decolonial agenda through examples from nine countries: Puerto Rico, Perú, Chile, México, Cuba, Dominican Republic, Colombia, Guatemala, and Argentina. My hope is that future research on metal music in the region will continue to expand the notion of decolonial metal as a constantly evolving and changing endeavor, much like the strategies of colonial oppression in the region, which seem to be never ending.

NOTES

1. I would like to shed some light on the underlying rationale to frame my findings on metal in Latin America through a decolonial approach, and not a postcolonial one. I have elected to do so in light of several identified differences between decolonial and postcolonial approaches, related to the following: (1) the origin of these ideas, (2) positions on the need for intervention in the social sphere (e.g., different forms of activism) that transcend academic settings, (3) invitation to linguistic plurality, and (4) their positionality as a choice versus an inherited condition. I will explain these differences here, and then briefly reflect on what they mean for my study of metal music in Latin America.

   Following Mignolo (2010), I am informed by reflections on the differences between decolonial and postcolonial approaches as parts of a larger historical "genealogy of the thoughts and experiences of the scholars and intellectuals engaged in each of them" (2010: 16). Postcolonial thought emerges largely from thinkers in Europe and their reflections about Palestine/Israel and India/United Kingdom relations. Decolonial thought, on the other hand, is anchored in the reflections of Latin American and Caribbean scholars who extend the scope of their considerations back to fifteenth-century colonialism as experienced in their region (Acha 2018). Focusing on the particular experiences of the Latin American region is an answer to the call for engaging knowledge production as a geopolitical endeavor. These are ideas generated by people whose bodies and experiences are embedded in the regions they describe, and they speak to these realities through their own voices. They aim to break with Western and Eurocentric theories, including postcolonial theories, which very frequently have universalist undertones.

   Mignolo (2011) also views decolonial thought as conjoined with the "aims of the political society for whom the decolonial is a question of survival rather than promotion" (2011: xxvii). Academia is not the epicenter of decolonial thought; the impetus for transformation it entails emerges from the oppressed communities from which it emanates. Decolonial ideas become a way to act upon the world, based on knowledges generated in those particular geographies by those who live through the colonial experience. This notion aims to distance itself from the academic-centered approach of postcolonial thought. Postcolonial authors have been aware of the critiques over institutionalization and their perceived lack of commitment to actual engagement in the fight against oppression (Loomba 1998). It seems to me that the criticisms posed to postcolonial framings have not been sufficiently addressed or at least not in a manner that allows authors identified with the decolonial perspective to feel its perusals meet the region's needs.

Authors have also noted the linguistic preferences of decolonial and postcolonial studies. For example, Stephen Lim (2019) has pointed out that decolonial thought has been concerned with the incorporation of different languages into its reflective process, particularly Spanish, in comparison with the English centeredness of postcolonial studies. This invitation to plurality in decolonial thought, and particularly through its different languages, is important as it highlights the intent to bring together more people whose knowledges might otherwise be excluded or erased.

Finally, postcolonial studies' reification of disciplinary approaches and academic institutionalization has separated the concept from engaging in more radical decolonial activism. This position stresses the idea that postcoloniality is a "condition, a certain human existential situation which we have often no power of choosing." On the other hand, decoloniality is "an option, consciously chosen as a political, ethical, and epistemic positionality and an entry point into agency" (Tlostanova 2019: 165). This may be one of the reasons why Puerto Rican author Ramón Grosfogel (2011) has called for the decolonization of postcolonial studies.

In light of these differences, I have elected to explain the relevance of metal music in Latin America in relation to coloniality through the lens of decolonial thought. This has allowed me to understand the phenomenon, a global movement that has been regionalized, mostly through theories developed by individuals in Latin America, through their historically anchored experiences, and in their own language. It has also allowed me to understand how metal music in the region has incorporated, on many occasions, an activist approach that aims to challenge coloniality and modify its present-day effects. Much like decoloniality is a choice, metal's engagement in social justice issues in the region is also a choice, amidst a musical environment that calls for easily digestible music that addresses unproblematic realities. Therefore, my endeavor echoes the call made by Chilean musicologist Juan Pablo González (2018) to engage in a "critical gaze at coloniality" through music and understand the world, in this case our world, through the political act of "listening to it" (2018: 40). This is not to say that decolonial and postcolonial thoughts are completely at odds with each other. In fact, Mignolo (2011) has argued that they are "complementary trajectories with similar goals of social transformation" (2011: xxvi). I see this position exemplified in the use of postcolonial theory in rock music research carried out by Jeremy Wallach and Esther Clinton (Wallach and Clinton 2019; Wallach 2020). In fact, it has been their call to "recolor the metal map" and to look for metal through a global lens

(Wallach et al. 2012; Clinton and Wallach 2015) that has fostered much of the Global North scholars' interest in the Global South. My work in Latin America has been influenced by their reflections, and Wallach has described my decolonial approaches toward metal music as an important contribution to "decolonizing" the field of metal studies (Wallach 2019). Therefore, decolonial and postcolonial studies can find common ground in the study of metal music. My selection of a decolonial approach rests mostly on my adherence to the Latin American region, the scholarship carried out there, and the decolonial efforts that transcend academia.

2. Aníbal Quijano's idea of coloniality of power has been expanded to address the many dimensions of life impacted by the colonial experience. Two main concepts have stood out: coloniality of knowledge and coloniality of being. The first has been used to describe the ways in which coloniality has aimed to devalue the knowledge produced by local communities while holding Eurocentric knowledge as a universal standard of excellence. Edgardo Lander (2000) has written about this problem and presented how authors linked to decolonial thought have challenged these Eurocentric perspectives in the social sciences. In this view, knowledge production becomes a potentially decolonial endeavor, as it aims to challenge established notions of objectivity, neutrality, and universality, which can hide the underlying power dynamics of coloniality. Also, in a closely linked endeavor, Nelson Maldonado-Torres has argued for the need to understand the "lived experience of colonization" (2007: 242). The term coloniality of being has been used to account for how the colonial experience marks the everyday lives of people, and more importantly, their ability to see themselves as fully human. Following Descartes's notion of "I think, therefore I am," coloniality of being explains how racialized people are deemed irrational, or non-thinkers, and therefore not fully human. Maldonado-Torres relies heavily on similar concerns raised by Frantz Fanon (1952, 1965) over the idea that Black people are not beings, not fully human, under the White gaze. As Maldonado-Torres mentions, "invisibility and dehumanization are the primary expressions of the coloniality of being" (2007: 257). Coloniality of knowledge and being are closely linked, as subjects who are deemed incapable of knowing, are thus, incapable of being.

3. I am not arguing that decolonial metal bands address the plights of all of these populations simultaneously. I have not encountered one band that engages in decolonial reflections toward all of these populations throughout their musical output. On the contrary, one band might decide to focus on indigenous issues, while another on the plight of farmers, based on their personal experiences or areas of interest. Still, taken together as a collective, decolonial metal bands address this wide-ranging set of topics.

4. For a more in-depth discussion on metal in Ecuador, the reader can examine the work of Olaf Kaltmeier (2019), which addresses the bands Curare and Aztra. Although the work does not include direct interviews with the band members, which I find somewhat problematic from a decolonial approach, it is still an important contribution to understanding

metal music in Ecuador, a country in which very little research on the matter has been carried out.

5. These are a handful of examples of bands and songs that have addressed historically anchored subject matters as part of decolonial agendas: *colonization* – Aggressive (Colombia), "Predator's Mind"; A.N.I.M.A.L. (Argentina), "Gritemos Para No Olvidar"; Dremis Derinfet (Colombia), "Cruz, Corona y Guerra"; Huinca (Chile), "América Letrina"; Hermética (Argentina), "La Revancha de América"; Ratos de Porão (Brazil), "Amazônia Nunca Mais." *Nineteenth- and twentieth-century regional wars and battles* – Custom71 (Argentina) – "Alas de Gloria"; Tren Loco (Argentina), "Acorazado Belgrano"; Abäk (Costa Rica), "Santa Rosa"; Gillman (Venezuela), "La Batalla de Carabobo." *Local massacres* – Corpus Calvary (Colombia), "El Aro"; Azeroth" (Argentina), "Campaña del Desierto"; Demolición (Ecuador), "Noviembre Negro." *Indigenous perspectives* – Kranium (Perú), "El Obraje"; Puya (Puerto Rico), "Areyto"; Werken (Argentina), "Sangre India"; Yanaconas (Argentina), "Tupac Amaru"; Malón (Argentina), "Grito de Pílaga"; Ch'aska (Perú), "Pururauca"; Sepultura (Brazil), "Roots Bloody Roots". *Social justice movements* – Leprosy (México), "Llora chispas"; Socavón (Colombia), "Cenizas en el Palacio"; Gillman (Venezuela), "F27"; Curare (Ecuador) – "Yaku."

6. Throughout Latin America the idea of "solidarity" has different meanings and interpretations. In my ethnographic work I witnessed how in some countries the idea is met with skepticism and distrust, as it is perceived to be condescending. It is equated with charity and the embodiment of a savior complex towards the oppressed. My use of the word is completely different. I deploy the notion of solidarity throughout this book as an expression of unity and mutual support, highlighting the communal aspect of decolonial metal music. This use of the term is reflective of the most frequent interpretations I found in my interviews.

7. This adoption of local instrumentation in metal music is an important part of understanding its decolonial intent. Music scholars have explained that during the 1990s some artists, specifically within the genre of rock, saw the integration of these instruments (specifically the *charango*) as a "symbol of cultural dogmatism" (Pacini Hernández et al. 2004: 11). Some of these instruments were too closely linked to local traditions and the politics-laden music of the *Nueva Canción,* and therefore, musicians could see them as obstacles to finding new ways to express their concerns in a manner that was closer to their generation and the times they lived in. For example, while writing about rock in Chile, Pino-Ojeda (2004) quoted a local musician who stated that some wanted to "get as far away from Canto Nuevo as possible" (2004: 293). In contrast, metal artists have returned to the use of these instruments, unconcerned about how linking their sounds to local traditions might seem dogmatic, but rather seeing them as liberatory.

8. The use of the image to understand the colonial experience has been championed by Bolivian scholar Silvia Rivera Cusicanqui (2015, 2020). She proposed a sociology of the Image to explain how these can help us understand the oppressive dynamics of colonialism.

She places trust in the image for this agenda and states that "It is evident that in a colonial situation, that which goes unsaid contains the most meaning; words mask more than they reveal, and symbols take center stage" (Rivera Cusicanqui 2020: 6). In her view words can "conceal" the plights of the colonial experience, as these are "plagued with euphemisms" (Rivera Cusicanqui 2020: 12–13). It is no surprise then that other authors, like Boaventura de Sousa Santos (2020) have also called for the use of artistic practices, which are closely linked to the image, in challenging coloniality and developing epistemologies of the South. I pose throughout this book that decolonial metal music uses images (e.g., album artwork, t-shirt messages) as ways to elucidate and challenge coloniality within metal scenes.

9. This use of emotions to address issues of hope and optimism contrasts sharply with findings from research done with metal proponents of extreme subgenres (i.e., death metal, grindcore) in other parts of the world, where their manifestation is sometimes interpreted by scene members as an affront to masculinity and, thus, to the music's "brutal disposition" (Overell 2014: 95). These differences could be attributed to diverse expectations placed by performers and listeners on more "extreme" subgenres of metal, but I understand that is not enough to explain the role of emotions in decolonial metal referencing the *Nueva Canción* movement. In fact, some of the Latin American bands that have revisited these songs actually belong to some of the most extreme subgenres of metal music. Here emotion is not frowned upon or seen as problematic, but rather interpreted as an ally to move forward in a scenario plagued by oppression. These metal artists have seen in the *Nueva Canción* an example of how emotions transmitted through music can help people feel connected to the experience of oppression in the region.

10. This stems from personal communications with band member Berny Santos on December 26, 2019.

11. It should be noted that some metal bands circumnavigate these types of external restrictions placed on their decolonial imagery. For example, the use of similar traditional masks has also made its way into metal music outside of Puerto Rico. The Dominican hardcore metal band *La Armada* (located now in Chicago, USA) uses the *lechón mask* (a local representation of devils or monsters) in their promotional t-shirts as a way to highlight their Dominican roots, while living in the United States. Their latest album, released in 2018, is entitled *Anti-Colonial*. Research on the band has highlighted the importance they place on Dominican culture and decolonial reflections in light of the band's migration to the United States (Nevárez Araújo, 2021). The mask portrayed in their shirts is used during the yearly *Festival de los Lechones* ("Festival of the Pigs"), held in the city of Santiago, Dominican Republic. Although the masks are distinctly different from those used in Puerto Rico, they have similar shapes with protruding horns and extravagant colors. The origins of the festival are thought to be closely linked to slave celebrations in the country and, therefore, to the region's Afro-Caribbean roots.

12. It should be noted that as other metal scholars engage in research throughout the Global South, the benefits of participation in metal culture continue to emerge. For example,

Paula Rowe has contributed to a better understanding of how youth use metal in Australia to foster a sense of community. She also notes how they engage in "positive self-talk," a mechanism that promotes mental health by providing them with some stability in their navigation of identity formation in the "less reliable social conditions and structures of late modernity" (Rowe 2018: 133–34). Unfortunately, these more positive uses of metal music have not permeated social discourses in Latin America.

REFERENCES

Acha, Omar (2018), "The places of critical universalism: Postcolonial and decolonial approaches in context," in C. Roldán, D. Brauer, and J. Rohbeck (eds.), *Philosophy of Globalization*, Berlin: De Gruyter, pp. 95–106. doi: 10.1515/9783110492415-008.

Actualidad (2018), "Guatemala prohíbe la entrada a una banda sueca de metal por 'inmoral' y 'satánica'," *Actualidad RT*, September 27, https://actualidad.rt.com/actualidad/290024-guatemala-prohibir-banda-marduk-suecia-satanico?fbclid=IwAR2PgvIlHjKH9CgqcYkweMtp41ZhXKrKN2HA6QJSp53kYU1hxNINF0lzqgk. Accessed December 8, 2019.

Almeida, Paul and Cordero Ulate, Allen (2016), *Handbook of Social Movements across Latin America*, New York: Springer.

Arraigo (2012), "Fronteras y Horizontes," CD, Buenos Aires: Mondo Tunes.

Avelar, Idelber (2003), "Heavy metal music in postdictatorial Brazil: Sepultura and the coding of nationality in sound," *International Journal of Phytoremediation*, 21:1, pp. 329–46. doi: 10.1080/13569320310001629496.

Avelar, Idelber (2011), "Otherwise national: Locality and power in the art of Sepultura," in J. Wallach, H. M. Berger, and P. D. Greene (eds.), *Metal Rules the Globe: Heavy Metal Music Around the World*, Durham, NC: Duke University Press, pp. 135–58.

Azevedo, Claudia (2012), "Metal in Rio de Janeiro, 1980–2008: An overview," in N. Scott (ed.), *Reflections in the Metal Void*, Oxford: Inter-Disciplinary Press, pp. 89–100.

Banchs, Edward (2016), *Heavy Metal Africa: Life, Passion, and Heavy Metal in the Forgotten Continent*, PA: Word Association Publishers.

Banchs, Edward (2016), "Swahili-tongued devils: Kenya's heavy metal at the crossroads of identity," *Metal Music Studies*, 2:3, pp. 311–24. doi: 10.1386/mms.2.3.311.

Barandiaran, Javiera (2016), "The authority of rules in Chile's contentious environmental politics," *Environmental Politics*, 25:6, pp. 1013–33. doi: 10.1080/09644016.2016.1218156.

Biddle, Ian and Knights, Vanessa (2007), *Music, National Identity and the Politics of Location: Between the Global and the Local*, Surry, England: Ashgate Publishing Ltd.

Calamity (2015), "Imminent Disaster," CD, San Juan, PR: Independent Release.

Calvo, Manuela Belén (2016), "Acerca de la heterogeneidad del rock: El 'aguante' en el heavy metal en Argentina," *El Oído Pensante*, 4:2, pp. 1–19.

Calvo, Manuela Belén (2016), "Almafuerte: Metal pesado argento and its construction of Argentinian nationalism," *Metal Music Studies*, 2:1, pp. 21–38. doi: 10.1386/mms.2.1.21.

Calvo, Manuela Belén (2017), "Metal extremo y globalización en América Latina: Los casos de Hermética (Argentina), Masacre (Colombia) y Brujería (México)," in M. C. Dalmagro and A. Parfeniuk (eds.), *Reflexiones comparadas Desplazamientos, encuentros y contrastes*, Buenos Aires, Argentina: Universidad Nacional de Córdoba, pp. 170–89.

Calvo, Manuela Belén (2018), "Perspectiva indigenista en la música metal de Argentina," *Metal Music Studies*, 4:1, pp. 147–54. doi: 10.1386/mms.4.1.147.

Camisassa, Elena and Moreno, María Laura (2004), *Recuperando la memoria: La historización como posibilidad de superar el fatalismo*, Buenos Aires, Argentina: XI Jornadas de Investigación. Facultad de Psicología – Universidad de Buenos Aires.

Campos Garza, Luciano (2018), "Denuncian en Monterrey censura religiosa contra concierto de rock," *Proceso*, October 14, https://www.proceso.com.mx/555326/denuncian-en-monterrey-censura-religiosa-contra-concierto-de-rock?fbclid=IwAR37oHtS-MYXKblzZc2Ow1XyGeXKNH3jnLPfA12Wl0fc1j5kAiwDm2j0XNo. Accessed December 8, 2019.

Campos Medina, Fernando and Campos Medina, Luis (2012), "The environmental institution in Chile: A political representation of the ecological crisis," *2012 Berlin Conference on the Human Dimensions of Global Environmental Change*, Berlin, pp. 1–20.

Caouette, Dominique and Kapoor, Dip (2016), *Beyond Colonialism, Development and Globalization: Social Movements and Critical Perspectives*, London: Zed Books.

Cervantes, Marco Antonio and Saldaña, Lilliana Patricia (2015), "Hip hop and nueva canción as decolonial pedagogies of epistemic justice," *Decolonization: Indigeneity, Education & Society*, 4:1, pp. 84–108.

Charner, Flora (2019), "Rock music is linked to abortions, says new Brazilian culture official," *CNN*, December 5, https://edition.cnn.com/2019/12/05/americas/bolsonaro-funarte-abortion-intl/index.html?utm_source=fbCNNi&utm_term=link&utm_content=2019-12-05T17%3A32%3A11&utm_medium=social&fbclid=IwAR16DFotf6XZKb5qPT9qYy3RqVonJxqJ8USn23cjVAZPNL6XbGT7ZWoGa8U. Accessed January 21, 2021.

Cheshire, Lynda and Lawrence, Geoffrey (2005), "Neoliberalism, individualisation and community: Regional restructuring in Australia," *Social Identities*, 11:5, pp. 435–45. doi: 10.1080/13504630500407869.

de la Corte Ibáñez, Luis (2000), "La psicología de Ignacio Martín-Baró como psicología social crítica: Una presentación de su obra," *Revista de Psicología General y Aplicada*, 53:6, pp. 437–50.

Clifford-Napoleone, Amber (2015), *Queerness in Heavy Metal Music: Metal Bent*, New York: Routledge.

Clinton, Esther and Wallach, Jeremy (2015), "Recoloring the metal map: Metal and race in global perspective," in T.-M. Karjalainen and K. Kärki (eds.), *Modern Heavy Metal: Markets, Practices and Cultures*, Helsinki, Finland: Department of Management Studies, Aalto University, pp. 274–82, http://iipc.utu.fi/MHM/Clinton.pdf. Accessed April 2, 2019.

Clinton, Esther and Wallach, Jeremy (2019), "Theories of the post-colonial and globalization: Ethnomusicologists grapple with power, history, media, and mobility," *Theory for Ethnomusicology: Histories, Conversations, Insights*, 2nd ed., H. M. Berger and R. Stone (eds.), Upper Saddle River, NJ: Prentice Hall, pp. 114–39.

Dawes, Laina (2013), *What Are You Doing Here?: A Black Woman's Life and Liberation in Heavy Metal*, Brooklyn, NY: Bazillion Points.

Díaz Vergara, Fabiana (2006), *El Duelo y la Memoria, en la Primera y Segunda Generación de Familiares de Detenidos Desaparecidos en Chile*, Santiago, Chile: Universidad Academia de Humanismo Cristiano.

Domínguez Prieto, Olivia (2017), *Transhumancias Musicales y Globalización: El Metal No Tiene Fronteras*, Ciudad de México, México: Plaza y Valdez Editores.

Dos Santos Silva, Melina Aparecida (2018), "Letters, cassette tapes and zines: The circulation of Brazilian heavy metal as a gift system," *Metal Music Studies*, 4:1, pp. 241–49. doi: 10.1386/mms.4.1.241.

Drinot, Paulo (2009), "For whom the eye cries: Memory, monumentality, and the ontologies of violence in Peru," *Journal of Latin American Cultural Studies*, 18:1, pp. 15–32. doi: 10.1080/13569320902819745.

Dunn, Sam and McFayden, Scott (2009), "Global Metal," DVD, USA: Warner Home Video.

Dussel, Enrique (1985), *Philosophy of Liberation*, OR: Wipf and Stock Publishers.

Escobar, Arturo (2010), "Worlds and knowledges otherwise: The Latin American modernity/coloniality research program," *Globalization and the Decolonial Option*, New York: Routledge, pp. 33–64.

Eyerman, Ron and Jamison, Andrew (1998), *Music and Social Movements: Mobilizing Traditions in the Twentieth Century*, New York: Cambridge University Press.

Fanon, Frantz (1952), *Black Skin, White Masks,* New York: Grove Press.

Fanon, Frantz (1965), *The Wretched of the Earth*, New York: Grove Press.

Flórez Flórez, Juliana (2015), *Lecturas Emergentes: El Giro Decolonial en los Movimientos Sociales*, Bogotá, Colombia: Pontificia Universidad Javeriana.

Freire, Paulo (2000), *Pedagogy of the Oppressed*, 30th anniv. ed., New York: Bloomsbury Academics.

González, Juan Pablo (2018), *Thinking about Music from Latin America: Issues and Questions*, London: Lexington Books.

González-Sepúlveda, Osvaldo, Varas-Díaz, Nelson , Mendoza, Sigrid and Rivera-Segarra, Eliut (2015), *The Distorted Island: Heavy Metal Music and Community in Puerto Rico*, Puerto Rico: Puerto Rico Heavy Metal Studies.

Grosfogel, Ramón (2011), "Decolonizing post-colonial studies and paradigms of political-economy: Transmodernity, decolonial thinking, and global coloniality," *Transmodernity – Journal of Peripheral Cultural Production of the Luso-Hispanic World*, 1:1, doi: 10.5964/jspp.v3i1.143.

Grosfogel, Ramón and Cervantez-Rodríguez, Ana (2002), "Unthinking twentieth-century Eurocentric mythologies: Universal knowledges, decolonization and developmentalism," in R. Grosfogel and A. Cervantez-Rodríguez (eds.), *The Modern/Colonial/Capitalist World-System in the Twentieth Century: Global Processes, Antisystemic Movements and the Geopolitics of Knowledge*, Westport, CT: Praeger Press, pp. xi–xxix.

Hill, Rosemary (2013), *Representations and Experiences of Women Hard Rock and Metal Fans in the Imaginary Community*, York: University of York.

Hill, Rosemary Lucy (2016), " 'Power has a penis': Cost reduction, social exchange and sexism in metal – reviewing the work of Sonia Vasan," *Metal Music Studies*, 2:3, pp. 263–71. doi: 10.1386/mms.2.3.263.

Iglesias Saldaña, Margarita (2005), "Trauma social y memoria colectiva," *Historia Actual Online*, 6, pp. 169–75.

James Díaz, Cristhian (2010), "Hacia una pedagogía en clave decolonial: Entre aperturas, búsquedas y posibilidades," *Tabula Rasa*, 13, pp. 217–33.

Kahn-Harris, Keith (2007), *Extreme Metal: Music and Culture on the Edge*, London: Bloomsbury Academic.

Kahn-Harris, Keith (2012), " 'You are from Israel and that is enough to hate you forever': Racism, globalization, and play within the global extreme metal scene," in J. Wallach, H. Berger, and P. Greene (eds.), *Metal Rules the Globe*, New York: Duke University Press, pp. 200–26.

Kaltmeier, Olaf (2019), "Rockin' for Pachamama," in O. Kaltmeier and W. Raussert (eds.), *Sonic Politics: Music and Social Movements in the Americas*, London: Routledge, pp. 179–204.

Karjalainen, Toni-Matti (2018), *Sounds of Origin: In Heavy Metal Music*, Newcastle: Cambridge Scholars Publishing.

Karmy Bolton, Eileen (2014), " 'Remembrance is not enough …': The cantata popular Santa María de iquique forty years after its release," in P. Vila (ed.), *The Militant Song Movement in Latin America: Chile, Uruguay and Argentina. 2*, Lanham, ML: Lexington Books, pp. 45–70.

Lander, Edgardo (2000), *La Colonialidad del Saber: Eurocentrismo y Ciencias Sociales – Perspectivas Latinoamericanas*, Buenos Aires: CLACSO.

LeVine, Mark (2008), *Heavy Metal Islam: Rock, Resistance, and the Struggle for the Soul of Islam*, New York: Three Rivers Press.

Loomba, Ania (1998), *Colonialism-Postcolonialism*, London: Taylor & Francis.

Maldonado-Torres, Nelson (2007), "On the coloniality of being: Contributions to the development of a concept," *Cultural Studies*, 21:2&3, pp. 240–70.

Marrero, Mayi (2018), *Prohibido Cantar*, Ponce, PR: Mariana Editores.

Marsh, Hazel (2017), *Hugo Chávez, Alí Primera and Venezuela: The Politics of Music in Latin America*, London: Palgrave Macmillan.

Martín-Baró, Ignacio (1994), *Writings for a Liberation Psychology*, Cambridge, MA: Harvard University Press.

McFarland, Pancho (2018), *Toward a Chican@ Hip Hop Anti-Colonialism*, New York: Routledge.

McSherry, Patrice J. (2015), *Chilean New Song: The Political Power of Music 1960s–1973*, Philadelphia, PA: Temple University Press.

Mendoza, Sigrid, Varas-Díaz, Nelson, Rivera-Segarra, Eliut and Vélez, Carlos (2018), "Media representations of metal music in the Dominican Republic: Between oppression and social resistance," *Metal Music Studies*, 4:1, pp. 197–208. doi: 10.1386/mms.4.1.197.

Metallica (1988), "And Justice for All," CD, New York: Elektra.

Mignolo, Walter D. (2000), *Local Histories/Global Designs: Coloniality, Subaltern Knowledges, and Border Thinking*, NJ: Princeton University Press.

Mignolo, Walter D. (2010), "Introduction: Coloniality of power and de-colonial thinking," *Globalization and the Decolonial Option*, New York: Routledge, pp. 1–21.

Mignolo, Walter D. (2011), *The Darker Side of Western Modernity: Global Futures, Decolonial Options*, Durham and London: Duke University Press.

Mignolo, Walter D. and Walsh, Catherine E. (2018), *On Decoloniality: Concepts, Analytics, Praxis*, Durham, NC: Duke University Press.

Miquian (2015), "Tlaltecuhtli," CD, Mexico City: Heart of Steel Records.

Mojica, Julio (2010), "Neoliberalism, civic participation and the salmon industry in southern Chile: Spatial patterns of civic participation on the island of Chiloé," Stanford, CA: Stanford University, Spatial History Lab, pp. 1–6.

Molinero, Carlos and Vila, Pablo (2014), "Atahualpa Yupanqui: The Latin American precursor of the militant song movement," in P. Vila (ed.), *The Militant Song Movement in Latin America: Chile, Uruguay and Argentina. 2*, Lanham, ML: Lexington Books.

Morris, Nancy (2014), "New song in Chile: Half a century of musical activism," in P. Vila (ed.), *The Militant Song Movement in Latin America: Chile, Uruguay and Argentina*, Lanham, ML: Lexington Books, pp. 19–44.

Negrón-Muntaner, Frances (2017), "Introduction," in *Sovereign Acts: Contesting Colonialism Across Indigenous Nations & Latinx America*, Tucson, AZ: University of Arizona Press, pp. 3–36.

Negrón-Muntaner, Frances (2017), "The look of sovereignty: Style and politics in the Young Lords," in F. Negrón-Muntaner (ed.), *Sovereign Acts: Contesting Colonialism Across Indigenous Nations & Latinx America*, Tucson, AZ: University of Arizona Press, pp. 254–84.

Neustadat, Robert (2004), "Music as memory and torture: Sounds of repression and protest in Chile and Argentina," *Chasqui*, 33:1, pp. 128–37.

Nevárez Araújo, Daniel (2021), "Metal migration: The Latin American diasporic experience in heavy metal," in N. Varas-Díaz, D. Nevárez Araújo, and E. Rivera-Segarra (eds.), *Heavy Metal Music in Latin America: Perspectives from the Distorted South*, London: Lexington Press, pp. 305–31.

Nuñez, María de la Luz and Rivas, Arturo (2018), " 'Musical representation in times of violence': The origins of Peruvian metal music during the general crisis of the eighties," *Metal Music Studies*, 4:1, pp. 219–29. doi: 10.1386/mms.4.1.219.

Ocaña, Alexander Ortiz, López, Arias, Pedrozo Conedo, Maria Isabel, and Esther, Zaira (2018), "Hacia una pedagogía decolonial en/desde el sur global," *Revista Nuestra América*, 6, pp. 195–222.

Overell, Rosemary (2014), *Affective Intensities in Extreme Music Scenes*, London: Palgrave Macmillan.

Pacini Hernández, Deborah, Fernández L'Hoeste, Héctor, and Zolov, Eric (2004), "Mapping rock music cultures across the Americas," in D. Pacini Hernández, H. Fernández L'Hoeste, and E. Zolov (eds.), *Rockin' Las Américas: The Global Politics of Rock in Latin/o America*, Pittsburgh, PA: University of Pittsburgh Press, pp. 1–21.

Pack, Christian (2018), " 'Severed Reality': Representations of reality in Salvadoran tribal metal," *Metal Music Studies*, 4:1, pp. 187–96. doi: 10.1386/mms.4.1.187.

Pavón, Michelle (2019), "Artistas hondureños condenan censura de película 'Slayer'," *Conexihon*, November 8, http://www.conexihon.hn/index.php/libertad-de-expresion/1287-artistas-hondurenos-condenan-censura-de-pelicula-slayer?fbclid=IwAR07yHiRPvk4IF21 Dvs587RnAl9cKVkIu2__MBQXc1YEaZN6K7ajF7SKt6w. Accessed December 8, 2019.

Phillipov, Michelle (2012), *Death Metal and Music Criticism: Analysis at the Limits*, MD: Lexington Books.

Pino-Ojeda, Waleska (2004), "A detour to the past: Memory and mourning in Chilean post-authoritarian rock," in D. Pacini Hernández, H. Fernández L'Hoeste, and E. Zolov (eds.), *Rockin' Las Americas: The Global Politics of Rock In Latin/o America*, Pittsburgh, PA: University of Pittsburgh Press, pp. 290–311.

Pizarro, Angélca and Wittebroodt, Ingrid (2002), "La impunidad: Efectos en la elaboración del duelo en madres de detenidos desaparecidos," *Castalia – Revista de Psicología de la Academia*, pp. 115–35.

Quijano, Aníbal (2000), "Colonialidad del Poder, Eurocentrismo y América Latina," in E. Lander (ed.), *La Colonialidad del Saber: Eurocentrismo y Ciencias Sociales – Perspectivas Latinoamericanas*, Buenos Aires, Argentina: CLACSO, pp. 122–51.

Quijano, Aníbal (2010), "Coloniality and modernity/rationality," in *Globalization and the Decolonial Option*, New York: Routledge, pp. 22–32.

Raheja, Michelle (2010), *Reservation Reelism: Redfacing, Visual Sovereignty, and Representation of Native Americans in Film*, Lincoln, NE: University of Nebraska Press.

Ratner, Carl (2015), "Recuperación y promoción de las ideas de Martín-Baró sobre psicología, cultura y transformación social," *Teoría y Crítica de la Psicología*, 6, pp. 48–76.

Rivera Cusicanqui, Silvia (2015), *Sociología de la Imagen: Miradas ch'ixi desde la Historia Andina*, Buenos Aires, Argentina: Tinta Limón.

Rivera Cusicanqui, Silvia (2020), *Ch'ixinakax utxiwa: A Reflection on the Practices and Discourses of Decolonization*, Cambridge, UK: Polity Press.

Robaina, María Celia (2015), *Impactos psicosociales en los hijos de detenidos – desaparecidos percibidos en su vida actual como adultos*, Uruguay: Universidad de la República.

Rowe, Paula (2018), *Heavy Metal Youth Identities: Researching the Musical Empowerment of Youth Transitions and Psychosocial Wellbeing*, Bingley: Emerald Publishing.

Sabbath, Black (1970), "Paranoid," LP, UK: Vertigo.

Sánchez, Jaime (2005), "El fatalismo como forma de ser en el mundo del latinoamericano," *Psicogente*, 8:13, pp. 55–65.

Sánchez, Maximiliano (2014), *Thrash Metal: Del Sonido al Contenido*, Santiago, Chile: RIL.

Santos, Boaventura de Sousa (2018), *The End of the Cognitive Empire: The Coming of Age of Epistemologies of the South*, London: Duke University Press.

Santos, Boaventura de Sousa (2020), "Toward and aesthetics of the epistemologies of the south: Manifesto in twenty-two theses," in B. de Sousa Santos and M. P. Meneses (eds.), *Epistemologies of the South: Knowledges Born in the Struggle – Constructing the Epistemologies of the Global South*, New York: Routledge, pp. 117–25.

Scaricaciottoli, Emiliano (2016), *Se Nos Ve de Negro Vestidos: Siete Enfoques sobre el Heavy Metal Argentino*, Buenos Aires, Argentina: Ediciones La Parte Maldita.

Scaricaciottoli, Emiliano (2018), *Parricidas: Mapa Rabioso del Metal Argentino Contemporaneo*, Buenos Aires, Argentina: La Parte Maldita.

Schwarzstein, Dora (1995), "La historia oral en América Latina," *Historia, Antropología y Fuente Oral*, 14, pp. 39–50. doi: 10.18234/secuencia.v0i01.98.

Scott, Niall (2012), "Heavy metal and the deafening threat of the apolitical," *Popular Music History*, 6:1, pp. 224–39. doi: 10.1558/pomh.v6i1/2.224.

Scott, Niall, (2016), "Heavy metal as resistance," in B. G. Walter, G. Riches, D, Snell, B. Bardine and B.G. Walter (eds.), *Heavy Metal Studies and Popular Culture*, New York: Palgrave, pp. 19–35.

Snaza, Nathan and Netherton, Jason (2016), "Community at the extremes: The death metal underground as being-in-common," *Metal Music Studies*, 2:3, pp. 341–56. doi: 10.1386/mms.2.3.341.

Soto, Evelyn (2008), "Canciones y memoria: El caso de los detenidos desaparecidos," *Isla Flotante*, pp. 49–61.

Stephen Lim, Chin Ming (2019), *Contextual Biblical Hermeneutics as Multicentric Dialogue*, *Contextual Biblical Hermeneutics as Multicentric Dialogue*, Netherlands: Brill. doi: 10.1163/9789004399259.

Thibodeau, Anthony J. (2014), *Anti-Colonial Resistance and Indigenous Identity in North American Heavy Metal*, Bowling Green, OH: Bowling Green State University.

Tlostanova, Madina (2019), "The postcolonial condition, the decolonial option, and the post-socialist intervention," in M. Albretch (ed.), *Postcolonialism Cross-Examined: Multi-directional Perspectives on Imperial and Colonial Pasts and the Newcolonial Present*, New York: Routledge, pp. 165–78. doi: 10.4324/9780367222543-9.

Tren Loco (2006), "Sangresur," CD, Buenos Aires: Yugular Records.

Turner, Joe (2018), "Review of the books 'Global Metal Music and Culture: Current Directions in Metal Studies' and 'Connecting Metal to Culture: Unity in Disparity'," *Popular Music*, 37:3, pp. 509–12. doi: 10.1017/s0261143018000314.

Varas-Díaz, Nelson, Mendoza, Sigrid, Rivera, Eliut, and González, Osvaldo (2016), "Metal at the fringe: A historical perspective on Puerto Rico's underground metal scene," in B. Gardenour Walter, G. Riches, D. Snell, and B. Bardine (eds.), *Heavy Metal Studies and Popular Culture*, London: Palgrave Macmillan, pp. 99–120.

Varas-Díaz, Nelson, González-Sepúlveda, Osvaldo, and Rivera, Eliut (2016), *The Metal Islands: Culture, History and Politics in Caribbean Heavy Metal Music [Film]*, San Juan, PR: Puerto Rico Heavy Metal Studies.

Varas-Díaz, Nelson, Rivera, Eliut, González, Osvaldo, Mendoza, Sigrid, and Morales, Eric (2017), "Heavy metal as a vehicle for critical culture in Latin America and the Caribbean: Challenging traditional female gender roles though music," in *Connecting Metal and Culture: Unity in Disparity*, London: Intellect, pp. 57–80.

Varas-Díaz, Nelson, Rivera-Segarra, Eliut, Mendoza, Sigrid, Díaz, Xaymara, Vélez, Carlos, Morales, Eric, Bracero, Rafael, and Morell Fausto, James (2018), *Songs of Injustice: Heavy Metal Music in Latin America*, San Juan, PR: Puerto Rico Heavy Metal Studies.

Varas-Díaz, Nelson, Azevedo, Claudia, and Nevárez, Daniel (2018), "Metal in Latin America," *Metal Music Studies*, 4:1, pp. 131–35. doi: 10.1386/mms.4.1.131.

Varas-Díaz, Nelson, González-Sepúlveda, Osvaldo, and Rivera Amador, Andrés (2018), "From the 'Patio' to the 'Agency': The emergence and structuring of metal music in revolutionary Cuba," *Metal Music Studies*, 4:1, pp. 137–46. doi: 10.1386/mms.4.1.137.

Varas-Díaz, Nelson and Mendoza, Sigrid (2015), "Ethnicity, politics and otherness in Caribbean heavy metal music: Experiences from Puerto Rico, Dominican Republic and Cuba," in T. M. Karjalainen and K. Kärki (eds.), *Modern Heavy Metal: Market, Practices and Culture*, Helsinki, Finland: Department of Management Studies, Aalto University, pp. 291–99.

Varas-Díaz, Nelson and Mendoza, Sigrid (2018), "Ancestral morbid fascination: Reformulating local culture through metal music in Puerto Rico," *Metal Music Studies*, 4:1, pp. 175–86. doi: 10.1386/mms.4.1.175.

Varas-Díaz, Nelson, Mendoza, Sigrid, and Morales, Eric (2016), "Porous communities: Critical interactions between metal music and local culture in the Caribbean context," in N. Varas-Díaz and N. Scott (eds.), *Heavy Metal Music and the Communal Experience*, London: Lexington Books, pp. 101–23.

Varas-Díaz, Nelson and Morales, Eric (2018), "Decolonial reflections in Latin American metal: Religion, politics and resistance," *Theologiques*, 26:1, pp. 229–50.

Varas-Díaz, Nelson, Rivera-Segarra, Eliut, and Nevárez, Daniel (2019), "Coloniality and resistance in Latin American metal music: Death as experience and strategy," *Hispanic Issues Online*, 23, pp. 226–51.

Varas-Díaz, Nelson and Rivera, Eliut (2014), "Heavy metal music in the Caribbean setting: Politics and language at the periphery," in E. Abbey and C. Helb (eds.), *Hardcore, Punk and*

Other Junk: Aggressive Sounds in Contemporary Music, Lanham, MD: Lexington Press, pp. 73–90.

Varas-Díaz, Nelson and Scott, Niall (2016), *Heavy Metal Music and the Communal Experience*, London: Lexington Books.

Vila, Pablo (2014), "Introduction", in P. Vila (ed.), *The Militant Song Movement in Latin America: Chile, Uruguay and Argentina*, Lanham, ML: Lexington Books, pp. 1–18.

Wallach, Jeremy (2003), " 'Goodbye my blind majesty': Music, language, and politics in the Indonesian underground," in H. M. Berger and M. T. Carroll (eds.), *Global Pop, Local Language*, Jackson: University Press of Mississippi, pp. 53–86.

Wallach, Jeremy (2005), "Underground rock music and democratization in Indonesia," *World Literature Today*, September, pp. 16–21.

Wallach, Jeremy (2019), "Decolonizing metal studies: The documentary films of Nelson Varas-Díaz and Puerto Rico heavy metal studies," *MUSICultures2*, 46:1, pp. 163–66.

Wallach, Jeremy (2020), "Global rock as postcolonial soundtrack," in A. Moore and P. Carr (eds.), *Bloomsbury Handbook for Rock Music Research*, New York: Bloomsbury, pp. 469–85.

Wallach, Jeremy, Berger, Harris M., and Greene, Paul D. (2012), *Metal Rules the Globe: Heavy Metal Music around the World*, Durham, NC: Duke University Press.

Wallach, Jeremy and Clinton, Esther (2019), "Theories of the post-colonial and globalization: Ethnomusicologists grapple with power, history, media, and mobility," in H. M. Berger and R. Stone (eds.), *Theory for Ethnomusicology: Histories, Conversations, Insights*, 2nd ed., NJ: Prentice Hall, pp. 1114–39.

Walser, Robert (1993), *Running with the Devil: Power, Gender, and Madness in Heavy Metal Music*, Hannover, NH: University Press of New England.

Weinstein, Deena (1991), *Heavy Metal: The Music and Its Culture*, Boston, MA: Da Capo Press.

Weinstein, Deena (2011), "The globalization of metal", in J. Wallach, H. M. Berger, and P. D. Greene (eds.), *Metal Rules the Globe: Heavy Metal Music Around the World*, Durham, NC: Duke University Press, pp. 34–60.

Williams, Justin A. (2017), "Rapping postcoloniality: Akala's 'The Thieves Banquet' and neocolonial critique," *Popular Music and Society*, 40:1, pp. 89–101. doi: 10.1080/03007766.2016.1230457.

2

Colonialism Is Still Here/Metal Is Still Here – Puerto Rico

I was aware that engaging in ethnographic work in Puerto Rico would represent a challenge, particularly because of my proximity to the setting. At the time I had lived most of my life on the Island, and as a teenager I had been part of the local metal scene for some time. More than 25 years had passed since my engagement with it and many things had changed, but I still remembered the names of important musicians and bands. Although this information would help me regain access to the local scene, things had changed so much in my absence that sometimes it felt like a completely different setting. My initial outings were mainly to concerts hosted by local bands, mostly in the San Juan metropolitan area. Eventually, my presence there allowed me to engage in interviews with fans and musicians to document the history of the scene.[1]

Community formation via heavy metal music was probably the very first subject matter that local contacts wanted to talk about. I was intrigued about this thematic choice, as I initially expected them to talk mostly about music and local bands. However, contrary to my expectations, almost all scene members constantly spoke about the communal nature of the local metal scene, how it served as a protective space for them, and how solidarity was a major staple shared among them. As a researcher I was immediately intrigued by this issue, particularly with the potential limits of this communal endeavor they described. I knew that understanding how the scene came together was important, but being aware of the challenges to that unity was also crucial. What were the major tensions within this communal experience? This question was a guiding consideration in my research process, although, as I would soon find out, scene members would become evidently tense about discussing it in detail.

Several months into the project, people in the local scene became more accustomed to my presence and opened up about subject matter they initially did not want to talk about (Varas-Díaz et al. 2016). Tensions within the scene finally came to the forefront the longer I conversed with its actors. Some of the most frequently mentioned tensions included problems between bands, the firing of band members, and the competition between local promoters who booked international bands on similar dates, thus impacting each other's potential income. Although these tensions initially dominated our conversations, in time a deeper debate began to emerge. Specifically, tensions related to each respective scene member's political opinions regarding Puerto Rico's colonial relation to the United States. Where some scene members saw a colonial and oppressive relation, others saw a link between nations that needed to be maintained and valued.

Some scene members were quick to point out that the debate over Puerto Rico's political status had made it into the music of some local bands. For example, at the time of my ethnographic work, the local band Tavú released their album entitled *Clamor Victorium, Clamor Silentii,* which included the single "Sin Miedo" ("Without Fear"). The song directly addressed Puerto Rico's colonial relation with the United States, its lyrics inherently warning listeners: "The winds from the North are crushing your way of life, and nobody protects your right to exist." It goes on to describe the challenging nature of confronting the colonial situation and the stresses it amplifies: "It's not easy being the first one. It's not easy breaking the ice. It's not easy to bear the weight of walking without fear!" Upon listening to these lyrics, I immediately thought that the band was courageous in tackling this subject so explicitly, particularly because many members in the local scene would not share this political position. It seemed to me that communal formation was important to them, but not at the expense of silencing their political views regarding Puerto Rico. This explicit political position, one challenging Puerto Rico's colonial political situation via metal music, merits attention. Before doing so in this chapter, I will first provide a brief summary of Puerto Rico's colonial history.

The shadow of Puerto Rican colonial history

The Commonwealth of Puerto Rico is an archipelago that consists of various islands, which have an estimated population of 3.6 million. The largest of these islands, comprising an area 114 miles long and 42 miles wide, is in turn the smallest of the Greater Antilles located in the Caribbean. Puerto Rico has never been a politically independent nation since its encounter with the Europeans. Spain ruled it for over four centuries beginning in 1493. This all changed at the very end of the Spanish-American War in 1898. Through the Treaty of Paris, Puerto Rico was ceded to the United States as part of the spoils of war (Rivera Ramón 2001; Varas-Díaz and Serrano-García 2003). As a result of this process, Puerto Rico became a non-incorporated territory of the United States. In 1952, the Commonwealth of Puerto Rico (*Estado Libre Asociado* in Spanish, or Free Associated State as a literal translation to English) was established to allow for a locally administered government, still under complete supervision of the United States. This entails that the US Congress holds total control over areas such as the applicability of federal law and the jurisdiction of federal courts, citizenship, commerce, currency, migration, patent laws, communications, mail, customs, air and sea transportation, military service, international relations, and treaty development.

Throughout the more than 120 years of the United States control over Puerto Rico, there have been evident efforts to integrate Puerto Ricans into the US melting pot. Some of the methods used for this purpose include: (1) the imposition of English as the official language of the public education system for over 40 years, (2) compulsory participation in US military conflicts since 1917, and (3) the systematic political persecution of pro-independence advocates (Seijo Bruno 1989; Picó 2005). This last example is probably the most dramatic. For example, in 1948 the US government, in collaboration with local politicians, imposed Law 53 (also known as the Gag Law), which made it a crime for any person within the territory to sing tunes that could be considered patriotic. This extended to the possession or the act of displaying a Puerto Rican flag, among other actions that were considered subversive at the time (Acosta 1987). Law 53 existed until 1957, when it was declared unconstitutional. After the establishment of the Commonwealth of Puerto Rico in 1952, there have been various efforts to change the colonial status of the archipelago, mainly via referendums. None of these efforts have had any significant effects on the current colonial status.

The colonial nature of the US-Puerto Rico relationship has been widely researched and documented in the social sciences literature. In general it highlights the challenges of a country with distinctive Hispanic cultural influences, confronted with a vague integration into the United States (Varas-Díaz and Serrano-García 2003). Puerto Rico finds itself deeply submerged in what academics have labeled the "colonial dilemma" (Meléndez and Meléndez 1999). It is a Caribbean community absorbed as a non-incorporated territory into a larger and culturally different nation. This, in turn, has led to the rejection, degradation, and devalorization of its history and what is perceived as local or endemic to it. Still, it is vitally important to explore how these negative interpretations of the colonized are challenged and brought into question. Metal music in Puerto Rico has played an important role in this process.

In order to understand the role of metal music in challenging its social context, and in this case coloniality, we must highlight some of the specific characteristics of the colonial experiences described in Chapter 1. These characteristics specifically tackle how the colonial power addresses the colonial subject and what the latter comes to understand as true and immutable about this group. Only then can we really understand how these visions are in turn challenged through metal music. Colonial discourse aims to devalue the characteristics associated with the local. This has historically included forcing changes upon local language, customs, and overall culture. The colonial experience has also sought to isolate communities from interaction with others that share similar historical backgrounds and potential parallel interests as a way to erase their collective memory (and avoid any type of collective upheaval). Finally, it has sought to use violence against the population as a way to control its future and potential avenues of development.

Two seminal Puerto Rican bands have incorporated a decolonial challenge in their musical output. Throughout my work, I had the opportunity to interview members of the bands Puya and Dantesco on several occasions. Although these bands come from opposites ends of the metal genre spectrum (Nu Metal and Doom, respectively), they share a concern for the colonial situation of the Island. In this process, I came to understand how their music challenged negative portrayals of colonized subjects. Each of these bands warrants its own close examination, which will be addressed below.

Puya's role in Puerto Rico's heavy metal scene

Puya was formed in 1992 out of the remnants of the experimental trio Whisker Biscuit. With the addition of a singer, Puya adopted a heavier musical style while also increasingly moving toward integrating local instrumentation and arrangements in their music. For some people in the local scene, Puya became the most successful band to emerge from Puerto Rico. For example, they are the only local band to have played at the Ozzfest festival. They also toured alongside names such as Slipknot, Pantera, Red Hot Chili Peppers, Sepultura, and KISS (Varas-Díaz and Rivera 2014). The band is still the only local group to have been signed by a major record label in the United States. However, restricting a description of the band to their success would limit an in-depth understanding of their decolonial contributions. To understand Puya's role in Puerto Rico's metal scene, one needs to take into account the context in which they emerged.

The band originated in what I have described elsewhere as the second period in the development of Puerto Rico's metal scene (Varas-Díaz, Mendoza, Rivera, and González 2016). After an initial period in the development of the local scene, this 7-year "survival period" (1993–2000) was characterized by cultural debates on the Island that would influence the development of metal music. For example, the emergence of the *Rock en Español* ("Rock in Spanish") movement in Latin America had a great impact in Puerto Rico's metal scene as many Spanish-speaking bands took over the local airwaves. With the slogan *rock en tu idioma* ("rock in your language"), they seemed to validate local national identities and their ties to the Latin American region. Metal sung in English was then positioned as a foreign artifact, while Rock in Spanish would represent a way to appropriate those musical styles and infuse them with a local flare (Varas-Díaz et al. 2016). This movement echoed larger ongoing cultural and political debates in Puerto Rico that were simultaneously taking place. For example, during this period Puerto Ricans voted twice in referendums whose intention was to determine the island's relation to the United States (1993 and 1998). Also, the Puerto Rican legislature would open a space for the debate on the use of Spanish or English as the official language for the Island. Finally, Puerto Ricans would engage in massive protests to close US military bases throughout the Island. It is in this context of cultural debates over national identity, culture, and politics that Puya surfaced as a force to be reckoned with.

Puya directly challenged the colonial situation in Puerto Rico via four distinct mechanisms: (1) the integration of local instrumentation and musical genres into metal music as a reaffirmation of the importance of local identity discourses, (2) the consideration of the direct effects of the colonial experience via music (i.e., military practices carried out by the United States in Puerto Rico), (3) the establishment of linkages to metal scenes throughout Latin America and the Caribbean, and (4) the critical exploration of the diversity found within metal music via the integration of discussions on race and ethnicity into lyrical content and embodied practices (i.e., dancing styles). Let us address each of these mechanisms in detail.

Integration of local instrumentation and musical genres into metal music

One of the most salient differences between Puya and a prototypical metal band has to do with their musical arrangements and the integration of salsa music into their sound. This mixture of musical styles would inevitably entail changes to how metal songs are created and played. The addition of new instrumentation would quickly follow, and two elements would stand out: wind and percussive instruments. For example, the inclusion of trumpets and trombones would help link them with the deep history of salsa music, which was endemic to the Island. Melodies that would usually be carried out by an electric guitar would be assigned to these wind instruments, infusing the heavily distorted guitar-driven background with local elements. More importantly, percussion instruments like *conga*, *bongó*, and *timbales* would further cement the hybrid[2] nature of their music, adding textures previously absent in the genre (see Figure 2.1).

Exploring the integration of these rhythmic instruments in metal music needs to be understood in all its complexity. On the one hand, it allowed for new sounds to emerge within the realm of metal music. On the other, it linked the band to

FIGURE 2.1: Puya's rhythm section during a concert in Puerto Rico. Photo provided by Nelson Varas-Díaz.

geographical spaces that were inherently different to those with which metal had been traditionally associated, specifically Europe and the United States. Several of these instruments are of Afro-Caribbean descent. Therefore, their presence connects the music to the deep histories of the African slave trade and African culture's presence in the Caribbean region in general (i.e., *congas* and *bongos*). Others instruments also present were more recent in development and particularly linked to the neighboring island of Cuba (i.e., *timbales*).[3] In time, these instruments would find their way to Puerto Rico and influence local Afro-Caribbean music. In choosing the instruments they would use to create their music, Puya would help change metal music to recognize the African and Caribbean roots that were part of their histories.

When I asked about the integration of these rhythmic instruments in Puya's music, drummer Eduardo Paniagua mentioned the following:

As a drummer, I believe it's been a blessing being able to incorporate traditional Latin instruments and rhythms to our music. It has helped me grow as a musician, and it has brought me closer to my roots. The new musical arrangements have also given our music an edge that metal music has never had before.

An even more challenging integration of local instrumentation to metal music would come in Puya's use of the *cuatro*, Puerto Rico's national instrument (see Figure 2.2). Shaped like a small guitar, the instrument has ten strings separated into five pairs. It is commonly used to play Puerto Rican traditional music, which is closely linked to life in the countryside or the inner part of the island. The instrument was incorporated into Puya's music during the band's later albums, specifically their release entitled *Areyto*[4] (Puya 2019). The song "Ni Antes Ni Después" (Neither Before Nor After) skillfully uses the instrument to infuse the heavy distorted guitars with an almost whimsical melodic accompaniment. The instrument would be even more prominent in guitarist Ramón Ortiz's subsequent projects, which include Ankla and his solo project Ortiz. In an interview, he mentioned the following regarding the use of the instrument:

FIGURE 2.2: Puya's guitarist Ramón Ortiz playing the *cuatro* atop his electric guitar. Photo provided by Nelson Varas-Díaz.

I wanted to reinvent it to make it sound exciting, and one of the elements I hadn't truly explored with Puya was *jíbaro* music[5] and the use of the *cuatro*. So, around 2002, I got my first *cuatro*; I bought it, I had it at home [...] it was mine. I said to myself, "I'm going to explore [sounds] with it." It was great timing: I started incorporating it to what I was doing for Ankla, even though the songs were very heavy and extremely dense melodically speaking; I tried to make it fit, I tried to feature the sound of the *cuatro* because it gave [the music] an exotic twist.

During my multiple conversations with Ramón Ortiz, he explained that the *cuatro* was part of his early years, when he played local music with his family members in Puerto Rico. Although the guitar was his main instrument, consuming most of his playing, the *cuatro* was there as a reminder of local culture and the ties to his Puerto Rican identity. Ramón was not shy to recognize that his father did not approve of his devotion to the electric guitar and metal music over local music. Still, later in his life, Ortiz would integrate the *cuatro* to his music as a way to meld these two worlds. I spoke to multiple metal guitarists in Puerto Rico that started out playing the *cuatro* and then moved on to the electric guitar; none, however, had integrated its sound into metal music at the time. When asked about the integration, Ortiz explained the following:

I understand that giving a cultural identity to the music is important. It is what makes you different from the sea of bands throughout the world looking to do exactly the same thing. I believe this is why Sepultura [the Brazilian metal band] became one of the largest bands in metal. They made that choice: "We will integrate our cultural identity to our musical fusion." That makes it even heavier and larger, because you are linking it to an issue of culture, an identity, and a country. You are linking it to a history. When you combine that with music, it can give you a lot of strength. [...] It is interesting for those who are open minded and who accept it, because there will always be people who say, "This is not traditional metal." Whatever [...] that has never concerned me much.

Puya aimed to integrate local instrumentation and arrangements to their music as a way to highlight Puerto Rican culture within the world of metal music. Although the mixture of instrumentation was problematic for some who perceived it as too experimental to be considered metal, Puya is still credited in the local scene (and beyond) for their musical experimentation. Their discussion of local identities was also manifested in their lyrical content, which addressed coloniality explicitly.

Addressing the direct effects of coloniality via music

Another important characteristic of Puya's music is its immediate connection to the Puerto Rican colonial experience via its lyrics. While most bands on the Island would shy away from directly addressing the colonial situation and its consequences, Puya would do so directly. Among the several instances in which they have done so, their defense of the island of Vieques stands out.

Vieques is a small island located to the southeast of Puerto Rico. It is one of the municipalities of the larger island, inhabited by approximately 9301 individuals who are of Puerto Rican descent and, therefore, US citizens (Census Bureau 2010b). The small municipal Island has served as a metaphor for US colonialism during the past decades. The navy controlled the western and eastern ends of the Island between 1941 and 1950, claiming for itself about two thirds of the territory. Almost all of the western territory was used primarily as a naval ammunition depot (Rourke 2001). The remaining eastern section of the Island was used by US military forces, beginning in the early 1940s, for training exercises involving ship-to-shore gunfire, air-to-ground bombing by naval aircraft, marine amphibious landings, and live-fire exercises (i.e., exercises with explosive ammunition). Throughout the years, a wide array of military weapons have been tested in Vieques lands and waters, causing damage to the Island's natural environment, historic resources, and archeological sites. This damage has extended to the people themselves, as the remains of these exercises have impacted the residents' health (i.e., higher incidence of cancer and other diseases, when compared to other populations) and overall safety. The civilian population was basically landlocked between two testing ranges, making their homes a de facto prison. This unilateral decision to use Vieques as a shooting range evidences even further the colonial dimensions of the relationship between Puerto Rico and the United States. Even today, there are still parts of the Island that cannot be accessed due to the threat of potentially active explosives.

On April 19, 1999, an accident in one of these shooting ranges killed a local security guard by the name of David Sanes (Ruiz Kullan 2010). The death lit the fire of an island-wide movement that sought to force the US Navy out of Vieques. International attention was placed on the small island. Many locals penetrated these restricted shooting ranges as an act of protest, with many facing arrest in the process. A mix of international pressure and reduced interest in the Caribbean region after the end of the Cold War fostered the decision by the US Navy to leave Vieques completely on May 1, 2003 (Faul 2003). Yet to this day, Vieques has not been properly decontaminated and its inhabitants continue to suffer the health consequences of military testing.

International pressure placed on the US Navy to leave the island of Vieques during the late 1990s and early 2000s relied heavily on individuals who used culture to bring attention to the dilemma. Artists, writers, and painters lent their work to the protests and managed to bring attention to the situation. Of course, this artistic support for Vieques would bring to the surface one important question: What did metal fans and musicians think and do in the midst of this struggle? Puya made their position explicit.

As part of their second release with a major label, Puya's album *Union* included a song entitled "Pa'ti, Pa'mi." The song addressed the plight of the people of Vieques calling for the protection of nature and a granting of power back to the people. The song mixed traditional metal distorted guitar riffs with funk-tinged arrangements, continuing with Puya's style of fusing musical genres. It quickly became one of Puya's most recognized tunes from their second album and a favorite among locals. The video released for the song was eye catching as it included photos and videos of the military tactics that had been at play on the Island. The disastrous ecological consequences of the bombing ranges, as well as the plight of local fishermen, were portrayed. The video also included shocking images of local and federal law enforcement agencies arresting protestors that crossed over to the shooting ranges in order to stop the military exercises.

The song's lyrics would directly address the colonial nature of Puerto Rico's relation to the United States (see lyrics in Box 2.1). In them, the United States is portrayed as *un imperio que va en caída* ("a crumbling empire"), which is taking away the power from the local people. *Poder para la gente* ("power to the people") is a chant that takes over the song during its final verses. Puya used its music as a call to action to challenge Puerto Rico's colonial dilemma, a dilemma that was seen in full display during the 1990s, particularly in the municipal island of Vieques.

Establishing linkages to metal scenes throughout Latin America and the Caribbean

As mentioned earlier in this chapter, the colonial experience isolates communities from interaction with others that share similar historical backgrounds and potential parallel interests. This isolation is both instrumental and ideological. For example, Puerto Rico is limited in its ability to establish economic international collaborations based on restrictions placed by the United States on its trade and ports of entry. This isolation also manifests in more ideological ways. For example, many islanders highlight their association to the United States with more frequency

Box 2.1 "Pa'ti, Pa'mi," Union, *composed by Puya (Puerto Rico) – 2001.*

Pa'ti, pa'mi	Get it, got it
Pa'ti – ¡lluvia!	Get it – rain!
Pa'ti, pa'mi	Get it, got it
Pa'ti – ¡lluvia!	Get it – rain!
Oye que te está llamando	Calling you out loud
Mira que te está llorando	Crying their heart out
Porque de ellas está abusando	You're wearing 'em out
La máquina viene a destruir	The machine's here to drown
Tierra, agua y aire	The earth, the water, the sky
Sin ellos tú no eres nadie	You'll be damned if they die
Humo, cemento, brea	Smoke, concrete, and tar
Progreso que envenena	Progress won't take you far
Destrucción a fuerza de billete	Tear them down to make a buck
Y amigo nos quedamos sin verde	Drowning the green off the shore
El mar es para los peces	Let the fish own the sea
La Marina, ¡fuera de Vieques!	Get out of Vieques, Marine!
Pa'mi, pa'ti	Get it, got it
¡Fuera!	Out!
Pa'ti, pa'mi	Get it, got it
Pa'ti – ¡fuera!	Get it – Out!
Buscando la verdad escondida	Looking for the hidden truth
Natural, simple, sencilla	Pristine, clear, and pure
Ante un imperio que va en caída	The empire's crumbling down
Viva que viva la vida	Rejoice in a new dawn
Cultiva, cría y siembra	Nurture, harvest, and grow
La bendición para toda la selva	Blessed be the land that you sow
Porque somos gente decente	'Cause we are honest people
Y el poder pertenece a la gente	And the power belongs to the people

Poder para la gente	Power to the people
Poder para la gente	Power to the people
Poder para la gente	Power to the people
Poder para la gente	Power to the people
Pa'mi, pa'ti	Get it, got it
¡Poder!	Power!
Pa'ti, pa'mi	Get it, got it
Pa'ti – ¡poder!	Get it - Power!
Yo te veo pasando	I see you walking on by
Sonrisa buscando	Trying to squeeze out some smiles
¿A cambio qué me das?	What do I get back?

than their historical and cultural ties to Latin America. Consequently, the trajectory of a band of Puya's caliber would invite Puerto Rican fans to reflect on their connection to Latin America.

Puya has garnered attention from fans in Latin America who saw in them a musical representation of manifest ethnicity. Even though Puya was clearly linked to Puerto Rican culture in particular, their inclusion into what the US media labeled Latin metal served to peak the interest of other minority groups in that country. The same happened in other countries of Latin America. For example, Puya was one of the headliners of the Argentinian festival Rock en el Parque in May 1996 (Puya 2014). This is one of the largest rock and metal festivals in the region, and playing there is considered a great honor for musicians. Events like this one would bring Puya, and therefore Puerto Rican fans, to mingle and exchange music and ideas with the rest of Latin America.

This link to Latin American countries continued in 2014 when Puya headlined the Cuban rock and metal festival *Patria Grande* ("Large Nation"). The festival would mark the first time a Puerto Rican metal band would play in the socialist country, which has been under a US embargo for more than 50 years (Amnesty International 2009). The meaning of such an event was not lost on the members of Puya and its fans. After all, the band was invited as a headliner to the one country in the Caribbean region that is still seen as politically and culturally resistant to the United States. In the act of merely showing up and visiting the sister island of Cuba, Puya would inevitably be seen as making a political statement.

The poster for the event (see Figure 2.3) would be comprised of Latin American imagery focusing on the message of the region, a message promoting the region as one large nation. Puya would print event shirts marking the occasion, shirts that

FIGURE 2.3: Poster for the Cuban festival entitled Patria Grande in 2014. Image provided by Eduardo Paniagua.

boasted the Cuban flag prominently in the center and that were sold in Puerto Rico as a way for them to garner travel funds. This decision by the band is emblematic of their efforts to use artistic artifacts as a cultural resistance tool in Puerto Rico and abroad. On the Island, most individuals and organizations that support activities in Cuba, including changes to the current embargo laws, are associated with supporters of Puerto Rico's independence movement. In fact, to be called a socialist or communist there is tantamount to the worst kind of insult. Although they represent a minority on the Island, they are still highly stigmatized and have been systematically persecuted. Eduardo Paniagua, Puya's drummer, described their decision to visit Cuba:

> To have played in Latin American countries such as Colombia, Chile, Argentina, Brazil, Mexico, and most recently Cuba is one of Puya's most important accomplishments. We've been given the chance to interact with Latin American audiences and share our music with them, and we have been welcomed with open arms. We feel proud to have been to these places representing our Island, and we couldn't have done so without our music. The power of music knows no limits.

Puya's participation in these international events on Latin American soil has an important place in their history as a band and on how local fans perceive them. Part of Puerto Rico's colonial dilemma has included a systematic devaluation of the island's link to Latin America and the Caribbean. Puya has made an open effort to connect Puerto Rico, and its local fans, to other countries in the Americas in more ways than one.

Discussing race and ethnicity in musical content and embodied practices

One final characteristic of the colonial experience that needs to be discussed here is related to the active devaluation of local culture. Race and ethnicity are not exempt from this endeavor. In fact, the history of colonialism in Puerto Rico is full of instances in which discourses emanating from the US mainland are plagued, most times purposefully, with racism and disdain for the customs of local individuals. In this colonial exchange, the aim is to foster the devaluation of the local as a mechanism to generate self-identification with the colonial power and self-doubt regarding the self's actual context. It is not surprising, then, to see that in one of the more recent demographic censuses, 75.8 percent of the total population self-identified as racially White (Census Bureau 2010a). Of course, a simple look at the population on the Island would prove otherwise and shed light on the actual presence of individuals of African descent there, for example. Puya would aim to highlight the Afro-Caribbean roots present in the Island's history as a way to promote self-awareness and cultural awakening.

During my ethnographic work, I was able to attend at least two Puya concerts. Their concerts are usually opened by local bands that play *bomba* and *plena* music. These are musical styles heavily influenced by the forced African presence in the

61

FIGURE 2.4: *Bomba* and *plena* artists opening a Puya concert in Puerto Rico. Photo provided by Nelson Varas-Díaz.

Caribbean as part of the Spanish slave trade (*bomba* in particular). The music is mostly based on rhythmic patterns played on drums to which singers respond via a call-and-answer structure, which allows them to transmit a message related to their status in life. Descendants of African slaves used *bomba* to share stories and capture meanings related to their common descent and experiences. Performers usually dress in colorful garbs and, as the reader can attest from Figure 2.4, they engage in visual aesthetics that are distant from what one would expect at a local metal show. When asked about this practice, Eduardo Paniagua explained the following:

> Puya has always been known for being diverse and for fusing different rhythms. Having *bomba* and *plena* groups as opening acts for Puya allows musical universes to converge. It brings us closer to our roots, and it helps us bring this particular music to a younger audience that typically doesn't listen to it. It allows us to educate them about our culture and to show them the place where Puya is coming from.

Ramón Ortiz described this decision as part of a larger framework where the band retains the freedom to explore linkages to a rich past of musical traditions in Puerto Rico. He mentioned the following:

> I believe that studying our music history – the rhythms of Puerto Rico – has been crucial in my mission to fuse the heaviness of metal music with local trends. I believe

that Puerto Rico has a rich musical heritage, especially when it comes to rhythms, and there's plenty to learn from Puerto Rico's music masters; there's *salsa*, *rumba*, Latin jazz. [...] Rock and heavy metal musicians from the Island can tap into those rhythms and come up with new music. One can take a local rhythm, blend it skillfully with something totally different, and brew something new, something unique, something no one has heard before. Our music taps into plenty of sources: *danza*, *mazurka*, *rumba*, *salsa*. [...] [In Puerto Rican music] there are polyrhythms, syncopations, tunes, and chord progressions that are very interesting. They could be reinterpreted, reinvented, modified, or adapted to find new [musical] formulas.

Puya has also integrated a discussion on race and ethnicity into their music via embodied practices, particularly the act of dancing at their concerts. It has been well documented that metal music has particular embodied practices associated to this style of music. Moshing and head banging are probably the most commonly known practices associated with this genre in terms of the spectators' physical reactions. Research has documented that these practices, which are closely linked to the particular music style, have important uses for spectators. Some of these include catharsis via simulated violence as well as the promotion of solidarity among metal fans (Riches 2011; Rivera-Segarra et al. 2015). Due to their integration of salsa arrangements into metal music, Puya concerts are more varied in terms of these embodied practices.

Given their incursion into other musical genres, a song might commence with a traditional metal arrangement and sound, only to rapidly shift to a salsa-infused breakdown. As I witnessed during their concerts, this rapid change in musical genres forces listeners who are familiar with both to shift from head banging to salsa dancing.[6] This happens almost seamlessly among local fans that know their songs, but these shifts can be outright confusing for foreigners and new listeners. The embodied practices displayed at a Puya show will inevitable look strange to both metal and salsa purists, who would consider these shifts to be unnatural. Still, Puya fans manage the change with outstanding ease. Ramón Ortiz explained this integration in one of our interviews:

> I think that for the Puerto Rican metal scene to expand, evolve, and thrive, up-and-coming artists and the next generations must develop the desire to learn about other genres, just like we've been doing, but to also explore Puerto Rico's musical heritage, so they can stand out internationally. To explore and incorporate our heritage, that cultural blending of Spanish, African, and native elements, will breed sounds never heard before. We've inherited a musical universe like no other: we have the sounds of the great Spanish guitar masters, the rhythms of Africa, and the Taínos'[7] percussive elements. We just need imagination and courage [to explore them].

Although fans might not be aware of it, the integration of salsa dancing into a metal song has implications beyond body movements. Of course, it challenges the traditional flow of a metal song and its expected structure, but I would argue that this is far from being the most important issue here. Instead, the importance resides in the purposeful integration of race and ethnicity into the performance. That is, Puya willfully brings forth their ethnic influences, with an attention to the roots that derive from the Island's historical relation to Spain and Africa. The outcome is their own brand of metal music that can no longer be solely associated to the mostly White experience of Europe or the United States. Puya brings to the forefront the music of the Island's African and Spanish history, this in a genre of music that has mostly avoided or even prevented this type of incursion.

For an outsider, the decolonial manifestations in Puerto Rican metal music might seem to have stopped with Puya's work. After all, their presence was overwhelming during the 1990s and very few other bands have achieved their level of recognition, but this is far from being the case. Decolonial reflections through Puerto Rican metal have continued to emerge, particularly in light of more recent manifestations of coloniality embedded in the US-Puerto Rico relation. Specifically, the metal band Dantesco has delved into the island's historical past to reflect on more recent manifestations of coloniality.

"La Tierra de los Míos Nadie la Violará"[8]: *Dantesco's examinations of the colonial past and the constant battle against historical colonization*

To some readers and local scene members, the examples provided here focusing on Puya's reflections on Puerto Rico's colonial situation might seem like a thing of the past. After all, some of the current scene members were not alive to witness the struggles against the US Navy in Vieques. Yet this is not the case given that Puerto Rico's colonial dilemma seems to be ongoing.

In 2017, the United States imposed the Financial Oversight and Management Board for Puerto Rico on the island. This governing board (or *la Junta* as locals refer to it) would be tasked with taking control of the Island's crumbling economy, for many a reflection of the economic consequences of colonial rule. The board would have power over the island's budget, lands, and local laws. All elected government officials would respond to the board's members as the new ultimate authority on the Island. Puerto Ricans had no say as to who composed that board. Colonialism was alive and well in Puerto Rico and probably in a more flagrant manner than had been experienced by more recent generations. How would metal music reflect on this newest colonial entanglement? One way would be to look to the past and local folk tales as a way to reflect on this present-day manifestation of coloniality. More specifically, it would do so through an engagement with the legendary death of Spanish *conquistador* Diego Salcedo.

Although there are variations in the details of Salcedo's death, the overarching story is commonly used on the Island as a tale promoting a decolonial conscious-ness among the local population and serving as a cautionary tale for colonial oppressors. In the story, two Taíno *caciques*, or indigenous chiefs, ordered some of their subjects to test the supposed immortality of conquistadors. Thus, those tasked with the job took Salcedo to a river and proceeded to drown him. They watched over his body for three days to see if he would come back to life, as the scriptures from the *conquistadores* suggested of their own god. If Salcedo could be killed, so the logic went, it would show that these individuals were mere invaders and not god-like figures. This folk tale has made its way into local metal through the music of the band Dantesco and its singer, Eric Morales.

In order to explore this theme, I met with Eric Morales on many occasions. At the time of our initial meeting, the band had released five full-length albums: the self-titled *Dantesco* (Dantesco 2004), *De la Mano de la Muerte* (Dantesco 2005), *Pagano* (Dantesco 2008), *The Ten Commandments of Metal* (Dantesco 2010), *Seven Years of Battle* (Dantesco 2011), and *We Don't Fear Your God* (Dantesco 2013). Dantesco has been signed to international labels such as Cruz del Sur (Italy) and Inframundo Records (México). The band was very well respected in Puerto Rico and stood out due to Morales' ability to compose intricate lyrics and its brazen challenge of religious conservatism on the island. The lyrics themselves are a direct product of Morales' education, which includes a master's degree in history from the University of Puerto Rico.

In one of our many conversations, we began to reflect on Eric's decision to tackle political and cultural subjects in his music, specifically the ways that he had integrated decolonial sentiments into the lyrics. He employed the use of the country's historical past as a strategy to foster a reflection on the ongoing colo-nial situation on the Island. For example, with the newly appointed *Junta*, colo-nialism seemed to reveal its power and influence over the Island once again. Eric would rely on the use of folk legends to reflect on this most recent manifestation of coloniality. In his latest release entitled *El Día que Murieron los Dioses* ("The Day the Gods Died") (Dantesco 2021), the band would use the story of Salcedo's death as its main lyrical inspiration (see lyrics in Box 2.2).

We took the song "The Day the Gods Died" and relate it to the reality of Puerto Rico today, with the Fiscal Control Board, for example. The song can be a perfect symbol of how, after centuries of being under a colonizing empire, the superiority of the invader has been accepted as normal. The moment of truth arrives, and the people have to fight for their rights, which, in the song, are their lives and their lands. Today, we demand

Box 2.2 "*El Día que Murieron los Dioses,*" El Día que Murieron los Dioses, *composed by Dantesco (Puerto Rico) – 2021.*

En una noche de luna	On a moonlit night
El fuego nos habló y nos hizo ver el mal	Fire spoke to us and exposed evil
Como lloraba la abuela luna	Oh, how Grandma Moon wept
Un nuevo sol en nuestra sangre ancestral	A new sun in our ancestral bloodline
En una noche de luna	On a moonlit night
El fuego nos habló y nos hizo ver el mal	Fire spoke to us and revealed evil
Como lloraba la abuela luna	Oh, how Grandma Moon wept
Un nuevo sol en nuestra sangre ancestral	A new sun in our ancestral bloodline
Han llegado del mar en un navío infernal	They came from the sea in their infernal ship
Dioses de blanca piel vestidos como su maldad	White-skinned gods vested in evil
Armas brillantes hechas con el aliento del sol	Shinning weapons forged from the sun's breath
Bañadas en nuestra sangre, cubriendo su resplandor	Our blood dousing and hiding their glint
Y en su nombre – Esclavizar	And in His name – Slavery
Y en su nombre – Divina maldad	And in His name – Holiest of evils
Y en su nombre – Y por su rey	And in His name – And by his king
¡Que en el cielo esta!	Who art in heaven!
Se ha reunido el consejo supremo	The High Council has assembled
Han decidido a los dioses probar	They've decided to put the gods to the test
Hemos visto que duermen, comen y beben	We've seen them sleep, eat, and drink
¿Y si no son dioses los que llegaron del mar?	What if they're not gods, the ones who came from the sea?
Calla, que reine el silencio	Quiet, let silence reign
Pedían caciques llenos de temor	The Caciques begged in fear
Debemos saber y debemos ver	We must know, we must see
Si es que la tierra se traga su dolor	If the soil can swallow his pain

Cacique de Yagueca, viejo sabio taíno	Cacique of Yagueca, old taíno sage
Ha dado la orden de a un dios ahogar	Gave the order to drown a god
Así veremos si es que son inmortales	Then we'll know whether they are immortal
o si son hombres y se pueden matar	Or mere men, as mortal as us
Y en la noche – Agüeybaná	And in the night – Agüeybaná
Y en la noche – Encendió la pasión	And in the night – Lit the passion
Y en la noche – Urayoán	And in the night – Urayoán
Y en la noche – Tomó la decisión	And in the night – Made his choice
Este es el día en que murieron los dioses	This is the day when the gods died
Cuando la luz se hizo canción	When light became song
Liberados todos del miedo a la noche	No longer enslaved by our fear of the night
El momento en que suspira el temor	The moment when fearfulness sighed
Este es el día en que murieron los dioses	This is the day when the gods died
Cuando la carne lo divino abandonó	When flesh abandoned divinity
Se derramó la más pura sangre	The purest of blood was shed
Hasta la muerte mi pueblo luchó	To their death my people fought
Urayoán ha enviado a sus hijos	Urayoán has sent his sons
Que al joven Salcedo sirvan como a dios	Let them treat young Salcedo like a god
Ofrecieron manjares dignos de los reyes	Presented him with foods fit for a king
Ha sido cargado como enviado del sol	Paraded him around like the emissary of the sun
(solos)	(solos)
Al cruzar el rio llamado Goaorabo	Upon crossing the river Goaorabo
A Diego han hundido y lo han ahogado	They submerged Diego, drowned him there
Velaron tres días el cuerpo sin aliento	Set eyes on his lifeless body for three days
Maquetaure guayabaª se lo ha llevado	Maquetaure Guayaba took him home

Lucha! Griten mis hermanos!	Fight! Scream, my brothers!
Bailen al fuego	Dance with the fire
Con la tortuga tambor	Sound the turtle drums
Guasábara … guasábara …	Guasábara … guasábara …
Si hemos de morir	If we are to die,
Compartamos el dolor	Then let us share the pain
Ser contra ser que sangran iguales	Human against human, they all bleed the same
Cruda batalla al amanecer	Ruthless battle till dawn
Aurora de opías que cubren los valles	Hupia[b] aurora cloaked the valleys
Y las montañas las cubren también	Covering the mountains too
Mueren los hombres por libertad	Men die for freedom
Mueren los hombres por el poder	Men die for power
Mueren los hombres – Enloquecer	Men die – Madness
Mueren los hombres por un sueño real	Men die for a legitimate dream
Este es el día en que murieron los dioses	This is the day when the gods died
Cuando la luz se hizo canción	When light became song
Liberados todos del miedo a la noche	No longer enslaved by our fear of the night
El momento en que suspira el temor	The moment when fearfulness sighed
Este es el día en que murieron los dioses	This is the day when the gods died
Cuando la carne lo divino abandonó	When flesh abandoned divinity
Se derramó la más pura sangre	The purest of blood was shed
Hasta la muerte mi pueblo luchó	To their death my people fought

[a]Taíno god of the dead. *Guayaba* is the Arawak word for the guava fruit, which taínos believed to be the fruit of the dead.

[b]Spirit of the dead. They were believed to come out at night to feed on guava fruit, but were also capable of taking anyone who dared venture out in the dark.

that the board report its work, address poverty, and audit the debt of the people of Puerto Rico. All this is demanded with marches and protests, which are comparable to the uprising of the natives after the death of Salcedo. It is finally seeing the truth. Those who arrived from the sea also die. They are men! It is the same thing as we have realized that the board did not come to help, but to protect the interests of the rich and the empire. There is revolution in both examples, as people ultimately open their eyes.

Eric pointed to the fact that they had used these tales of the past consistently throughout their songs to reflect on colonialism in Puerto Rico. He was referring to the song "Morir de Pie" ("Die on Your Feet") that was included in the band's first album. In my many ethnographic outings to shows in which Dantesco was included in the bill, I would see how people reacted to the song. It was one of those songs that people knew the lyrics to, leading them to sing together as part of the concert experience. The song addresses the need to stand up to an aggressor and defend what is yours. Morales positioned this reflection during the Spanish colonization of the Island and the extermination of the native Taíno population. Morales explained the logic behind the song.

> The practical absence of a nationalistic sentiment in Puerto Rico has lifted songs that address issues of freedom and struggle and turned them into hymns. "Die on Your Feet" is one of those songs that people are expecting to hear at a Dantesco show. People sing along with the band. The song isn't properly a retelling of a historical event, but it does address a particular moment when indigenous people rebelled against Spaniards. I use poetic references to explain how they came and took away our freedom and land. The underlying message is that, even today, some of us are ready to die before kneeling to either tyrants or the empire. We will never give in, for the sake of the freedom of our children.

In one of my very last visits to a frequently used venue by metal fans in Puerto Rico, called *La Respuesta* ("The Answer"), a street artist had painted the legend of Salcedo on the walls. The large mural showed two indigenous people drowning the Spanish conquistador. It seems like everybody in this colonial context had someone to drown, and metal music presented them with a symbolically important way of doing so.

NOTES

1. Those initial interactions were very positive, and I published several academic papers on Puerto Rico's metal scene, particularly focusing on how the island's social context had helped shape this largely ignored community (Varas-Díaz et al. 2014, 2015, 2016; Varas-Díaz and Mendoza 2015).

2. During my interviews, participants used the term "hybrid" as a way to describe the emergence of something new out of two seemingly distinct and contradictory sources. I have continued to use the term throughout the book in respect for their voices. Still, I am keenly aware of the underlying tensions entailed in the use of this term in reflections over culture in Latin America, and decoloniality as a strategy. For example, Argentinian anthropologist Néstor García Canclini understood hybridization as a process in which "discrete structures or practices, previously existing in separate form, are combined to generate new structures, objects, and practices" (1995: xxv). In this scenario, something new emerges from the mixture of what previously existed. This position has been criticized by Bolivian scholar Silvia Rivera Cusicanqui when writing about decolonial efforts. She states that discourses related to hybridity are "essentialists" and can "obscure and renew the effective practices of colonization" (Rivera Cusicanqui 2020: 56). She criticizes Canclini's idea of hybridity for being a "genetic metaphor that connotes infertility" (Rivera Cusicanqui 2020: 66) and goes on to explain her distrust of the idea that the emerging new entity can exist in a "harmonic" manner. She proposes, instead, that what emerges should be best interpreted as a "parallel coexistence of multiple cultural differences that do not extinguish but instead antagonize and complement each other" (Rivera Cusicanqui 2020: 66). Therefore, it seems to me that she understands this new entity as one I constant tension. This idea is useful to understand decolonial metal music, particularly in its tensions with metal scenes in Latin America and in the Global North, as I explained in Chapter 1.

3. Personal communication with Angel Quintero, author of the seminal book on the genre *Salsa, Sabor y Control* published in 1998.

4. *Areyto* is the term used for ceremonies held by indigenous populations on the Island who were present before the Spanish colonial presence.

5. *Jíbaro* music is mostly sung by individuals living in the mountainous part of the Island. It is characterized by the use of guitar, *cuatro*, and percussion.

6. This shift between headbanging to metal and dancing to salsa music has an embedded decolonial undertone. Scholar Ángel Quintero Rivera (1998, 2020) has written extensively about salsa music in the context of the Caribbean and Latin America, and thus, his analysis has addressed the role of bodies in dance and their significance. He interprets dance styles heavily influenced by Black communities as anticolonial gestures, as these surpass the focus on the "erect torso" (2020: 418) from which other body parts would then follow in movement (characteristic of Europe). He argues that "the mulatto dance, poli-centric and decentered, brought into space a different sentimental structure" (Quintero Rivera 2020: 419). He sees these movements in dance as "anticolonial democratizing breaks in the terrain of hegemony" (Quintero Rivera 2020: 419).

7. Taínos were the indigenous local population of the Island before European presence in 1492. The population was destroyed via outright war or exposure to disease.

8. "No one shall rape the land of my people." This line comes from Dantesco's song "Morir de pie."

REFERENCES

Acosta, Ivonne (1987), *La Mordaza: Puerto Rico, 1948–1957*, San Juan, PR: Editorial Edil.

Amnesty International (2009), The US Embargo against Cuba: Its Impact on Economic and Social Rights, London: Amnesty International.

Census Bureau, US (2010a), *Profile of General Population and Housing Characteristics in Washington, D.C.*

Census Bureau, US (2010b), *Profile of General Population and Housing Characteristics in Vieques, Puerto Rico.*

Dantesco (2004), *Dantesco*, Demo CD, USA: Independent.

Dantesco (2005), *De la Mano de la Muerte*, CD, USA: TDNE.

Dantesco (2008), *Pagano*, CD, Italy: Cruz del Sur Records.

Dantesco (2010), *The Ten Commandments of Metal*, CD, USA: Jurakan.

Dantesco (2011), *Seven Years of Battle*, CD, USA: Stormspell Records.

Dantesco (2013), *We Don't Fear Your God*, CD, México: Inframundo Records.

Dantesco (2021), *El Día que Murieron los Dioses*, CD, USA: Independent Release.

Faul, M. (2003), "U.S. Navy leaves Vieques bombing range," The Intelligencer, https://www.theintelligencer.com/news/article/U-S-Navy-Leaves-Vieques-Bombing-Range-10588628.php. Accessed 23 February 2020..

García Canclini, Néstor (1995), *Hybrid Cultures: Strategies for Entering and Leaving Modernity*, Minneapolis, MN: University of Minnesota Press.

Meléndez, Edwin and Meléndez, Edgardo (1999), *Colonial Dilemma: Critical Perspectives on Contemporary Puerto Rico*, Boston, MA: South End Press.

Picó, Fernando (2005), *History of Puerto Rico: A Panorama of Its People*, Princeton, NJ: Markus Wiener Publishers.

Puya (2014), *Puya Online Bio*, https://www.theintelligencer.com/news/article/U-S-Navy-Leaves-Vieques-Bombing-Range-10588628.php. Accessed August 26, 2020.

Puya (2019), "Areyto," CD, USA: PeopleMusic Entertainment.

Quintero Rivera, Ángel (1998), *Salsa, Sabor y Control: Sociología de la Música Tropical*, Spain: Siglo XXI.

Quintero Rivera, Ánegl (2020), *La Danza de la Insurrección: Para una Sociología de la Música Latinoamericana*, Buenos Aires: CLACSO.

Riches, Gabrielle (2011), "Embracing the chaos: Mosh pits, extreme metal music and liminality," *Journal for Cultural Research*, 15:3, pp. 315–32.

Rivera Cusicanqui, Silvia (2020), *Ch'ixinakax utxiwa: A Reflection on the Practices and Discourses of Decolonization*, Cambridge, UK: Polity Press.

Rivera-Segarra, Eliut, Mendoza, Sigrid, and Varas-Díaz, Nelson (2015), "Between orden and chaos: The role of moshing in Puerto Rico's heavy metal community [In Spanish]," *Revista de Ciencias Sociales*, 28, pp. 104–20.

Rivera Ramón, Efrén (2001), *The Legal Construction of Identity: The Judicial and Social Legacy of American Colonialism in Puerto Rico*, Washington DC: American Psychological Association.

Rourke, R. O. (2001), "Vieques, Puerto Rico Naval Training Range: Background and Issues for Congress," Congressional Research Service Report for Congress.

Ruiz Kullan, G. (2010), "De víctima inocente a héroe póstumo," April 17, *El Nuevo Día*, https://www.elnuevodia.com/noticias/locales/notas/de-victima-inocente-a-heroe-postumo/. Accessed 23 February 2020.

Seijo Bruno, Miñi (1989), *La Insurrección Nacionalista en Puerto Rico, 1950*, San Juan, PR: Editorial Edil.

Varas-Díaz, Nelson, Mendoza, Sigrid, Rivera, Eliut, and González, Osvaldo (2016), "Metal at the fringe: A historical perspective on Puerto Rico's underground metal scene," in B. Gardenour Walter, G. Riches, D. Snell, and B. Bardine (eds.), *Heavy Metal Studies and Popular Culture*, London: Palgrave Macmillan, pp. 99–120.

Varas-Diaz, Nelson and Serrano-Garcia, Irma (2003), "The challenge of a positive self-image in a colonial context: A psychology of liberation for the Puerto Rican experience," *American Journal of Community Psychology*, 31:1 & 2, pp. 103–15.

Varas-Díaz, Nelson, Rivera-Segarra, Eliut, Mendoza, Sigrid, and González-Sepúlveda, Osvaldo (2014), "On your knees and pray! The role of religion in the development of a metal scene in the Caribbean island of Puerto Rico," *International Journal of Community Music*, 7:2, pp. 243–57. doi: 10.1386/ijcm.7.2.243.

Varas-Díaz, Nelson, Rivera-Segarra, Eliut, Medina Rivera, Carmen, Mendoza, Sigrid, and González-Sepúlveda, Osvaldo (2015), "Predictors of communal formation in a small heavy metal scene: Puerto Rico as a case study," *Metal Music Studies*, 1:1, pp. 87–103. doi: 10.1386/mms.1.1.87.

Varas-Díaz, Nelson, Mendoza, Sigrid, Rivera, Eliut, and González, Osvaldo (2016), "Methodological strategies and challenges in research with small heavy metal scenes: A reflection on entrance, evolution and permanence," *Metal Music Studies*, 2:3, pp. 273–90.

Varas-Díaz, Nelson and Mendoza, Sigrid (2015), "Ethnicity, politics and otherness in Caribbean heavy metal music: Experiences from Puerto Rico, Dominican Republic and Cuba," in T. M. Karjalainen and K. Kärki (eds.), *Modern Heavy Metal: Market, Practices and Culture*, Helsinki: Department of Management Studies, Aalto University, pp. 291–99.

Varas-Díaz, Nelson and Rivera, Eliut (2014), "Heavy metal music in the Caribbean setting: Politics and language at the periphery," in E. Abbey and C. Helb (eds.), *Hardcore, Punk and Other Junk: Aggressive Sounds in Contemporary Music*, Lanham, MD: Lexington Press, pp. 73–90.

3

The Experience and Sound of Ethnic Extermination – Perú

It is no secret that the sounds and lyrics found in music frequently reflect, and are transformed by, their contexts. In Peruvian metal this transformation has happened as a result of local experiences of systematic violence, which have been embedded within historically entrenched mechanisms of racism and which have disproportionately impacted indigenous populations. This process of transformation in metal's sounds and lyrics has subsequently spread from Perú to other countries in the region. Peruvian metal has understood the plight of the local oppressed communities that faced violence, transformed its sounds and lyrics to reflect their subject's complex and particular situation and, thus, engaged in some of the most effective and *extreme decolonial dialogues*.

Terrorism, racism, and metal music

I was walking through the streets of Lima in order to meet up with Eloy Arturo, the guitarist for Kranium, one of Perú's oldest and most important metal bands (López Ramírez Gastón and Risica Carella 2018; Nuñez and Rivas 2018). Prior communication via social media with Eloy had been scarce; my first impression was that he was a reserved man, not keen on long conversations via impersonal channels. We met at a corner street in *Miraflores*, one of the most affluent sectors in Lima. He had chosen the meeting place, and I was oblivious as to the underlying reasons. Eloy greeted me warmly; still, I sensed in him some level of disbelief at the idea that someone would be interested in discussing his legacy in the local metal scene. I would come to understand that he is, in fact, a very humble man who had great difficulty talking about himself or his band's achievements. This, however, was not the case when you asked him about the local metal scene; that conversation could go on for hours. As we walked through *Miraflores*, Eloy pointed out that during the 1980s, just a few blocks away, a car bomb had destroyed many buildings. He explained the event's importance, emphasizing the fact that before that event "nobody cared about terrorism in Perú." It was only when events like this one reached the affluent populations in the city that, as he stated, "people began to pay attention." We continued to walk through the streets, with intermittent moments of silence. The tone of this conversation, both reflexive and mournful, would stay with me throughout my trips to Perú.

Eloy and I grabbed a taxi and went to *Galerías Brasil*, where many quaint metal record shops abound. He wanted to show me one of the places where members of the local metal scene would hang out and got their music and clothing. As with many other places in Latin America, the small stores share space with people selling a variety of products. This time around the space was shared with vending stalls, where copy machines were plentiful and people seemed to be constantly making duplicates of legal documents. We walked past them toward the music stores. I immediately started to look for a Kranium album entitled *Testimonios* ("Testimonies") (see Figure 3.1), which has become an important collector's item in the country as well as other places in Latin America. After some time digging through boxes of CDs, I finally found a copy, an original pressing, no less. The storeowner wanted USD 100 for the copy. In shock at the scandalous amount, we went back and forth on the price until a deal was reached. Eloy's presence there probably helped, as the storeowner seemed uncomfortable negotiating in front of him. With my CD in hand, the seller proceeded to explain why Kranium was such a legendary band in the country, emphasizing as one key element the fact that the band integrated local indigenous sounds and themes into their music. I agreed with him, which moved the conversation toward a discussion on how their work was probably the first to infuse metal music with folk sounds in Latin America. Everyone around us seemed to agree, and no one could think of another metal release before *Testimonios* that blended metal with indigenous sounds in such a seamless way. This fact highlighted the importance of Kranium for the metal scene in Perú and the rest of Latin America. Still, during one quick glance at Eloy's face, I could tell that something was not sitting well with him. I was missing something, and it was making him uncomfortable. We walked through other stores and decided to grab a bite to eat.

We walked over to a Hindu temple that served vegetarian food. The building seemed majestic, its wood looked very old and heavily carved by hand, and the calmness it instilled in me made the sensation stick out like a sore thumb in the busy streets of Lima. Now in a more impoverished part of town, Eloy seemed more at ease with himself and his surroundings. He explained that he came here frequently to practice Hinduism, a routine that began several years ago. He described the much-needed calmness it provided to his life and context. After a brief tour of the place, we had a great vegetarian meal and Eloy played the sitar for me. It was a surreal moment to see this metal guitarist play the instrument with such ease and joy. The restaurant owner grabbed a set of handheld drums and played along. For

FIGURE 3.1: Artwork for the album *Testimonios* (1999) by the Peruvian band Kranium. Image provided by Eloy Arturo.

a moment everyone forgot we were there to talk about metal music, but it seemed that Eloy was happy in the moment, in that space, and I became, consequently, all the more eager to know the man behind the sitar.

After a few songs, our conversation returned to metal music. He asked, "Do you really want to know why I did it?" While a bystander might have found the question to be confusing, I was well aware that his query was in reference to the integration of local indigenous instrumentation into metal music, which we had begun to discuss earlier. I nodded affirmatively, to which he followed: "I did it because of the racism in this country." His rationale, seemingly simple at a first glance, was both historically profound and significant for anyone who knows about Perú's past.

During the 1980s and 1990s, Perú was ravaged by the armed struggle between local terrorists groups and the local government (Barrientos Hernández and Church 2003). *Sendero Luminoso* ("Shining Path") has probably become the best known of these groups, or at least the one mostly associated with the violent events that took place during those two decades (Barnhurst 1991; Harmon 1992; Casallas and Padilla Piedrahita 2004; Burt 2007). Led by university professor Abimael Guzmán, the group aimed to take power from the local government by force, considering the latter to be a completely corrupt institution. *Sendero Luminoso* professed communism as an alternative social and political approach. Their worldview came to be known as the *Pensamiento Gonzalo* ("Gonzalo Thought or Doctrine"). The doctrine was to be imposed by force and at any cost (Starn 1995). The group was well known for its ruthlessness; farmers in the countryside who refused to join their ranks would be either murdered or denied access to their harvest. While these violent events took place in Perú's countryside, the government seemed to turn its head, knowingly avoiding any opportunity at becoming fully involved. Once the car bombs reached Lima, specifically the *Miraflores* sector, the government and the army had no choice but to become engaged in the struggle. The effects were dire. Lacking a strategic plan to curtail the spread of *Sendero Luminoso*, the army would enter communities and kill local farmers randomly and at will, oftentimes using them as human shields during skirmishes (Taylor 1998). Unable to identify *Senderistas*, they would murder large numbers of people in order to "catch" a few terrorists. The murder of poor people in the countryside by both *Sendero Luminoso* and the government took a heavy toll on local communities. Perú's Truth and Reconciliation Commission has stated in their final report that during those two decades more than 69,000 people disappeared or were murdered. The sheer number seems simply unimaginable, and the suffering that it entailed for Peruvian society, particularly the poor and oppressed, is still felt today. One number stands out as particularly striking: 75 percent of those that disappeared or died were indigenous Quechua speakers (Laplante and Theidon 2007). As a whole, the two decades took a disproportionate toll on people of indigenous descent.

Eloy was well aware of this number and the disproportionate impact of these two decades on indigenous populations. He also vividly remembered how the situation was experienced in Lima at the time. He described living in constant fear of car bombs and the local police. He explained that the police were very harsh with the local people and would "plant drugs on you if they saw you on the streets having a drink." The police would also "plant terrorist flyers on you." As a result, Eloy explained, "many people who were innocent ended up in the *Castro Castro* penitentiary, simply for being poor or unable to defend themselves." These were the populations mostly impacted by the war on terror. Eloy seemed haunted by those who were wrongly imprisoned, and repeated once and again that "they were innocent" and "people knew they were innocent."

The consequences for the indigenous population were harsher than for those in the capital city. Eloy was particularly concerned about the people in the countryside. He described the farmers as "those who paid the price" of the conflict between *Sendero Luminoso* and the local government. Although great attention was paid to this group's role in the process of victimizing local communities, Eloy was keen on emphasizing the role of the local government in the process as well. To him, both sides were responsible for the murders in the country, and he described them all as terrorists. He brought up the following as a harrowing description of government-sponsored brutality:

> Here in Lima many people were murdered. They raped girls that had nothing to do with terrorism, just for being from *Ayacucho*. Some of them had their arms and breasts cut off. Everybody knows this! Aren't they terrorists too? Well, then, the government at the time was also a terrorist. People want to say that they were defending the population. What were they defending? They were killing people that had nothing to do with it! Somebody had to pay the price. Who did? The farmers.

In the middle of this conflict, the local metal scene emerged. Its members were also impacted by the strategies implemented by the local government to address the terrorist threat. For example, curfews were established in order to avoid having people walk the streets of Lima. This had a direct effect on the local metal youth who were perceived as problematic due to their musical preferences and accompanying metal-related attire. The stories told by local metal fans about police harassment at the time were startling. They were frequently stopped, frisked, and taken to jail for no other reason than looking different and, consequently, being suspected of terrorist activity. Concerts were also affected by these curfews, as they had to take place and end in early hours of the afternoon. Concertgoers from outside Lima, or the peripheries of the city, had to stay at friends' houses until the next day in order to avoid being stopped by the police and taken to jail. The effects of the war on terrorism during these two decades indubitably influenced the development of the local metal scene, which was driven to the underground in a more extreme manner than others in Latin America.[1]

The effects of this social context would immediately find their way into Kranium's music (Nuñez and Rivas 2018). They would sing about the impact of terrorism, the imprisonment of innocent people, and the persecution of metal fans. Eloy expressed disdain for metal bands that, at the time, sang about issues he saw as less pertinent. He explained:

Let's stop playing around! Some metal bands sang about superficial things or legends. Even worse, some sang about legends from other countries. It's not our history. If it's a band from another country, it's OK. I can respect that; black metal, for example. But with what is happening in Perú, how can you be singing about the devil? They are killing people in Perú! Terrorism has reached Lima, so let's stop talking about fantasies. Many people are dying. We are dying of hunger here. When will this stop? Let's sing about reality.

Eloy's vision of what metal should address in its lyrics was a direct critique to other metal bands in the country and the region, who were more concerned with subject matter that did not address the plight of the country. This explains the choice of lyrical content in their songs. Songs like "Castro Castro" describe the prison that housed political prisoners and innocent people who were labeled as terrorists (Kranium 1992b). "Bleed Out" is a song that addresses terrorism and the murder of the people in Perú (Kranium 1992a). This critical outlook is also levied at the treatment of young rock and metal fans in songs like "¿Sociedad o Suciedad?" ("Society or Dirtiness?"), which addresses the marginalization of youth in the country (Kranium 1992b). I was interested in Eloy's position regarding the need for *realismo* ("realism") in metal lyrics as a reflection of its context. He was well aware that this call was ill received by many in the metal scene. It clashed with the ever-present calls for authenticity in metal music (Laurin 2012; Anttonen 2016; McCombe 2016), which can sometimes steer the genre away from political content. In this scenario, metal's common call for authenticity or, as one could describe it, an adherence to particular sounds and themes was in direct conflict with Eloy's lyrical and musical path. This need for *realismo* in metal music, which felt like a call for sociopolitical positionalities within the metal scene, emanated from his personal experiences and would eventually impact Kranium's metal sound.

Expanding metal's sound and content within the Peruvian context

Eloy described in detail his travels through Perú's countryside as a young man. He seemed particularly impacted by one event in which he met an older woman of indigenous descent, who ran a small convenience store. He would visit the store on several occasions and notice that the house above it had, what he believed to be, multiple bullet holes. Eloy, who was very curious about the story behind them, asked the woman about their origin on several occasions. He mentioned feeling irked by her silence and on one occasion asking more vehemently about them. In that instance, and probably because of his insistence on the matter, the old woman replied that "some things were best unspoken." Eloy would explain in our conversations that, in time, he would come to understand that these were the consequences of terrorism in the countryside, evidence of the reasons why local communities would keep silent in order to avoid retaliation. For Eloy, his travels showed him how Perú's countryside had been severely impacted by terrorism and how indigenous communities had carried the burden of this process.

After his description of this particular event, and its importance in his personal life, Eloy's rationale for his endeavors in metal music would finally begin to make sense to me. When he described the country's racism as a motivating factor behind the type of metal music he created, he was talking about these types of experiences. Coming face to face with the indigenous populations in the countryside and seeing the impact of terrorism on their daily lives would motivate him to integrate indigenous sounds and subject matter into metal music. Kranium's lyrics had already taken a sociopolitical bent in the band's early years, but now Eloy's attention would be turned toward the band's sound. He would integrate indigenous instruments, like the *quena*, as a way to pay his respects to those impacted communities in his country. He described the process in detail in one of our conversations:

> It all happened throughout the process. You grow, and see things. [...] There are things that you don't like, and people usually stay silent. [...] There is a lot of racism in Perú. So [...] I don't care who is offended but metal needs to address this. An old band like Kranium could, you know. Why not? Like I told you, I traveled a lot through the countryside and that is how it came to be. I told my friend Mito, a guitarist, who also played wind instruments, to come and join me by the river and in nature. I told him to bring his *quena*. He was into very extreme death metal. I had an acoustic guitar and asked him to play along to the chords. That is how it came about. I asked, "How about we do a song like this?" He said, "No, you are crazy. This is not metal." I said, "Let's do it!" We took it to rehearsal and it came out great.

Kranium would be changed forever. The band would go from sounding like a traditional thrash/death metal band to a more refined outfit merging a doom-oriented approach with local indigenous instrumentation. This change in direction would not happen without challenging the above-mentioned calls for authenticity in metal's sound. Kranium had faced backlash for their realist approach in their lyrics; now they would experience the same backlash with their new sound, in this case even from within the band. Concerns over the notion that this new music was "not metal," as Eloy recalled one bandmate stating, would not deter the band from their new agenda. The resulting album, *Testimonios*, would be a completely new direction for the band and, I would argue, metal music in the region (Kranium 1999). The songs are full of Andean sounds, provided in great measure by wind instruments like the *quena* and string instruments like the *charango*. The transformation did not stop there. The lyrical content throughout the album would directly address the plight of indigenous peoples in the Americas, focusing heavily on their extermination during the fifteenth-century colonial period. One song, entitled "El Obraje" ("The Workshop"), stands out above the rest for its inclusion of lyrics sung in Quechua, an important language among the indigenous peoples in the Americas (Manley 2008). To the foreign interpreter, this might seem like a simple stylistic choice, but given Perú's historical context, it is a more complex situation. As mentioned earlier, 75 percent of those that disappeared or were murdered during the two decades of terrorism in Perú were Quechua speakers. Also, in the Peruvian context, other languages, including Spanish and English, are sometimes seen as more prestigious and interrelated to economic prosperity (Hornberger 1988; Nino-Murcia 2003). Therefore, Kranium's integration of the language into its song was in and of itself a politically reflexive and decolonial act, as it recognized the plight of the indigenous people in Perú. Eloy explained the subject matter of the song, and its use of Quechua in it, in detail:

> El Obraje is a place where Spaniards took rebel Indians. They would tie you to a tree trunk and bleed you out. They would place the Bible on you. Then they would throw you to the river when you were almost dead. That's what they did. Bleeding out with open wounds. When they told an Indian that they were taking him to the *Obraje*, it's because he was going to die. Our song is called "El Obraje" and we are singing about Inca culture. You asked why we sing in Quechua. Because we speak Quechua! I'll translate one part for you. It says, "It will be reborn. It will return. We will return." *Kutimunkan Ari* [...] "It will be reborn. It will return."

Throughout the conversations with Eloy, it became clear to me that his experiences traveling through the countryside, along with his knowledge of the events that took place during those two harsh decades in Perú, had marked him as an individual and as a musician. Kranium had used metal to denounce the injustices experienced by the population in general, but most importantly, the indigenous people. Their songs evidence how they perceive more recent exploitative practices as a continuation of the legacy of fifteenth-century colonialism. As such, "El Obraje" might seem like a distant memory from Spanish times, but it still served as an examination of the recent, and ongoing, ethnic extermination of the indigenous populations in Perú. When Eloy mentioned he had created this music because of the racism in his country, he was not exaggerating. The pervasiveness of racism in Perú has been an ardent topic of discussion (Cadena 1998; Laurie and Bonnett 2002; Drzewieniecki 2004), even though some would rather deny its existence (Manrique 1995; Golash-Boza 2010; Sue and Golash-Boza 2013). Kranium had transformed metal in the region and its influence would be felt in younger bands, as I will show below. Eloy put it plainly during our last meeting in Perú:

> We had no idea we were among the first to do folk metal. We had no idea. It was casual and unplanned. It was mostly due to racism, our inferiority complex. People don't love their roots. It's a reflection. You have to say things like they are. You don't have to hide them simply because it is metal music.

Metal as memory and warning in the Peruvian experience

It never ceases to amaze me how frequently conversations with cab drivers in Latin America become moments of enlightenment and clarity. Maybe because of their willing interaction with people from multiple countries and backgrounds, I have frequently found them to be very knowledgeable of regional mores and, more importantly, how the locals interpret their history. Perú would be no exception. I jumped in a cab to visit the *Lugar de la Memoria, Tolerancia y la Inclusión Social* ("Place of Memory, Tolerance and Social Inclusion"). The site was inaugurated in 2015 as a space that fosters reflections about the effects of terrorism in Perú. As soon as I told the driver where I was headed, he asked, "You are not Peruvian, right?" I was surprised by his question and inquired about what prompted his curiosity. He mentioned that Peruvians "don't usually come to this place." He went on to explain, "Most people just want to forget the traumatic experience of those two decades." Furthermore, he said that some people "simply don't believe this happened" and that the "reports of the number of dead are seen as grave exaggerations," an idea that has been documented via previous social research (Drinot 2009). I was surprised by his explanation, but remembered facing a similar experience when visiting the *Museo Nacional* ("National Museum"), which houses the first photographic exhibit of the armed conflict. When I visited that space, the security guards asked me where I was going, and upon giving them my answer, one of them stated, "It only had the exposition on terrorism," as if that were not interesting enough. Another guard said there was "not much to see here, really." And thus, I visited both sites, which aim to capture and preserve the memory of these tragic events, this despite the discussions taking place out in the streets being characterized by tense silences.

Kranium had sparked a deep reflection about the effects of terrorism on the country and the underlying thread of racism that ran though these attacks. Their influence would not go unnoticed by younger generations of metal fans, who would later become musicians themselves. To explore this connection, and the more recent reflections about terrorism and racism in Perú, I met with Alonso

Herrera, singer and guitarist of the progressive metal band Flor de Loto. He was a teenager during the 1990s and witnessed the effects of terrorism in Lima. He remembered that during that decade, international metal acts would avoid Perú over fears for their security. Still, he vividly remembered when the Swedish heavy metal band *HammerFall* visited the country during that same period, an act that he described as "very brave of them." Kranium opened that show and Alonso mentioned being "completely impressed with how they integrated metal and Andean music." "They even had a *queinista*!," he emphasized as an important fact. He also highlighted the fact that Kranium was the first band to "mix metal with Andean music, and to sing in Quechua." It was evident that he felt heavily influenced by Kranium. This was an important event for young Alonso, as he offered that metal in the country had "not addressed our origins in its sound" and had, for the most part, "tried to imitate the sounds of foreign bands."

This process of imitation was clearly of concern for Alonso. His band had made an attentive effort to integrate local sounds and subject matter into its content as a way to distance itself from the convention. Much like Eloy, he remembered living concerned over the impact of terrorism on the country. Although he experienced it as a young man, he recognized that addressing this issue was still a "polemic subject" due to the government's involvement in the process of ethnic extermination and the attendant racism underlying the disproportionate targeting of indigenous communities. Alonso described in detail how racism in Perú had served as a motivating agent for this extermination. Regarding this last detail, he stated the following:

> One of the effects of being a very fragmented country is that we live in a country that likes to think of itself as an elite and that Perú is limited to that elite. The roots of what we are have to do with the indigenous. We are Indians! We are a mix between Indians and Spaniards, but we can't deny our indigenous origin. I think our indigenous origin makes us very angry. It makes us angry. We want to uproot it from our past and uproot it from our history. We feel ashamed of it. It is a source of discrimination when confronting somebody with more power than ourselves.

This denial of the country's indigenous roots was of great concern for Alonso, who saw in this psychological distancing a pathway toward violence. It was easy for the *Senderistas* and the local government to "randomly kill," as Alonso stated, those that were perceived as worthless or less Peruvian. The indigenous fell right into that category; therefore, the violence exerted toward them seemed unimportant to some and even logical to others. Just like Eloy, he saw these racist practices as an extension of the devaluation of indigenous people stemming from fifteenth-century colonialism. He explained:

It is a reflection that we are, from our very origins, a very divided country. Very divided. The scars from the colonial conquest have not healed. I think we are a very classist society. Very discriminatory. Racism exists everywhere, but in such a fragmented country like Perú, I think we experience institutionalized discrimination. That discrimination goes hand in hand with aggression and extermination, as it has happened throughout the history of humanity. Therefore, Perú has not been the exception. The most excluded peoples are the indigenous groups. The people that pay the consequences of illegal mining exploitation are indigenous groups. The people that pay the consequences of indiscriminate deforestation, or of oil spills in the Amazon, are indigenous groups. Not us who live in Lima. It's very easy for us to feel in a different dimension to all of that. And feeling that away [...] the emergence of the indigenous reminds you of your origins, and generates a lot of anger. A need to exterminate, exclude, and discriminate.

Alonso was clear that Flor de Loto's music was created with this context as a background. When asked to describe his music, he stated that the band's output aimed to "integrate, recognize, and give a space to the indigenous in our identity." He stressed that music, and metal in this particular case, was "a call to reflect on these issues." This seemed to be an ongoing reflection, given that Alonso pointed out on many occasions that terrorism in Perú was always around the corner. He saw it as a violent option taken up by those who had been left behind, both socially and economically, by a society that had neglected to address structural problems like poverty and racism. This idea is present in one of their early compositions entitled "Imperio de Cristal" ("Crystal Empire"), in which the lyrics reflect on the fragility of the current time of peace (Flor de Loto 2011). "Terrorism is always around the corner in Perú," he stated in one of our conversations. This sentiment was echoed in one of the band's songs entitled "Tempestad" ("Tempest") (see lyrics in Box 3.1), where concerns over terror "coming back" were directly addressed by the band (Flor de Loto 2019).

Alonso emphasized during our multiple conversations the importance of Flor de Loto's sound in actively considering the origins of the music. For him, this meant recognizing that the band's sound had changed throughout the years, becoming ever more linked to Andean elements. Alejandro Jarrín, the band's bass player, stressed how the group had gone from using the *flauta traversa,* which he described as "more of a universal wind instrument," to using *quenas* and *zampoñas*, which he saw as more "characteristic of Andean music." A close examination of the band's musical output evidenced the ever-growing presence of these indigenous wind instruments. In their latest release, the *quena* would play a vital role and even take the place of the electric guitar in moments where one would expect to hear electric guitar solos. This sound, which Alonso described as "melancholic," was

Box 3.1 *"Tempestad,"* Eclipse, *composed by Flor de Loto (Perú) – 2018.*

La gente no comprende la violencia y el dolor	People cannot comprehend the violence and the pain
Que invade mi mente cada día que pierdo la razón	that invade my mind each day that I lose my sanity
Mi cabeza explota cuando trato de pensar	My head explodes whenever I try to think
La incertidumbre es mi destino y mi pesar	Uncertainty is my destiny and my curse
Ilusiones nada más	Illusions and nothing more
Mi rencor y mi verdad	My resentment and my truth
Y la vida se diluye en mi soledad	And life disintegrates into my own solitude
Mis deseos volverán	My desires will return
El terror regresará	But the terror will come back
Y mis miedos se potencian en mi tempestad	And my fears they swell and turn into a tempest
Imágenes perdidas me marean confusión	Lost images make me dizzy in confusion
Tu fantasma me seduce y pierdo la razón	Your ghost seduces me and I am reasonless
Mis músculos se deshacen y no existe sensación	My muscles vanish and I have no sensation
Mis latidos se dispersan en la imaginación	My heartbeats are dispersed in imagination
Ilusiones nada más	Illusions and nothing more
Mi rencor y mi verdad	My resentment and my truth
Y la vida se diluye en mi soledad	And life disintegrates into my own solitude
Mis deseos volverán	My desires will return
El terror regresará	But the terror will come back
Y mis miedos se potencian en mi tempestad	And my fears they swell and turn into a tempest

conceived as a reflection of the suffering experienced in the region. Alonso mentioned the following about the intersectionality of their lyrics and sound:

> As far as our musical aspirations are concerned, we strive to showcase the presence of Andean elements. But in terms of our lyrics, we propose a questioning of and

a reflection on what it means to carry out that musical fusion. The lyrics account for what it means to become one with our roots. [...] I think that the possibility of expressing a critical perspective in a fusion with Peruvian music makes me gravitate more toward Andean music. It has a melancholic tone. We could even call it a scream. It's a call for help. It calls for attention. That is characteristic of this zone in our country that has been so hardly hit.

For Alonso, this intersectionality of critical lyrics and local sounds served as the materialization of a need to address the historical violence faced by local communities in Perú. What became interesting in our conversations was the fact that he immediately linked the more recent violent events that took place in the 1990s to the country's colonial past. These were not separated events, but rather a continuum. He interpreted his music as a way to find alternatives to the colonial experience and the disdain it helped foster toward their indigenous roots. He also made it clear that his approach had little to do with negating the experience of colonialism or denying its influence on Peruvian society. In fact, there is a greater recognition of the role this cultural clash played in creating the Perú he sees today. He explained:

Our lyrics have that direct challenge. They challenge an imposition, a contempt for our origins. It is an inverse process to colonialism. I would say it's more of a syncretism. It's not about denying the colonization, and that we are a product of colonization. We also have foreign influences, which have been creolized and have become part of our country and our current society. But I think syncretism provides an alternative to colonialism. Syncretism entails that in light of the meeting of these two worlds, we establish an identity. You process and elaborate an identity. But that is not possible without some questioning.

This process of questioning the country's recent history of violence, and its link to fifteenth-century colonialism, was not described as unproblematic. The band was keenly aware that they were inevitably embarking on reflections that were political in nature and that some members of the metal scene would see as a problematic endeavor. Far from limiting their critical reflections, Alonso seemed to reinterpret the political role of their music. He conceived of a difference between "talking strictly about politics" and seeing their music as having potential "political consequences." He described a "way of being political through art," a way in which they would not "take sides with a political view" traditionally ascribed to the left- or right-wing movements. Rather, he saw music as having "political consequences" as it could help "shape political thought, a political logic, in the listener." This need to distance one's music from traditional politics was not new, as bands in many countries I visited throughout my travels did the same in order to avoid being labeled as a political metal band. Still, it was interesting that a band like Flor de Loto was reconceptualizing what it meant to be political in order to engage their listeners in critical reflections about their country and its history. For example, Alejandro saw their music as a "message for future generations about local culture." He stated that, although they did not do so directly, with the "music and these Andean elements, younger people who have not taken this into consideration in Perú or elsewhere can research a bit more about Perú's culture." It was, in fact, what they posited in their work: the use of metal for educational purposes about subject matters that are sometimes deemed too political for the traditional school classroom. They were both aware of the fine line they were threading, and Alonso made sure to mention that although varying perspectives on the matter could be argued, for him, this was "the objective of making music."

As I left Perú during one of my last trips there, Flor de Loto was playing at RoSfest, one of the most important progressive rock festivals in the United States. They would be the first Latin American band to play there and the only one to be invited 2 years in a row; such was the impact of their set at the event. The band began the show with an interpretation of the song "El Condor Pasa" ("The Condor Flies By"), a song by the Peruvian composer Daniel Alomía Robles. One of the most widely recognized songs from the country, the song was initially part of a *zarzuela*, or musical play addressing a conflict between local indigenous miners and foreign mine owners (Dorr 2007). The colonial undertones in the song, for those who know its origins, are undeniable. It made me wonder if the mostly US-based audience at the event understood what they were witnessing. The band had its work cut out for them, now bringing their decolonial reflection to the Global North.

NOTE

1. José Ignacio López Ramírez Gastón has written about the metal scene in Perú and how it faced the armed conflict. He has argued that scene members went into a process of "self-segregation" as a survival strategy. He describes that metal music "served as a social tool for the creation of secluded, sheltered, and private social spaces that helped them escape the political mayhem" (Ramírez Gastón 2020: 108). Although this process might have helped youth navigate troubled times, it is evident to me that they were not alienating themselves from the experience. On the contrary, they were still keenly aware of what was happening around them and these experiences made their way into their lyrics. Eloy Arturo and Kranium are an important example of this practice. Therefore, the idea of self-segregation is important, but should not be confused with the notion of alienation (so prevalent in early critiques of metal music in the Global North), as youth were still critically engaging their context via their musical production.

REFERENCES

Anttonen, Salli (2016), " 'Hypocritical bullshit performed through gritted teeth': Authenticity discourses in Nickelback's album reviews in Finnish media," *Metal Music Studies*, 2:1, pp. 39–56. doi: 10.1386/mms.2.1.39.

Barnhurst, Kevin G. (1991), "Contemporary terrorism in Peru: Sendero Luminous and the media," *Journal of Communication*, 41:4, pp. 75–89. doi: 10.1111/j.1460–2466.1991. tb02332.x.

Barrientos Hernández, Dora H. and Church, Adam L. (2003), "Terrorism in Perú," *Prehospital and Disaster Medicine*, 18:2, pp. 123–26.

Burt, Jo-Marie (2007), *Political Violence and the Authoritarian State in Peru*, New York: Palgrave Macmillan.

Cadena, Marisol (1998), "Silent racism and intellectual superiority in Peru," *Bulletin of Latin American Research*, 17:2, pp. 143–64. doi: 10.1111/j.1470–9856.1998.tb00169.x.

Casallas, Diego A. and Padilla Piedrahita, Juliana (2004), "Antropología forense en el conflicto armado en el contexto latinoamericano. Estudio comparativo Argentina, Guatemala, Perú y Colombia," *Maguaré*, 18, pp. 293–310.

Dorr, Kirstie A. (2007), "Mapping 'El Condor Pasa': Sonic translocations in the global era," *Journal of Latin American Cultural Studies*, 16:1, pp. 11–25. doi: 10.1080/ 13569320601156720.

Drinot, Paulo (2009), "For whom the eye cries: Memory, monumentality, and the ontologies of violence in Peru," *Journal of Latin American Cultural Studies*, 18:1, pp. 15–32. doi: 10.1080/ 13569320902819745.

Drzewieniecki, Joanna (2004), "Peruvian youth and racism: The category of 'race' remains strong," *2004 Meeting of the Latin American Studies Association*, Las Vegas, Nevada, October 7–9, http://hdl.handle.net/10535/1886. Accessed January 19, 2021.

Flor de Loto (2011), "Imperio de Cristal," CD, Buenos Aires: Pulmonar Recordables.

Flor de Loto (2019), "Tempestad," *Eclipse*, CD, Lima: Melodic Revolution Records.

Golash-Boza, Tanya (2010), " 'Had they been polite and civilized, none of this would have happened': Discourses of race and racism in multicultural Lima," *Latin American and Caribbean Ethnic Studies*, 5:3, pp. 317–30. doi: 10.1080/17442222.2010.519907.

Harmon, Christopher C. (1992), "The purposes of terrorism within insurgency: Shining Path in Peru," *Small Wars & Insurgencies*, 3:2, pp. 170–90. doi: 10.1080/09592319208423019.

Hornberger, Nancy H. (1988), "Language ideology in Quechua communities of Puno, Peru," *Anthropological Linguistics*, 30:2, pp. 214–35.

Kranium (1992a), "Mundo Interior," Cassette, Lima, Perú: Independent.

Kranium (1992b), "¿Sociedad o Suciedad?," Cassette, Lima, Perú: Independent.

Kranium (1999), "Testimonios," CD, Lima: Plasmatica Records.

Laplante, Lisa J. and Theidon, Kimberly Susan (2007), "Truth with consequences: Justice and reparations in Post-Truth Commission Peru," *Human Rights Quarterly*, 29:1, pp. 228–50. doi: 10.1353/hrq.2007.0009.

Laurie, Nina and Bonnett, Alastair (2002), "Adjusting to equity: The contradictions of neoliberalism and the search for racial equality in Peru," *Antipode*, 34:1, pp. 28–53. doi: 10.1111/1467-8330.00225.

Laurin, Hélène (2012), "Triumph of the maggots? Valorization of metal in the rock press," *Popular Music History*, 6:1, pp. 52–67. doi: 10.1558/pomh.v6i1/2.52.

López Ramírez Gastón, José Ignacio (2020), "*Sounds of exclusion and seclusion: Peruvian metal as a model for cultural self-segregation,*" in N. Varas-Díaz, D. Nevárez Araújo, and E. Rivera- Segarra (eds.), *Heavy Metal Music in Latin America: Perspectives from the Distorted South*, London: Lexington Press, pp. 107–29.

López Ramírez Gastón, José Ignacio and Risica Carella, Giuseppe (2018), *Espíritu del Metal: La Conformación de la Escena Metalera Peruana (1981–1992)*, Lima: Editorial Grafimag S.R.L.

Manley, Marilyn S. (2008), "Quechua language attitudes and maintenance in Cuzco, Peru," *Language Policy*, 7:4, pp. 323–44. doi: 10.1007/s10993-008-9113-8.

Manrique, Nelson (1995), "Political violence, ethnicity and racism in Peru in time of war," *Journal of Latin American Cultural Studies*, 4:1, pp. 5–18. doi: 10.1080/13569329509361843.

McCombe, John (2016), "Authenticity, artifice, ideology: Heavy metal video and MTV's 'Second Launch', 1983–1985," *Metal Music Studies*, 2:3, pp. 405–11. doi: 10.1386/mms.2.3.405.

Nino-Murcia, Mercedes (2003), "'English is like the dollar': Hard currency ideology and the status of English in Peru," *World Englishes*, 22:2, pp. 121–41. doi: 10.1111/1467-971X.00283.

Nuñez, María de la Luz and Rivas, Arturo (2018), "Musical representation in times of violence: The origins of Peruvian metal music during the general crisis of the eighties," *Metal Music Studies*, 4:1, pp. 219–29. doi: 10.1386/mms.4.1.219.

Starn, Orin (1995), "Maoism in the Andes: The Communist Party of Peru-Shining Path and the refusal of history," *Journal of Latin American Studies*, 27:2, pp. 399–421. doi: 10.1017/S0022216X00010804.

Sue, Christina A. and Golash-Boza, Tanya (2013), "'It was only a joke': How racial humour fuels colour-blind ideologies in Mexico and Peru," *Ethnic and Racial Studies*, 36:10, pp. 1582–98. doi: 10.1080/01419870.2013.783929.

Taylor, Lewis (1998), "Counter-insurgency strategy, the PCP-Sendero Luminoso and the civil war in Peru, 1980–1996," *Bulletin of Latin American Research*, 17:1, pp. 35–58. doi: 10.1016/S0261-3050(97)00059-4.

4

Dictatorship/Resistance/Inspiration – Chile

A close look at Chile allows us to examine two characteristics of decolonial metal. First, decolonial metal's commitment to siding with the stories of oppressed populations by showcasing the collective memory of the latter's experiences. Second, decolonial metal's affinity for finding inspiration in other Latin American decolonial artists as a way to infuse the lyrical content of metal music with social justice-oriented perspectives. This chapter will explore the relation between Latin American metal music and dictatorships through the case of Chile. The local metal scene in Chile emerged in the midst of the Pinochet dictatorship, and the music created by the country's youth (during that time and, arguably, still today) reflects the effects of that political process. I examine the implications of the Pinochet dictatorship for the development of metal music, some of the ongoing tensions within the metal scene with regard to this experience, and how the long-term effects of this political process are still being addressed through metal music today.

I had been to Chile before, mainly during my years as a student. I was and am still keenly aware of one undeniable reality: the topic of the dictatorship is an ever-present one. People talk about it incessantly and with good reason. The dictatorship in Chile, which I will describe later in the chapter, was a harsh one (as most are), leaving deep scars that have not yet healed, even to this day. I, of course, wanted to understand this experience through the voices of metal musicians and fans. In order to start this process, I met with local musician Chris Irarrázaval, guitarist for the metal band Nimrod B.C. He was one of the older members of the metal scene there, and his work was very well-known abroad. We met at the *Paseo de la Ahumada*, a central street in Santiago, which on any given day is full of people rummaging through its small shops. We talked for a bit and I explained the purpose of my visit. He seemed enthused about the idea of documenting some aspects of Chile's metal scene and, more directly, the relation between metal and politics. We began to walk through the city and talk about music.

About half an hour into our conversation, we stopped at a local street booth and Chris introduced me to a couple of older men in their seventies, men who were part of a group protesting the mismanagement of pensions and its potential detrimental impact on the elderly in Chile. In introducing me, Chris told the men that I was "Puerto Rican [...] so he knows about colonialism." I found his introduction to be somewhat funny, but they, perhaps sensing my impression, immediately explained that Chileans were deeply aware of the colonial plight experience in my home country. Without losing a beat, the men veered the conversation toward comparing the similarities between traditional colonialism and dictatorships. I asked them why so many people in Chile spoke incessantly about the dictatorship era, and one of them immediately replied that "the dictatorship will never be forgotten, as it marked us all." He stated that they had passed on that concern to their children and grandchildren. He stressed that "Pinochet and his people got away unscathed," making it clear for me that some of the individuals who participated in that era's government were still active in present-day Chilean politics. They described this as an "open wound" for the country. The conversation, which had a fast pace and a sense of urgency for them, evidenced the ongoing need to deal with the consequences of the dictatorship. I was aware of the role of music (specifically folk music) in helping Chileans in this process, but I was more eager to understand how metal had been involved in this endeavor, if at all.

Our walk through the streets of Santiago continued as Chris decided to take us to a space where metal had a greater presence, specifically a shopping mall called the *EuroCentro*. The five-story building was small, but had many small shops inside. On the lower levels, which are basically located underground, there were about eight metal-themed shops selling albums and shirts. The metal stores were mixed with other stores geared toward youth culture or which focused on video games, comics, and Japanese manga. As I engaged in a conversation with one of the shop owners, he immediately stated that the "local metal scene is waning." He explained that it was "nothing as big as Argentina's scene." I found this comparison with the local Argentinian scene at every destination in my travels throughout Latin America. That scene seems to be the great referent against which all other scenes are measured. After complaining for a bit, the shop owner explained that some of the stores were closed during most of the day as they could not afford to open for extended hours. He explained that "this is the only way to survive," as they could not "compete with a traditional mall that asks you to stay open all of the time." Still, customer traffic was active and people came in asking for shirts and posters.

As we walked through the several metal-themed stores, Chris introduced me to some of the storeowners who were his friends. They immediately recognized him and joked around a bit about the local bands. One storeowner asked about my work and, before I could answer, Chris immediately said, "He is doing a documentary about Pinochet and metal." I was struck by this description as it was more specific than I anticipated; I simply decided to roll with the punches. More importantly, this pronouncement served as a window into Chris's conceptualization of metal in Chile. You could not discuss metal, it seemed, without addressing the dictatorship. The storeowner became a bit disgruntled and could not hide his reaction. I could see disdain on his frown, as he immediately explained that "all the suffering described by metalheads during those years was made up." He said this made him angry because "it is a way of idealizing the past." He went on to state, "At the time we the fans were only concerned with the music and the latest demo coming out. Nobody cared about politics. Now they want to make you believe they were always interested in the subject. Bullshit!"

Some of the other customers listening to the conversation were evidently in disagreement, as suggested by their disapproving looks. Still, they went about their shopping so as to avoid conflict. This dynamic is not new to Chileans. In fact, the debate over the implications of the dictatorship is ongoing with some sectors defending the Pinochet government for its "economic achievements," while others preferring to highlight its repressive tactics. This debate was present in Chilean society, and the local metal scene was not exempt from its implications. Chris, who was listening to the conversation intently, pushed back on the ideas being expressed with concrete examples of bands in Chile that had addressed the experience of the dictatorship. He mentioned a song from his own band to drive the point home. The storeowner seemed unimpressed and stated, "I never saw anything […] I was never afraid," as if to put a capstone on the conversation. He quickly changed the subject and went back to talk about metal music in a more general manner. The experience was telling, despite leaving room for many uncomfortable moments of silence, which were oddly filled with the sounds coming from the store's sound system. As an outsider, it served as a stark proof that having conversations about the dictatorship represented an uncomfortable exercise in and of itself, an exercise that became even more complex for some metal fans when the topics of music and politics were merged. I was there to understand the role of metal born under a dictatorship, so I would need to handle this tension carefully on many occasions. A few days in Chile made it abundantly clear that metal had, in fact, addressed the experience of the dictatorship, even if it represented an unbearable subject of discussion for some members of the local scene.

Addressing the dictatorship through metal music

Although my experience with the storeowner described above revealed some of the lingering resistance regarding the discussion of the implications of the dictatorship via metal music, a more detailed examination of metal production in the country demonstrated how the musical genre had, in fact, addressed those difficult years. While walking with Chris through the streets of Santiago, this subject came up again in our conversation. He was quick to point out that metal musicians and fans, much like the rest of society in Chile, were divided in their opinions about the dictatorship and its actions. For some it was an instrument of torture, oppression, and death. For others it was a process needed to stop the emergence of socialism in the region.

It all began when Salvador Allende won the presidency in the 1970 election. He was a socialist, and his positions would clash with those of local conservatives and the political forces originating from the United States, which held a heavy influence in the region. In 1973, Allende faced a military coup and was ultimately killed in the government building called *La Moneda* (Padilla and Comas-Díaz 1987). This leadership vacuum was filled by a *Junta Militar* ("military board") made up of the leaders for the army, navy, air force, and carabiniers. Although it was the expectation that power would be given back to elected officials, this did not happen. Augusto Pinochet, one of the board members, took sole power and yielded it until 1990. Throughout the life of his regime, it is estimated that 30,000 individuals, comprised mostly of those who resisted the dictatorship as well as other non-involved bystanders, were captured, tortured, and murdered (Perez Sales and Navarro Garcia 2007; Soto 2008; Soto Castillo 2009). A plebiscite to remove Pinochet in 1988 was won by the opposition, and the dictatorship would end in 1990 amid great pressure from the international community observing the process. The repercussions of this experience have been addressed from multiple perspectives, including a focus on the psychological consequences (Díaz Vergara 2006; Cerutti 2015), the development of activism as a form of resistance (Guerrero 2014), and the mourning of death and loss by surviving family members (Robaina 2015), to name a few of the areas of professional inquiry. The dictatorship and its effects have also been addressed through metal music, and as we walked through the city, Chris began to discuss examples of this intervention. We began our perusal with his band, Nimrod B.C.

Nimrod B.C. is one of the oldest metal bands in Chile, continuing to play a brand of old school thrash metal even to this day. Chris is one of the remaining original members in the band, which he continues to nurture and through which he channels his creative energies. In the band's first demo recording entitled *Time of Changes* (Nimrod 1988), the musicians directly address the dictatorship and the need to challenge its permanence. The eponymous song was written in reference to the national plebiscite held in 1988 through which Chileans finally toppled Pinochet from power through a direct vote. The song's lyrics are clear and to the point:

> Let me tell you a story
> And it will be shown by us
> Happens in this place
> Where nobody can escape

It's about this dictator
Blood in his hands
Facing his fury
All in him is hate

War!! The end will bring destruction
The tyrant will try to win
Hate!! Killing your brothers
For an insane will
Perish!! By hands you know well

(Nimrod 1988)

The lyrics make reference to the many deaths experienced in Chile during the dictatorship and shed light on Pinochet's temperament, at least as interpreted by teenagers during that time. The song ends with a more hopeful approach by stating the need to "change the world without fear" and "change the world with me." Chris was evidently very proud of having addressed this subject matter in one of his albums. Not everyone within the metal scene had been courageous enough to do so directly, and Nimrod B.C. wore that song as a badge of honor. Considering that the musicians were teenagers at the time, it seemed to me like a very brave thing to do, even if it was done under the youthful aura of adolescent invincibility.

Other metal bands in Chile addressed the dictatorship process through pointed examinations of its consequences. The thrash metal band Warpath stands out as an important example in this regard. Their self-released demo from 1989 entitled *Torture* (Warpath 1989) could not be more direct and to the point. Its frontispiece shows a human figure inside a cage during the height of a torture session (see Figure 4.1). The lyrics contained in the titular song describe in detail this process. One of the main verses is written from the first person perspective and highlights the plight of those who were arrested and tortured, some despite not being directly linked to the political opposition:

Two shadows are chasing me
I've been caught and I never knew why
I've been tortured without a crime
Why did this happen to me?
They found I was to blame
Many years under prison
I never had anything to do in politics
I only want the truth to be known

FIGURE 4.1: Artwork for the album *Torture* (1989) by the Chilean band Warpath. Image provided by Marco Cusato.

The song subsequently takes a more interesting and problematic approach toward the dictatorship and the silent support it received from many sectors of society. The lyrics question how some people could believe these processes never took place when they were so plainly in sight. These lyrics echoed my initial meeting with the storeowner, described above, and showed how the tensions over discussing these matters were present then and could still be found today. To end the verse, the song takes a very dark turn in questioning the capacity of any political system to truly liberate individuals, equating the systematic treatment of people to that of the treatment of cattle.

I'm tired to live this day by day
Why can't anybody see
If this can be seen everywhere
However no one complains
Democracy the perfect technical lie
Dictatorship are worse so far
Why can the intelligent services
Treat us like cattle?
Yes, like cattle

I had the opportunity to speak with the band's leader, Marco Cusato. He explained the situation experienced by Chileans under the dictatorship as cruel and violent, which in turn inspired his writing and engagement in metal music. He was 17 years of age when the band came into existence. He explained that the decision to sing in English was made to avoid direct repression over the lyrics and also to allow people outside of Chile to know what was happening. He explained: "I understood I could contribute, since we sang in English and the tapes were sent abroad. Some consciousness could be raised outside of Chile and let people know what was happening." Marcos was realistic in his approach and mentioned that although bands like Warpath and Nimrod B.C. were very clear when it came to what they were singing about, other people in the scene were slower in understanding their lyrical content. As he stated, "Some people came to understand them five years after they came out." Still, time would allow Warpath to become more overtly political, and by 1988 the band was openly motivating listeners to vote against Pinochet in the plebiscite.

Another band that directly addressed the consequences of the dictatorship was Massacre. Led by singer and guitarist Yanko Tolic, the band released an EP in 1986 entitled "Pissing into the Mass Grave" (Massacre 1986) (see lyrics in Box 4.1). The band's notoriety in the local metal scene emanated from their combination of a relentless thrash sound with controversial lyrics. The band's biographer, Maximiliano Sánchez Mondaca (2014, 2016), explained in one of our interviews that many people initially saw the release of the EP as an affront to those murdered during the dictatorship. After all, the title could not be more forceful in its apparent invitation to desecrate the graves of the dead. However, he mentioned that the band's intent was actually the complete opposite. Although the title might have suggested an extremely disrespectful act, it was conceived from the perspective of the military members who had killed dissenters. It was meant to represent the soldiers who had pissed into the mass graves as a symbolic act meant to further disrespect the dead. A closer examination of the lyrics, sung in Spanish, reveals a more complex approach toward these events. The lyrics are sung from a first-person perspective of an individual inside the mass grave. The voice coming from the mass grave laments the "extermination of ideas" and warns the listeners that the "struggle continues." In an eerie passage, the dead call upon the listener to "place your ear to the ground" and listen to the words being pronounced for the rest of time. The song then mutates into chants of the phrase "mass grave" before warning the living to pray as retribution, or hell itself will come to avenge the dead.

Although Massacre was very direct in addressing one of the most tragic effects of the dictatorship, the band's interrelated story with that historical event was not limited to its lyrical content. According to Maximiliano, the band's lead singer had been himself subjected to torture as a teenager. He described the event as a gruesome encounter, with the *pacos* ("local police officers") taking Yanko to a local police station and torturing him severely. This included pulling out his hair with pliers and burning his back with lit cigarettes. Maximiliano described the event in detail:

> One glaring case of repression of thrash metal during the dictatorship occurred when Yanko, singer and guitarist for the band Massacre, was taken to prison for dressing differently. Basically for that. They saw him. A policeman said he had committed a crime or raised his voice at him while walking a few blocks away. They arrest him close to the National Stadium where there is a police station. They apprehend him and started to torture him. They beat him with sticks, took his clothes, pulled his hair out with pliers. He began to bleed and couldn't take the pain. The police were laughing at him. Saying things like "you won't make it out of here alive."

The effect on Yanko were long term, effects that had an impact on his health. Still, Maximiliano stressed one important and unintended consequence of that event. He explained that once musicians found out about what had happened, it "motivated some bands in Chile to have a more political perspective." He mentioned that the bands would make an effort to "face their situation and write lyrics making direct reference to the military government." Just as descriptions of the dictatorship's actions are still contested in Chile, some metal fans that I spoke with were skeptical about this event ever happening. There are pockets of entrenched denial regarding these events in every corner of Chile, and the metal scene seemed to be no exception. Still, my personal conversation with Yanko revealed an individual who was willing to explain his experience with utmost transparency, in vivid details, and who was keenly aware that some people would never believe him. Still, far from trying to make his experience the center of attention, he was intent on embedding his personal experience as one part of the repressions faced by the larger metal scene at the time. He stated the following in our interview:

Box 4.1 "Pissing into the Mass Grave," Pissing into the Mass Grave, *composed by Massacre (Chile) – 1986.*

Hemos muerto muchas veces	We have died many times
Luchando miles de veces	Struggling a thousand times
Fosa común, fosa común	Mass grave, mass grave
Entre llanto y ceniza	Amidst crying and ashes
Exterminio de ideas	Extermination of ideas
Fosa común, fosa común	Mass grave, mass grave
Y la lucha sigue y sigue	The struggle goes on and on
Aún estamos de pie	We are still on our feet
Acerca tu oído a la tierra	Place your ear to the ground
y escucharás las palabras	and you will hear the words
que pronuncio día y noche	that I pronounce day and night
ahora y siempre	now and forever
Mi descanso no es descanso	My rest is not peaceful
Y mi cuerpo ya no es cuerpo	And my body is a body no more
Las campanas doblan por mí	The bells chime for me
En esta fosa común.	In this mass grave
Fosa	Mass grave
La traición se paga	Treason is paid
Fosa	Mass grave
La venganza llega	Revenge will come
Fosa	Mass grave
El odio no muere	Hate does not die
Fosa	Mass grave
Sangre indomable	Indomitable blood
Fosa	Mass grave
Aún estamos de pie	We are still standing
Fosa	Mass grave
En esta fosa común	In this mass grave
El infierno viene	Hell is coming
Reza y reza	Pray and pray
El infierno viene	Hell is coming
Reza y reza	Pray and pray
Fosa común	Mass grave
Reza y reza	Pray and pray

It was a bit of everything. Sometimes we were playing and the police would arrive and dissolve the crowd by beating them. Since they were a police force under a dictatorship, they could fire at you and beat you. In fact, I was detained by the police, taken out of sight, and tortured. They burnt my back with cigarettes and performed the dry submarine technique on me. They place a bag over your head to asphyxiate you until you turn gray, and then they take it off. You can breathe again, colors come back to your face, and they do it once again. At the time, many things came to light. Atrocities like, for example, throwing those detained and disappeared into volcanoes. Some were tied to railroad tracks and thrown out of helicopters into the sea. Some were badly tied and actually reached the shores where they were identified by members of the opposition to the military regime. The murders were systematic in Chile. It makes me very angry when people older than me say that they didn't know about it, that they didn't understand what was happening, that they didn't see anything. That, to me, is abhorrent.

Yanko's account is very important as it links three themes that were present throughout many of my interactions with metal fans and musicians in Chile: these were the outright need to recognize the consequences of the dictatorship for the population at large, its implications for the metal scene and some of its members, and the pain still felt by many who face a social context that wants to deny these events ever happened. In this sense, metal music in Chile has served as a mechanism to keep those memories alive and remind the members of the community about what the country has lived through. Even today, it is not unusual to see images promoting metal shows with pervasive images making allusion to the dictatorship, urging people to "never forget." Metal music has served in Chile as a constant reminder of the country's past.

Until now, I have focused on examples in which metal music engaged in reflections about the dictatorship's action toward individuals that resisted. These have focused mostly on the experiences of torture and the disappearance of large groups of individuals. Still, reducing the scope of metal's reflection about Chile's experience to these two examples would prove limited and would, consequently, fail at providing a larger picture of the vast consequences the period had for the country. In the next section I will address another of these consequences: the effects on the environment. I will also describe how local metal continues to be inspired by Chile's musical past in fostering a critical stance toward the country's history and future.

The road less traveled: Environmental consequences of the dictatorship

The exploitation of local natural resources, the expropriation of land from indigenous communities, and the overall lack of concern for the protection of the environment have been a staple of the colonial experience in Latin America. These practices have been discussed at length as characteristic of fifteenth-century colonization, but it should be noted that they continued after many of the countries in the region became free and independent states. Therefore, environmental exploitation continued almost unaltered through the colonial process, was implemented later by local independent governments, and is still present today through widespread neoliberal practices (Gómez-Barris 2017).

Chile is an important example of the link between the colonial experience and environmental exploitation. It is the longest country in the region. Its access to the Pacific coast, vast stretch of land, and varied climates make the country one rich in resources. Some of these include valued minerals and extensive forests. The exploitation of those resources in more recent times is linked to the policies put in place during Augusto Pinochet's dictatorship. After the armed *coup d'état* against Salvador Allende's democratically elected socialist government, Pinochet ruled Chile from 1973 to 1990 (Manzi et al. 2004). During this period, Chile became a model for neoliberal policies in Latin America (Mojica 2010; Barandiaran 2016). The country was to become an example for others in the region of the economic growth that could happen once private entities were freed from the restrictions imposed on them by the State. In fact, under neoliberal policies Chile experienced an economic boom that would keep Pinochet in power and garner him supporters to this day. Still, these neoliberal policies would be detrimental to the country's environment, with dire consequences to its land, water, and air. Of great significance would be the accelerated rate of deforestation in Chile, a process that is estimated to consume half a million acres annually beginning in 1970 (Tockman 2005). It is not an exaggeration to state that the death of the environment in Chile is a major concern for the region and the world at large.

Metal music has captured this concern over Chile's environmental woes. Specifically, the progressive metal band Crisálida has vividly reflected on the consequences of environmental abuse in Chile. In their 20 years of existence, the band has released multiple albums, but it was in 2015 with their album *Tierra Ancestral* (Ancestral Land) when their concern over environmental exploitation and death came to the forefront of their musical output (Crisálida 2015). In their song "Morir Aquí" (To Die Here) (see lyrics in Box 4.2), the band reflects on Chile's environmental exploitation in a very direct and critical manner. The chorus stresses how the protagonist "does not want to die here," as the city's "cement does not speak to me." The video for the song is compelling as it follows a female protagonist during a walk through a city, one that we could assume is Santiago (Chile's capital city), but which could also represent any other city in Latin America. The protagonist has a depressed look on her face while she walks through the city, is jammed into public transportation, and manages to witness how the police beat an indigenous woman (see Figure 4.2). This last image echoes the violence that these

FIGURE 4.2: Artwork from the video for the song "Morir Aquí" by the Chilean band Crisálida. Image provided by Cynthia Santibañez.

communities have endured for defending their environment. The progress of the city is juxtaposed with the exploitation of the indigenous communities still present today in Chile. When she closes her eyes, memories of her ancestors come to her as a reflection of earlier times. In the ending sequence of the video, she climbs onto the balcony of her high-rise apartment, turns into a bird, and flies away. In this context, the excessive concrete constructions found in the city are equated to death and echo the exploitation of nature in Chile.

As part of my ethnographic work in Chile, I had the opportunity to interact with the band, which led to conversations about their music and worldviews. Cinthia Santibañez, the band's singer and lyricist, explained during one interview the following about the song:

> "Morir Aquí" is my life manifesto. I am from the north of Chile, closer to Bolivia and Perú. Arriving to the capital, where you have to come to achieve your goals, is difficult. I exchanged being close to the sea and the mountains [...] the tranquility of living in these regions. Something as simple as seeing the horizon every day, which in some parts of Santiago is impossible. That is what I experienced in Santiago. The amount of cement does not allow you to have a true sense of the temperature. It does not allow you to enjoy the wind. Some people can't even see the mountain range. What is that? That is terrible. There should be laws to restrict companies to a certain height for their construction. They have stolen the horizon and the Sun from us. How sad that companies can take that away from you [...] the benefit of seeing the Sun. That is "Morir Aquí." I will not die here [...] I'll die in my land, in the desert.

Box 4.2 "Morir Aquí," Tierra Ancestral, *composed by Crisálida (Chile) – 2015.*

Yo no quiero morir aquí	I don't want to die here
El cemento no me habla	The cement does not speak to me
No quiero morir aquí	I don't want to die here
Yo no puedo soñar	I can't dream
Aquí el alma no descansa	The soul cannot rest here
mientras la ciudad avanza	while the city moves
Cada noche enferma	Each sick night
se vuelve más eterna y caigo	becomes eternal, and I fall
Yo no quiero morir aquí	I don't want to die here
El cemento no me habla	The cement does not speak to me
No quiero morir aquí	I don't want to die here
Pensamiento vuela	Thoughts fly
Que el desierto me espera	The desert awaits
Y voy	And I go

The environmental plight faced by Chileans as a consequence of the dictatorship is not limited to deforestation. The control of other natural resources by private entities is similarly concerning. Even today, water is a privatized entity in light of laws enacted under the dictatorship (Gallagher 2016). This entails that private companies can control access to water, a basic resource that, under normal circumstances, should be a human right. Several interviewees mentioned this fact as examples of the continued legacy of Pinochet's dictatorship. Still, much like the effects of the dictatorship remain varied and diverse, so are the sources of inspiration that invite many Chileans to critically assess these effects through music. One of these sources was completely unexpected for me, as I describe below.

Chilean sources of inspiration in metal music

After having caught the band in concert at a local music hall, I had the chance to interview Crisálida at their rehearsal room. It was a small room located in an industrial building in the middle of Santiago. The floor was divided into many "boxes" that musicians used to rehearse. They seemed to have had the place rented out for a long time as it was very well decorated with posters ranging from their musical influences to those memorializing their previous concerts. Judging from their wall decorations, the band was equally influenced by heavy metal icons like Iron Maiden as well as more progressive bands like Anathema. They are well known in Chile and have opened shows for bands like Therion, King Crimson, Riverside, and Metallica, just to name a few. With this varied set of influences hanging on the walls, it quickly became evident in our conversation that they did not like labels. Rock, progressive, metal; it all seems secondary to, as Cinthia stated, "making people feel the music and the message."

During our interview it was readily evident that the lyrical message and conceptual direction of the band was mainly in Cinthia's hands. In general, they were concerned with the historical implications of oppression in Chile, ranging from the Spanish colonization to Pinochet's dictatorship, and the lasting consequences of each epoch's oppressive dominants. Cinthia spoke about Chile's indigenous populations and the protection of nature as key elements in their music. It seemed clear that she was actively seeking to address the implications of coloniality in Chile through their music. We spoke at length about using metal as a source for fostering critical thinking, and they all seemed to be quite aware of this agenda.

In one of my encounters with Cinthia, the topic of conversation took an unexpected turn, and we began to discuss the different sources of inspiration for their lyrical content. Without hesitation, she started to mention local protest singers associated to the *Nueva Canción Chilena* movement, which had played a key role in fostering critical thought during the 1960s and 1970s. This movement of protest singers would echo the sentiments of the local people who eventually elected Salvador Allende to the presidency, and would later serve as a critical voice against the dictatorship. She mentioned singers like Violeta Parra and Victor Jara as inspirations for their particular brand of metal music. I was aware of this connection prior to our conversation given that their latest album at the time included a song referencing Violeta Parra (the song is titled "Violeta Gris"). Still, I was not fully cognizant of the impact these singers had on metal artists like Cinthia until we had the opportunity to discuss the issue at length and in more detail. She linked her interest in their music to their critical role during the dictatorship. For her, it was evident that the dictatorship had horrible effects on individuals, indigenous communities, and the country's natural resources, but she took her analysis one step further. She expressed great concern over the elimination of local culture itself as part of the dictatorship's political and social strategy.

> Unfortunately, the dictatorship was such a grave and sad event in Chile's history that it marked a before and after, particularly in Chile's culture, particularly its

culture. Culture was eliminated! The military was capable of torturing people like Victor Jara. People who are part of world history! Transcendental figures. People who through their lyrics and music communicated peace, happiness, hope, sacrifice, and work. People who had culture. People who were pure poetry. Sung poetry. […] They were tortured and murdered. What is that? Horrible things happened here.

Cinthia was well aware of protest singers from the *Nueva Canción* movement from early in her childhood. She mentioned being aware of Violeta since she was a small girl, initially not liking her "ragged voice." She later became better acquainted with the singer during her adolescence and could "better understand her compositions." Cinthia stated that she then began to love her music, which opened the gates for exploring other folk artists, like Quilapayún. Cinthia described being entranced by their lyrics, which addressed, among other socially relevant subjects, the murder of more than 3000 people in the town of Iquique. She felt "motivated to find more information about those stories in Chile, but these were hidden for many years." Cinthia was well aware of the differences between the musical style she was describing and her metal-oriented approach. She mentioned that her metal music "was from elsewhere," but that the lyrical influences of local protest singers were "very much present." In her analysis, Cinthia was linking metal music with Chilean protest songs and linking her band to a long line of artists who had used music to reflect on the effects of the dictatorship (Neustadat 2004).

My conversation with Cinthia about the role of the *Nueva Canción* movement in her music led us to discuss important moments in which this particular subject matter had become an open conversation with other metal musicians and fans. I was intrigued with understanding if other actors in the local and international metal scene were aware of this connection between these two seemingly disparate worlds. She quickly mentioned a touring experience in Europe with the Israeli band Orphaned Land. Crisálida had joined the band's 2016 tour as an opening act. The experience was new for them and, as I gathered from our conversation, somewhat intimidating. Cinthia described feeling very fortunate for the opportunity and needing to "communicate a message to people from another part of the world." Although, as she put it, she "did not understand a word that people spoke," she wanted to find a way to "make them feel we came from afar, and that our proposal was not traditional metal music," but rather a different kind of proposal. She sang in Spanish throughout the whole European tour. When summarizing her touring experience, she stated that the goal was to "sing about the forgotten stories in Chile." She understood that the lyrical content of the *Nueva Canción*, now reimagined through metal music, was "a way to move forward into the future."

Although she was concerned that people would not understand the band's message throughout the tour, she used everyday opportunities to express it. One of these experiences stood out quite vividly for her. During one of the many tour stops, Cinthia began to have conversations about Victor Jara and the Chilean New Song movement with Orphaned Land's singer, Kobi Farhi. She recalled those conversations as being highly emotional and effective in transmitting to her new friend a general idea of who she was and where she came from. Kobi was no stranger to the *Nueva Canción* movement, having researched it himself for some of the lyrical content of his band. One night, they discussed Victor Jara's song "Manifiesto." In a nutshell, the song addresses the role songwriters have in fostering critical consciousness through their music. It is particularly poignant as it ends with an emotional lyrical phrase: *Canto que ha sido valiente, siempre sera canción nueva* ("Any song that is courageous, will always be a new song"). Cinthia mentioned crying over the meaning of this song, while explaining its importance to Kobi. The very same lyrics would make their way into Orphaned Land's (2018) album *Unsung Prophets and Dead Messiahs*, which deals with the importance of individuals who have strived for social change throughout the world. As the last song of the album plays, aptly entitled "The Manifest," a choir singing in Spanish comes into the fold to remind the listener that "*canto que ha sido valiente, siempre sera canción nueva.*" Cinthia had achieved her goal of transmitting the message of where she came from to her audience, the struggles Chile had gone through, by using metal music as a source of transformation.

My ethnographic visits to Chile and the conversations with band members and fans had revealed the tensions faced by metal musicians who had decided, even during their teenage years, to sing about the plights faced under the dictatorship. Even today, their message is met by some with skepticism. Still, an examination of their music and lyrical output evidences their engagement in critical reflections about the political reality they lived through, a reality whose long-term consequences they continue to face today. These artists continue to inspire local fans, and other international artists, while looking to their musical past for decolonial inspiration.

REFERENCES

Barandiaran, Javiera (2016), "The authority of rules in Chile's contentious environmental politics," *Environmental Politics*, 25:6, pp. 1013–33. doi: 10.1080/09644016.2016.1218156.

Cerutti, Amandine (2015), "La desaparición forzada como trauma psicosocial en Chile: Herencia, transmisión y memoria de un daño transgeneracional," *Multitemas*, pp. 35–47.

Crisálida (2015), "*Tierra Ancestral*," CD, Santiago: Mechanix Records.

Díaz Vergara, Fabiana (2006), "El duelo y la memoria, en la primera y segunda generación de familiares de detenidos desaparecidos en Chile," Ph.D. thesis, Santiago: Universidad Academia de Humanismo Cristiano.

Gallagher, Daniel (2016), "The heavy price of Santiago's privatized water," *The Guardian*, September 15, https://www.theguardian.com/sustainable-business/2016/sep/15/chile-santiago-water-supply-drought-climate-change-privatisation-neoliberalism-human-right. Accessed August 26, 2020.

Gómez-Barris, Macarena (2017), *The Extractive Zone: Social Ecologies and Decolonial Perspectives*, Durham: Duke University Press.

Guerrero, Manuel (2014), "De víctimas a activistas expertos: Marco conceptual para el estudio del devenir militante en la configuración del campo de derechos humanos en el Chile actual," *MERIDIONAL Revista Chilena de Estudios Latinoamericanos*, 2, pp. 133–49.

Manzi, Jorge, Ruiz, Soledad, Krause, Mariane, Meneses, Alejandra, Haye, Andrés, and Kronmüller, Edmundo. (2004) "Memoria colectiva del golpe de estado de 1973 en Chile," *Interamerican Journal of Psychology*, 38:2, pp. 153–69.

Massacre (1986), "Pissing into the Mass Grave," Tape, Santiago: Independent.

Mojica, Julio (2010), "Neoliberalism, civic participation and the salmon industry in southern Chile: Spatial patterns of civic participation on the island of Chiloé," Stanford, CA: Stanford University: Spatial History Lab, pp. 1–6.

Neustadat, Robert (2004), "Music as memory and torture: Sounds of repression and protest in Chile and Argentina," *Chasqui*, 33:1, pp. 128–37.

Nimrod (1988), "Time of Changes," Santiago: Independent.

Orphaned Land (2018), *Unsung Prophets and Dead Messiahs*, CD, n.l.: Century Media Records.

Padilla, Amado and Comas-Díaz, Lillian (1987), "Miedo y represión política en Chile," *Revista Latinoamericana de Psicología*, 19:2, pp. 135–46.

Perez Sales, Pau and Navarro Garcia, Susana (2007), *Resistencias Contra el Olvido: Trabajo Psicosocial en Procesos de Exhumaciones en America Latina*, Barcelona: Gedisa Editorial.

Robaina, María Celia (2015), *Impactos Psicosociales en los Hijos de Detenidos – Desaparecidos Percibidos en su Vida Actual como Adultos*, Uruguay: Universidad de la República.

Sánchez, Mondaca, Maximiliano (2014), *Thrash Metal: Del Sonido al Contenido*, Santiago: RIL.

Sánchez, Mondaca, Maximiliano (2016), *Massacre: 30 Años de Thrash Metal*, Santiago: Ajiaco Ediciones.

Soto Castillo, Evelyn Soledad (2009), "Detenidos desaparecidos: Ausencia y presencia a través de la imagen fotográfica," *Revista Electrónica de Psicología Política*, 7:21, pp. 1–21.

Soto Castillo, Evelyn (2008), "Canciones y memoria: El caso de los detenidos desaparecidos," *Isla Flotante*, pp. 49–61.

Tockman, Jason (2005), "Surviving the Chilean economic miracle," *Cultural Survival Quarterly Magazine*, 29:2, https://www.culturalsurvival.org/publications/cultural-survival-quarterly/surviving-chilean-economic-miracle. Accessed August 26, 2020.

Warpath (1989), "*Torture*," Tape, Santiago: Attic Records.

5

Social Movements and Hybrid Sounds – México

Metal musicians in México have engaged in reflections about organized social justice movements, a commitment that has been of utmost importance to the genre's involvement in decoloniality. This engagement has been inflected by one particular topic in the Mexican context: the Zapatista uprising in Chiapas and their fight for the visibility of indigenous populations and against neoliberal policies. Metal's lyrical and visual content has been used throughout this process to explain the link between fifteenth-century colonialism and neoliberalism's present-day exploitation of marginalized populations. Through a focus on the theme of transformation, I address the hybridization of metal music's sound via the use of local instrumentation while also shedding light on its practical/symbolic use as a tool capable of reflecting on the region's colonial past and present. This transformation of sounds and lyrical content, more than a simple aesthetic choice, positions metal music in México[1] as a prime example of *extreme decolonial dialogues*.

A social movement as an inspiration

México City's main plaza, *El Zócalo*, is one of the largest public spaces in all Latin America. Its sheer magnitude and size makes it seem endless, and the number of people walking through it at any given moment of the day can make anyone feel overwhelmed. Standing in the middle of the plaza with the sun beating down on me, I noticed people waiting in various lines. I counted at least twenty individuals in one of them. While walking to examine what was going on, I noticed multiple individuals dressed in indigenous attire performing rituals directly on bystanders. The use of flowers, plants, and water was evident in the process, an activity that was described on a nearby sign as a cleansing process. Those in line waiting to engage in the ritual were locals; it was difficult to identify any tourists in the vicinity. These indigenous practices in the middle of this Mexican plaza might be taken by some to be an unimportant, even trivial, touristic attraction, but the truth is they are far from it. In a country that has systematically neglected and failed to recognize its indigenous populations, this presence, out in the open, seemed to me as an affirmation. Indigenous communities are an important part of the Mexican population, even if some may want to deny this fact. Therein lies one important factor found in Mexican metal music; its contribution to the recognition of the indigenous and its continued efforts in sustaining that visibility.

One way in which metal music has promoted an engaged reflection regarding the indigenous populations of México comes by way of its constant attention to the Zapatista movement, be it through its lyrics or through its artwork. The Zapatista movement has been mentioned in the lyrical output of various US bands, including the album *Evil Empire* by the band Rage Against the Machine (1996). Zapatista-related imagery has graced the covers of albums such as *Raza Odiada* (Hated Race) by Brujería (1995). Given this knowledge, during my visit to México, I made it a point to explore this from a more local perspective, touching base with metal musicians who had lived in the country during the Zapatista uprising in the 1990s. One such figure is Alberto Pimentel, a renowned metal musician within the country and member of the seminal bands Transmetal and Leprosy.

Alberto and I met in an apartment I had rented, which was located a few blocks away from *El Zócalo*. Now in his early fifties but still sporting his characteristic long, curly black hair, he came across as a soft-spoken, heavily tattooed man. Within a local Mexican crowd, he easily stood out as different. By different, I do not strictly mean in his physical appearance; ideologically speaking, Alberto is also an entity unto himself. Back in 1998, Alberto, along with his bandmates in Leprosy, had released an album entitled *Llora Chiapas* (Chiapas Cries), an album focused on the Zapatista uprising. His decision to engage in such a profoundly political issue would place him in a position starkly different from the one taken up by most other metal musicians in the country. In order to understand why this decision made him stand out in the metal scene, it becomes necessary to offer a few words on the topic of Chiapas and the conflict that emerged there.

One of the 32 states that compose present-day México, Chiapas stands as a reminder of the existence of America's indigenous population. Its ruins evince the earlier presence of the ancient Maya civilization, which populated the region long before colonization made its effects known. Today, multiple indigenous groups conform the local population. The region, and its indigenous groups, became visible to the world outside México during the local rebellion that took place in the 1990s. The group's cause centered on the recognition of the existence and needs of the indigenous populations, which extended to the protection of their lands from the State and its officially sponsored multinational companies (Stahler-Sholk 2001).

Historically, the Chiapas region has been a site of tension within México for multiple reasons, which include conflicts over the use of land by the local people.

The adoption of neoliberal policies affecting the land and farming practices would serve as the breeding ground for the emergence of the Zapatista movement during the 1990s. The Zapatistas would be critical of the exploitation of the local indigenous population, which lacked the most basic of services from the Mexican government, including sewage, electricity, and education (Couch 2001). They would become a movement intent on echoing these concerns via military action, their presence dominating international press coverage of México for years (Martínez Espinoza 2008). The Mexican government could do little to stem the tide of support for the Zapatistas, support mainly coming from the indigenous populations, with Chiapas serving as a central locus of action.

On the morning of January 1, 1994, the Zapatista movement took up arms and gained control of several provinces. The movement, which would be an armed group for a short initial period of its existence, became savvy users of the internet, finding it ideal to spread their message against neoliberal policies and in defense of indigenous groups in the region (Martinez-Torres 2001; Pitarch 2004). The level of local and international support garnered by the Zapatistas exceeded that of many other similar groups in Latin America. One reason for this difference may be related to the message promoted by the group, which, far from focusing on violence as a strategy, fostered notions of solidarity among people (Olesen 2004). Some of these ideas included: (1) the notion that leaders should follow the will of the people, (2) an emphasis on the importance of community feedback over the imposition of rules, (3) the need for a communal perspective towards problem-solving, (4) the need to surpass and replace traditional forms of power, and (5) a call toward dialogue and the collective creation of a new world in an effort to bypass the traditional dominants of violence and revenge found in armed conflicts, among others (Meneses et al. 2012). Probably the most salient principle set forth by the Zapatistas became their call for *un mundo donde quepan muchos mundos* (a world where many worlds fit) (Stahler-Sholk 2000). It was evident that the Zapatistas were fostering diversity as a value and taking an important step toward the recognition of the indigenous in México and Latin American. This worldview highlighting diversity would also be manifested in the role of women as organizers and combatants in the uprising (Olivera 2005). The foresight of their proposals became one of the reasons why the Zapatistas, and by extension Chiapas, remain important icons in a critical reflection on neoliberalism and the exploitation of indigenous populations to this day.

At the onset of the age of the internet, where information flowed fast and visuals gained heightened importance, the Zapatistas tapped into the advantages of this new tool, thus making their leader, *Subcomandante Marcos*, a prominent presence online (see Figure 5.1). Marcos's presence and image became legendary and spread fast online. Dressed in military fatigues and sporting a mask, he would

FIGURE 5.1: *Subcomandante Marcos*, Zapatista leader (1996). Image by José Villa used under Creative Commons Attribution-Share Alike 3.0 Unported license.

fast become the voice of the movement. Living deep in the Chiapas jungle, hiding there along with members of the indigenous population, his words carried the weight of a man who lived what he preached. Through his anti-capitalist critique of neoliberal policies, and with the recently signed NAFTA agreement between the United States and México as his backdrop, he was able to explain in a very eloquent manner how such policies widened the gap between the rich and the poor. He was clever and able to put in plain words complex ideas that echoed those of authors like Paulo Freire (2000) and Eduardo Galeano (1971), to name just a few.

The message posed by the Zapatista movement and Marcos would not fall on deaf ears. In our conversations, Alberto mentioned that becoming aware of the group in 1994 left a "deep impression" on him. He remembered valuing their presence because "Marcos made the government take notice" of what was happening in the indigenous communities, which were "completely marginalized and with millions in extreme poverty." Alberto vividly remembered the Zapatistas, and Marcos in particular, becoming part of the 24-hour news cycle in México. His respect for Marcos came through loud and clear in our conversations. For him, Marcos was successful in making "everyone look" and understand that there was "another México" among them. Alberto described it as "the México that is marginalized," clearly present in "our backyards" but systematically forgotten.

Alberto helped found the metal band Transmetal, one of the most important metal groups in México, at least when one considers their productivity and dissemination throughout Latin America. Transmetal had addressed México's history in their music on multiple occasions, and their album *México Bárbaro* ("Barbaric México") stands out as an important example (Transmetal 1996). However, at one point Alberto became keenly aware of what was happening in the country at the time and decided that he needed a new band that would allow him to address these issues in a more direct manner. Thus, he formed the band Leprosy, whose name and sound were intended as a tribute to Florida's Death and their lead singer, Chuck Schuldiner, a musician Alberto admired for having influenced the creation of the death metal subgenre. Even before forming his new band, Alberto was aware of the direction it would take. He explained his thought process at the time: "Something is happening in my country and I want to make my album about it. I didn't have the music but I had the title. My album was going to be titled *Llora Chiapas*."

Leprosy's album is inarguably one of the most salient examples of metal music addressing the dichotomy of politics and social movements in México (Leprosy 1998). It describes the Chiapas experience from the perspective of the indigenous groups that inhabit the area (see Figure 5.2). Songs like "Residentes Olvidados" (Forgotten Residents) and "A Tomar las Armas" ("Take up Arms") make the album one of the most political musical statements in Mexican metal history. The lyrics position the listeners as witnesses to the Chiapas conflict, inform them about the origins of the situation, explain the logic behind the armed movement, and situate the latter as a reaction against the oppression of the Mexican State. Leprosy's contribution to Mexican metal proves vitally important given its successful bridging of reflections on neoliberal politics, indigenous oppression, and armed resistance.

The lyrics for the title song, "Llora Chiapas" ("Chiapas Cries"), read like a newspaper report taken from 1994. Less concerned with the aesthetics of rhyme and word complexity, the song narrates aspects of the Zapatista revolution much the same way a reporter would (see lyrics in Box 5.1). The song presents a problem

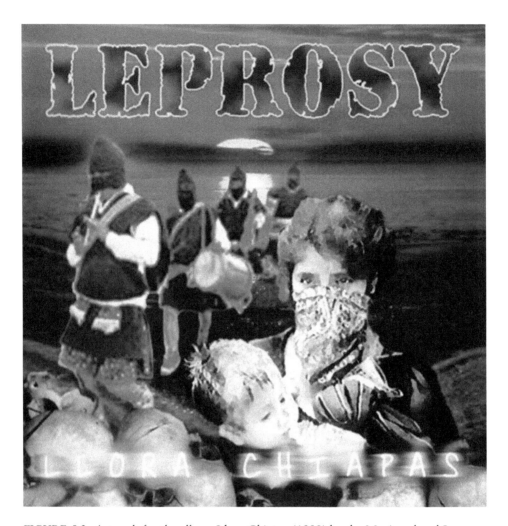

FIGURE 5.2: Artwork for the album *Llora Chiapas* (1998) by the Mexican band Leprosy. Image provided by Alberto Pimentel.

(hunger, fleeing peasants), it proposes a solution (Marcos and the Zapatistas), and it even offers the necessary historical context to allow the listener to come to a conclusion. Among the information presented, Leprosy includes a mention of the church's role during the failed negotiations between the revolutionaries and the State. While it may come across as simple, the chorus haunts the listener with its vivid visual descriptions. One need only hear "Chiapas cries, it rains blood" to get a sense of the urgency in display.

During our conversation, I pressed Alberto for a deeper dive into the motivations behind the album. This is when he brought up his notion of the existence of "another

Box 5.1 "Llora Chiapas," Llora Chiapas, *composed by Leprosy (México) – 1998.*

Llora Chiapas	Chiapas cries
Llueve sangre	It rains blood
Llora Chiapas	Chiapas cries
Llueve sangre	It rains blood
Campesinos huyendo	Peasants fleeing,
niños hambrientos.	children starving.
Una madre sufriendo	A mother suffering
se siembra el desconcierto.	bewilderment is sown.
Zapatistas vivos,	Living Zapatists
fundidos en sombras.	cast in shadows.
Luchan por la causa	They fight for the cause
de un pueblo olvidado.	of a forgotten people.
La iglesia media	The church negotiates
la paz entre hermanos	peace among brothers
y el obispado para el tornado.	but not even they can stop this tornado.
Un hombre aferrado	A man stands strong
su nombre es Marcos.	his name is Marcos.
Lucha por los hijos	He fights for the children
que dios ha olvidado.	that god has forgotten.
Pedazo de patria	Piece of homeland
te están pisoteando.	you are being stepped on.
Un pueblo olvidado	A forgotten people
es Chiapas llorando.	is Chiapas crying.
Llora Chiapas	Chiapas cries
Llueve sangre	It rains blood
Llora Chiapas	Chiapas cries
Llueve sangre	It rains blood

Nuestros indios	Our Indians
han sido olvidados.	have been forgotten.
Levanta la siembra	Harvest the land
que se ha cosechado.	that has been sown.
El odio y la muerte	Hate and death
es el resultado	are the result
de un pueblo que sufre,	of a people that suffer,
de un pueblo olvidado.	of a forgotten people.
Llueve sangre en Chiapas	It rains blood in Chiapas
Llueve sangre en Chiapas	It rains blood in Chiapas
Llueve sangre en Chiapas	It rains blood in Chiapas
Llueve sangre en Chiapas	It rains blood in Chiapas

México," that is to say, the idea that during their everyday practices, the people in the city have completely forgotten about "the marginalized." Alberto would constantly refer to them as "the forgotten people." He stated the following during one exchange:

In the north we have huge inequalities. It also happens in the center with indigenous communities. Sometimes they don't have the bare necessities. Things like drinking water, drainage, housing […] despite some of them having land, they can't even make ends meet to live a dignified life. It's social inequality. […] It's very difficult for me not to say or give my perspective on what is happening in my country. That is Leprosy and every week we do this live. I dealt with the subject matter but from a very particular perspective. It's not political in the sense of telling people to follow a system or support the Zapatistas. Instead, I call for support of our indigenous populations. Our people. That is what I did.

Alberto's conceptualization of his involvement in singing about the Zapatista movement was quite interesting to me. His statement that his dealing with the subject "was not political" seemed contradictory. After all, the Zapatistas were a social movement whose political dimensions were more than evident at plain sight. Even after singing about Marcos and the Zapatistas, Alberto seemed aware of the dangers of aligning oneself with a political party or group. The dangers of group-think, of having to fit one's ideas into a cohesive collective, worried him. This type of groupthink, primarily in the realm of politics, has frequently been considered dangerous for metal musicians and fans. Alberto found a way to address a political issue without tripping over the traditional pitfalls of what he perceived as engaging in traditional political reflections through political parties. His solidarity laid with the indigenous people, with the oppressed. His support was undivided for them. Everything else seemed like a strategy for action at the time, until another one was needed or took its place.

The influence of the Zapatista movement on metal music in México was not limited to Leprosy's album or Alberto's musical proposals. Younger bands, composed of individuals who were teenagers in 1994, also felt some level of solidarity with the movement. As children, they witnessed the emergence of the Zapatistas on live television. I had the opportunity to talk about this issue with Luis Oropeza, singer/guitarist for local band Acrania. Born in 1985, he remembered the emergence of the Zapatistas. He described that event as follows:

> That was in 94. I was 9 years old. Still, it was a commotion. I remember we were celebrating New Year's Day and watching the news. The "subcomandante" had taken San Cristobal and other municipalities. Although I experienced it as a child and couldn't be too critical at the time, it was still impactful. Even though I was a child, seeing those images and listening to what was being said [...] it shakes you and makes you think about and question what is happening.

Although experienced as a child, these events spurred a lifelong reflection about politics for Luis, one that he would eventually incorporate into metal music, as I will explain later in this chapter. What was different about his appreciation of the Zapatistas was his ability to see beyond the discussions about the indigenous populations. He was impacted by their denouncement of neoliberal policies and their impact on the poor. He mentioned that the Zapatistas "expressed a worldview that all of us shared," although he was quick to recognize that "their situation was even more fucked up." He added:

> Besides fighting for their dignity and making the indigenous world visible, which the Salinas government simply ignored [...] they also fought against this neoliberal worldview. We are all affected by that. We all continue to make less money, the country's economic situation worsens, natural resources get increasingly depleted. [...] We all live through that. So I think it was a real and honest movement. It expressed what many indigenous peoples, Mexicans, and Latin Americans thought. It was also a very intelligent guerilla. Of course, some of Marcos's political decisions would later be questioned, but people still love them. The last time Marcos spoke at the *Zócalo*, the place was packed. People supported him.

Echoing Luis's assessment regarding the average person in México, various taxi drivers and food vendors expressed their support for the ideas brought forth by the Zapatistas during many of my conversations with them. There is still an ongoing reflection about the Zapatistas role in standing up for the marginalized. I experienced this on many occasions while there. Nonetheless, Leprosy's decision to engage in a reflection about the Zapatista movement should not be taken lightly. These were subjects some people felt were too dangerous to tackle via their music. Maybe this is why other metal bands in the region rarely addressed the Zapatista uprising in such a detailed manner. Alberto, and Leprosy as a whole, found a way to address a very political dimension of their surroundings via their music, achieving this while also distancing themselves from traditional party politics. Reflections surrounding their solidarity with the marginalized indigenous communities had become the driving point of their thinking and their way of addressing the political. More importantly, those reflections impacted a new generation of metal musicians. As one young metal musician mentioned during one of my interviews: "[Marcos] sought to make the people wake up. He told them that there is no reason to submit to governments. [...] That idea became ingrained. That is why he has a lot of love from the Mexican people."

A band like Leprosy had engaged in decolonial reflections by using their lyrics and imagery to promote the need for discussion about the Zapatistas and the exploitation of indigenous populations in México. Still, this was not the only way in which local bands engaged in decolonial reflections. Before even traveling to México, I was already aware that other bands there were pushing the envelope on decolonial reflections through their choice of sounds. With this in mind, I set out to meet with local musicians engaged in this endeavor.

Hybrid sounds and inspirations

My conversations with Luis Oropeza about the Zapatista movement were very productive, so we decided to meet again to continue our discussion about metal music in México. He invited me to join Acrania in one of the rehearsal spaces they rented in the city. We met in the early afternoon and I watched the band set up their equipment. People came and went, and greeted them as they passed by. It was evident that they were well known among the other musicians there. Watching them set up their instruments was telling for, amid their electric guitars and amplifiers, one could also see *congas* and even a trumpet in its stand. For a newcomer, it would be hard to tell if the rehearsal room was being prepared for a band that played salsa or metal. They seemed to navigate comfortably within this apparent confusion.

The band began to play, and I could immediately tell I was witnessing something special. The crunch of the distorted guitars and Luis's singing in a death metal growling style were seamlessly integrated to passages marked by Afro-Caribbean rhythms coming from the *congas*. In the middle of their first song, the band segued into an interlude that owed more to jazz modes and structures than to any other genre. This digression eventually found them going back to their death metal riffs to close out the song, with Luis's trumpet filling the room with a flourish of even more diverse sounds. The final notes were the melody of the famous song "Tequila," recorded in 1958 by the US rock and roll band The Champs, and whose main rhythm is based on a Cuban mambo. It seemed to me like a fitting conclusion to a song that had run through many different musical styles, achieving it all without straying from its metal roots. We began to talk about the hybrid nature of their music, and Luis invited me to meet with him over the weekend to discuss this issue in detail.

We decided to visit the open market of *El Chopo* together. That day I took a cab and arrived on time to meet him where we had agreed. I found myself standing at a library next to the open market. The cab driver was somewhat confused by the closed-off streets that were bustling with metal fans. The number of black shirts making their way through the streets looked overwhelming from inside the car, and I had no idea where the market started or where it ended. The driver, knowing that we could not advance any more through the street, asked me to step out of the car and walk the rest of the way. I did and, after a few steps, met Luis at the public library.

Luis and I started to walk around *El Chopo* as he explained the place's history and role in the local metal scene. This was an open market that catered to rock and metal fans in México. The number of stalls selling merchandise seemed endless, as the market itself occupied several streets across three blocks. The sellers had the usual merchandise of interest to metal fans, including shirts, CDs, vinyl records, and books. Just as I began to think that this was simply another music market, like the many others I had seen throughout Latin America, I walked toward a crowd watching a guitarist provide a free seminar on metal solos. He used a small amplifier and a microphone to discuss guitar-playing techniques and their role in metal music. Luis immediately looked at me as if to make it clear that *El Chopo* was a cultural center, and not just a marketplace. The place has been active for more than 25 years and provides metal fans with both the music they loved and the sense of being participants of a shared space that was exclusive for them. After spending a few hours there looking for vinyl records and shirts, we headed over to a local bar to have an in-depth conversation about his band, Acrania.

Although I saw Acrania live for the first time at their rehearsal space, I had become aware of the band 2 years before, during my initial visits to México. I was intrigued by their inclusion of local sounds into their music and the political

FIGURE 5.3: Luis Oropeza and César Gallegos from the Mexican band Acrania. Photo provided by Nelson Varas-Díaz.

content of their lyrics. The band's sound could be best described as a mix of death metal with Latin music (see Figure 5.3). At the time of my interviews with Luis, they had already released three full-length albums. Their most recent one, *Fearless,* served as the catalyst to our discussion that day (Acrania 2015).

The seamless mix the band had been able to achieve between metal music and Latin rhythms intrigued me. Far from being a commercial strategy, Luis explained that the mixture was a reflection of how he approached metal music from a Latin American perspective. On several occasions during our conversation, he mentioned that metal music had foreign origins. He was keenly aware of the music's pedigree in the United Kingdom and the role of US musicians in its development. Nonetheless, he noted, he felt the need to transform it and make it local. It seemed to me that the rationale for this process had as much to do with Luis as with his listeners. For him, it was a way to "appropriate" something that his context had identified as alien. For his listeners, it was, at least he hoped, a way to understand the perspective and lived experiences of a Latin American musician. Luis expanded this idea when he stated the following:

> Metal is a genre that comes from elsewhere. It wasn't born here. When you see it that way, there are many bands that find it viable to have a gringo sound or have a European sound. I think, first, we need to appropriate our musical resources [...] and that applies to dimensions beyond music. For example, in México our resources are not even ours. They are sold to gringo and Canadian companies. It's the same thing with music. We have not fully gone through the process of appropriating our music [...] or whatever we want! Like metal. Metal wasn't born here, but I like it,

I want to play it, and now I'm going to appropriate it and process it. Make a type of metal that sounds like it came through a Latin American being.

Other band members echoed Luis's opinion about the importance of processing metal music through a Latin American experience. Johnny Chávez, the band's drummer, joined one of our conversations on the subject and seemed very intrigued with the discussion. He stated that it was impossible not to transform metal music, as he had grown up listening to music that was very different from what was characteristic of the regions traditionally associated to metal. He mentioned his love for musicians like La Fania All Stars and Rubén Blades, stalwarts of salsa music in the region. Interestingly enough, the latter is best known in the salsa world for incorporating themes of social justice into salsa music (Janson Perez 1987; Padilla 1989; Quintero Rivera 1998). As if to drive the point home, Johnny stated he did not grow up "listening to the things that somebody in Sweden or Norway would have listened to," and therefore, he would not play things that were "not an integral part" of him. The context in which these metal musicians had grown up was a clear influence on their music and decision to transform the sounds they loved. Still, this discussion always seemed to take directions that surpassed music and sound preferences. I always felt that something deeper was at play in this appropriation and creation of hybrid sounds.

As this discussion over metal's sound and the need to transform it continued, it became evident that the process of appropriation was not limited to musical tastes. It was not just a process of making the music sound regional. A limited analysis would approach this as a publicity stunt or a way to differentiate the band from other groups in the country. Still, that interpretation would be an incomplete analysis of a deeper approach highlighting the importance of contextual reflection. The use of trumpets and *congas* in metal music was strategic and aimed to draw the audience's attention to the setting in which the music was being made. To some extent, this hybridization process was being used as a tactic to communicate to others the plights faced by individuals living in their country and the region. The audience, once faced with these instruments not traditionally associated to metal music, would be forced to examine their use and linkages to the band's history and context and, almost unavoidably, the politics of their setting.

The band used both their sound and lyrics as carriers of a political message. Acrania conceptualized itself as a political entity, singing about politically relevant themes. As I continued to probe into the complexities of being a political metal band in México, Luis looked at me and asked: "What are we going to sing about? Carnitas? Dragons?" Everyone around us chuckled at his outburst, and yet, he was serious about what he was explaining. It was evident that this was an important matter. He drove the point home by stating that "with the social and

119

political violence that Latin America experiences, we have enough material to put out 10 years' worth of albums."

Luis was right, and I nodded in agreement, as we continued to talk about the plights of countries in Latin America. From his perspective, people have a hard time accepting the linkages between metal music and politics because they have a limited perspective on the later. For him, politics did not force you to become "part of a political party" or go vote. Instead, politics was a way of thinking about social relations in his environment. This became all the more clear when he said,

> I don't see a problem with bands being apolitical. But the way I see myself and conceive of my music is that (politics) is not alien to us. We are our music. Our music is linked to what we live through. We live in México City and that is our everyday reality. That reality is very political. Everything we live through, even the beers we drink, has to do with the political. Political decisions that influence our way of life, how we see the world, and relate to each other. If we take a step toward that notion, we can understand that politics is not alien to us. Politics is not about voting or being a member of the party. Politics is about understanding the reality in which you live and taking a position, or questioning. More than taking the position [...] questioning the social and economic relations you are creating. After the economy, politics dictates everything.

I was eager to understand the sources of inspiration that led the band to engage in such deep political reflections. I asked the band members about their latest release, in which the topic of Latin America is featured prominently in its lyrical content. One song in particular entitled "People of the Blaze" stood out as it addressed the implications of colonialism in the region. Chávez explained that an essay from Mexican writer Octavio Paz inspired the song. The essay, entitled *La Pirámide* ("The Pyramid"), explains how Mexican society still harbors organizational structures from colonial times (Paz 1970). The essay argues against the idea of unmitigated power, where a singular leader is given free, unchecked reign while he guides the lives of many. Octavio Paz uses this reflection to explain the permanence of the Institutional Revolutionary Party (PRI for its acronym in Spanish) in political positions of power for more than 75 years. Acrania, in turn, use Paz's essay to reflect on the ways in which that very same pyramidal structure is used to "prioritize foreigners before Mexicans" and "devalue" locals when compared to "people for other countries." The song positions colonialism in Latin America, and México in particular, as an ever-present process and definitely not a thing of the past. Its lyrics always remain hopeful, even when there is a recognition that surpassing colonialism, or as they label it "the night of 500 years," seems insurmountable. Their "invisible history" is made manifest by their decolonial brand of metal music. The song lyrics state:

> But what if they are right
> And we are condemned by the past?
> Freedom, let me not give up on you
> But I, challenging time
> I will survive the night of five hundred years
> I deny, I refuse
> This invisible history of usurpation and abuse

While walking through *El Chopo* with Luis, I was moved by the depth of our conversation, particularly with the band's effort to have listeners grasp a wider notion of "the political" that surpassed traditional party politics. The idea that politics mediated everyday life, including the drinks we consumed, challenged the apolitical tendencies of many other metal musicians. It was a more ample and profound perspective toward politics, to say the least. This was very evident in their conceptualization of colonialism as an ever-present phenomenon in the region. Luis was very careful about forcing this perspective on others. He even stated that they tried to promote this standpoint without sounding "too preachy." Still, I found their message refreshing and quite daring, even in the context of metal music. While listening to the band during one of their rehearsals, I reflected on Acrania's transformation of metal music and how it encompassed both its sound and message. The exchanges between the distorted guitars and Luis's trumpet seemed to drive the point home.

Transforming sounds – transforming politics

My ethnographic work in México fostered in me a reflection about one topic of importance for decolonial metal: transformation. Metal music in México has allowed itself to engage in a process of transformation in order to incorporate different sounds and thematic discussions into the genre. Although to some individuals this transformation might seem commonplace, I understand it entails an important reflection on how metal engages in decolonial strategies by adapting to its new context and helping individuals engage in critical reflections on coloniality.

The transformation of sound in Acrania's music, via the integration of local instruments, was not done solely for aesthetic reasons. This was a sonic manifestation of the reflections the band members had engaged in. As an extension of that work, they wanted their audience to become similarly involved and engaged. These deliberations are related to the idea of "being" from a different geographical location and the importance of legitimizing and respecting the vast diversity of place and cultural identity. During one of our conversations on Latin America per se, Luis mentioned that the region was "composed of many cultures, many races, and many worldviews" that can be related and have "inclusion." He used a musical metaphor to drive the point home; as he notes, in music "you can say that a double bass drum and a trumpet don't mix. But they do and we show it can be done!" This was his way of communicating discursively in a non-lyrical manner or, at the very least, sending a message that "another world is possible and that we don't have to fit into predetermined boxes." Acrania's transformation of metal music to challenge ideas of exclusion in México echoed the call of the Zapatistas for *un mundo donde quepan muchos mundos.*

Another transformation process that seemed important in the Mexican scene was the reconceptualization of the idea of politics. Metal music has found a way to rethink the political and distance itself from membership in political parties and engagement in traditional political acts as de facto modes of political practice. This includes entrenched ideas surrounding the act of voting. Echoing Zapatista principles, the issue of solidarity itself is seen as a political act, as it was evidenced in the concern over the current challenges faced by indigenous communities. Coming back to the example of Leprosy, one can see an underlying critical reflection on issues of solidarity directly addressed at indigenous communities in Chiapas. This is not the only evidence of this type of discussion through the mode of metal. Their subsequent album entitled *Llueve Sangre* ("It Rains Blood") released in 2013 would continue to address issues of importance to the local population, like the plight of migrants crossing into the United States (songs like "Corre por tu Vida" – "Run for Your Life") and the abuse of youth by drug cartels in Juárez (songs like "Juárez tiene el Poder" – "Juarez Has the Power"). All of these subjects, which have political dimensions and implications, are addressed by the band in a process that Alberto described as "solidarity with the marginalized." My contact with México and its metal musicians brought home one prominent fact: this solidarity Alberto speaks of, whether named so or otherwise, has become entrenched in decolonial metal music practices. Leprosy and Acrania made this abundantly clear.

As I was leaving México in one of my many trips there, the cab driver had the radio on and was listening to a news report. The Zapatista movement, for the very first time, expressed support for a candidate in the presidential elections. The candidate was a woman of indigenous descent running as an independent (Alire García 2017). Just like Alberto and Luis had mentioned in our conversations, the group's legacy and consciousness-raising agenda were still very much present in México. Alberto and Luis had their fingers on the pulse of the nation, and metal music had given them the means to remain engaged. Consequently, we can safely say that metal music continues to make the indigenous presence manifest, guarding it to this day.

NOTE

1. For other detailed accounts of the emergence of the local metal scene in México, see *Música del Diablo: Imaginario, Dramas Sociales y Ritualidades de la Escena Metalera de la Ciudad de México* by Stephen Castillo Bernal (2015). For a more detailed account of specific rock/metal subgenres, see *El Otro Rock Mexicano: Experiencias Progresivas, Sicodélicas, de Fusión y Experimentales* by David Cortés (2017). Finally, México has generated more general reflections on metal music and globalization worth examining, such as the book *Transhumancias Musicales y Globalización: El Metal No Tiene Fronteras* by Olivia Domínguez Prieto (2017).

REFERENCES

Acrania (2015), "*Fearless,*" CD, México City: Independent Release.

Alire García, David (2017), "Indigenous woman registers to run for Mexican presidency in 2018," *Reuters*, October 7, https://www.reuters.com/article/us-mexico-politics/indigenous-woman-registers-to-run-for-mexican-presidency-in-2018-idUSKBN1CC0T6. Accessed August 26, 2020.

Brujería (1995), "*Raza Odiada,*" CD, n.l.: Roadrunner Records.

Castillo Bernal, Stephen (2015), *Música del Diablo: Imaginario, Dramas Sociales y Ritualidades de la Escena Metalera de la Ciudad de México*, Ciudad de México: Instituto Nacional de Antropología e Historia.

Cortés, David (2017), *El Otro Rock Mexicano: Experiencias Progresivas, Sicodélicas, de Fusión y Experimentales*, Ciudad de México: Grupo Editorial Tomo.

Couch, Jen (2001), "Imagining Zapatismo: The anti-globalisation movement and the Zapatistas," *Communal/Plural: Journal of Transnational & Cross-Cultural Studies*, 9:2, pp. 243–60. doi: 10.1080/13207870120081514.

Domínguez Prieto, Olivia (2017), *Transhumancias Musicales y Globalización: El Metal No Tiene Fronteras*, Ciudad de México: Plaza y Valdez Editores.

Freire, Paulo (2000), *Pedagogy of the Oppressed*, 30th anniv. ed., New York: Bloomsbury Academics.

Galeano, Eduardo (1971), *Las Venas Abiertas de América Latina*, México City: Siglo XXI.

Janson Perez, Brittmarie Janson (1987), "Political facets of salsa," *Popular Music*, 6:2, pp. 149–59. doi: 10.1017/S026114300000595X.

Leprosy (1998), "*Llora Chiapas,*" CD, México City: Discos y Cintas Denver.

Machine, Rage Against the (1996), "Evil Empire," CD, n.l.: Epic.

Martínez Espinoza, Manuel Ignacio (2008), "Democracia para la dignidad. Movimientos políticos sociales y ciudadanía como aportes a las reflexiones sobre la democracia en América Latina. El caso del Movimiento Zapatista," *Revista Española de Investigaciones Sociológicas*, 123:1, pp. 151–83.

Martinez-Torres, Maria Elena (2001), "Civil society, the internet, and the Zapatistas," *Peace Review*, 13:3, pp. 347–55. doi: 10.1080/1366880012007904.

Meneses, Aldo C., Demanet, Alain, Baeza, Constanza, and Castillo, Javier (2012), "El Movimiento Zapatista: Impacto político de un discurso en construcción," *Revista Enfoques*, 10:16, pp. 151–174.

Olesen, Thomas (2004), "Globalising the Zapatistas: From third world solidarity to global solidarity?," *Third World Quarterly*, 25:1, pp. 255–67. doi: 10.1080/0143659042000185435.

Olivera, Mercedes (2005), "Subordination and rebellion: Indigenous peasant women in Chiapas ten years after the Zapatista uprising," *Journal of Peasant Studies*, 32:3 & 4, pp. 608–28. doi: 10.1080/03066150500267073.

Padilla, Felix M. (1989), "Salsa music as a cultural expression of Latino consciousness and unity," *Hispanic Journal of Behavioral Sciences*, 11:1, pp. 28–45.

Paz, Octavio (1970), *Posdata*, México City: Siglo XXI.

Pitarch, Pedro (2004), "The Zapatistas and the art of ventriloquism," *Journal of Human Rights*, 3:3, pp. 291–312. doi: 10.1080/1475483042000224851.

Quintero Rivera, Angel (1998), *Salsa, sabor y control: Sociología de la música tropical*, México: Siglo XXI.

Stahler-Sholk, Richard (2000), "A world in which many worlds fit: Zapatista responses to globalization," *Panel 384, Globalization in the New Millennium? Perspectives from/for Latin America, Latin American Studies Association (LASA)*, XXII International Congress, Miami, March 16–18.

Stahler-Sholk, Richard (2001), "Globalization and social movement resistance: The Zapatista rebellion in Chiapas, México," *New Political Science Latin American Perspectives*, 234:22, pp. 88–100. doi: 10.1080/0739314012009960.

Transmetal (1996), "*México Bárbaro*," CD, México City: Discos y Cintas Denver.

6

Decolonizing Space and Culture Amid Revolutionary Entanglements – Cuba

Metal music in Cuba needs to be understood with the country's revolutionary context always in mind. Initial reactions to this musical genre's manifestation on the Island, and the subsequent goals metal musicians have achieved there, make it an important case study for the Caribbean region in particular and Latin America in general. It is precisely because of Cuba's revolutionary history, serving as a flash point to the entire region, that metal artists and fans have engaged in so many decolonial acts. For example, metal music and its adherents have: (1) raised concerns over Americanization and its counterrevolutionary accusations, (2) revised traditional stereotypes of gender by recognizing the importance of a singular woman as the movement's point of origin, (3) engaged in communal actions to carve out a space for metal music as a legitimate cultural manifestation on the Island, and (4) adapted metal sounds to their setting through the integration of Afro-Caribbean rhythms. Metal has done a lot in and for Cuba, precisely because the genre faced adverse reactions that would ultimately yield strong communal organization.

Suspicion, scarcity, and time traveling

I placed my bags in the X-ray scanning machine used to screen all visitors' carry-on luggage. A loud sound rang across the hall and, without hesitation, security personnel grabbed my luggage. I was asked to state the purpose of my visit and explain the contents of the bags. The security guard, who seemed to me no older than 18 years of age, asked me if any of the camera and sound equipment had wireless technology. My initial thought was that all of the equipment had some sort of wireless system; however, after thinking for a second, it was evident to me that he had no idea of this fact. This technology seemed new to his eyes, and it immediately brought to light the limitations faced by most Cubans when it comes to access to this type of video-recording equipment. Before I could answer, he spotted a microphone and asked if it worked wirelessly. Upon my affirmative answer, the microphone was immediately confiscated. I was given a form to fill out and told that it could be picked up once I left the country. Of course, I would never see that equipment again. My small cameras also raised suspicion, but after a more heated discussion, they were given back to me. Later conversations with local contacts would shed light on this event, specifically, how a Cold War mentality was still alive and well in Cuba, a worldview that still carried with it lingering concerns over espionage, even to this day. My research trip had begun with the confiscation of an important part of my audio-recording equipment and a blow to my pocket. I left the airport hoping these hindrances would be the last.

Upon exiting the airport, I went to the only available currency exchange office, which was located right outside the airport exit. There, my US dollars would be exchanged for euros, then to the local currency for tourists, what have come to be known as "convertibles." In this exchange, I would lose approximately 30 percent of the value of my initial currency. At the time, US-based credit cards were not accepted in any Cuban establishment or hotel, so the money I had with me was my only means of sustenance. The "exchange" made me all the more aware that I had crossed a line into another geographical space where the facilities and comforts of home were absent: no credit cards, no ATMs at my disposal if I ran out of money, no cell phone, and very limited access to the internet. I may have been a few hundred miles from home, but in reality, I felt worlds away.

I arrived at the hotel and immediately went to the bar to drink some water and wait for my local contact. A large sign read *no hay hierbabuena* ("out of mint"). It was basically the hotel's way of telling tourists not to order mojitos. This pattern of scarcity would accompany me throughout the trip. Cubans have trouble getting the most basic necessities, including clothes, shoes, and food. Even though Havana receives many European tourists each year, restaurants are usually not prepared for their presence. You could have some nice pork one day and come back the next day to find they had run out. When they would replenish items like these was anybody's guess. Since many of the products are locally produced by the government, cured meats have become a staple and other options are lacking. After several days in Havana, I joked with local friends that I would not order anything with cheese, as it seemed to always be the same kind, regardless of what you ordered on the menu. The situation I experienced in 2015 seemed to turn for the better 4 years later when I visited the Island once more in 2019; however, this improvement was not by much. Still, this scarcity was nothing in comparison to what some of my contacts in Cuba faced on a daily basis. It would impact metal bands in diverse ways, as I would later discover upon conversations with various musicians.

Alfredo Carballo picked me up at the hotel. He is the bass player for the band Tendencia. We had met a few months earlier when he was a visiting professor at the University of Puerto Rico. Although our initial meeting back then was short, we struck up a good conversation on metal in the Caribbean. It was evident to me at the time that our chat felt a bit out of place, as fellow faculty members were unaware that he was also a metal musician in Cuba. They focused more on Alfredo's role as a professor of economics at the University of Havana. Still, this initial conversation had allowed us to plan my trip. After much planning, there we were in his car a few months after our first meeting.

Alfredo drove me to Old Havana, and we walked around the city. In the midst of our conversation about metal music in Cuba, I was in awe of the changes that Old Havana had gone through since my first visit back in 1995. Back then, Cuba was under what the local government called the "Special Period," a moment of extreme austerity after the fall of the Soviet Union. Cuba was left without its major supporter, and you could see and feel it everywhere. Alfredo immediately highlighted how things had changed since then, and it was evident. Newer cars roamed the streets, remodeling projects within Old Havana were under way, and tourists seemed to be everywhere. Parts of the city were getting a much-needed facelift. Still, visiting the city always feels like time traveling to the 1950s. Alfredo made sure I saw both the newly remodeled parts and those that were beyond the eyes of the tourists, where poverty and crumbling buildings remained in plain sight. I came to appreciate his openness, for it gave me access to a Cuba few encounter or see. We would meet some days later in Pinar del Río, where I would spend several days with his band. In the meantime, I would start interviewing other individuals to get a better sense of how metal was perceived in Cuba and the challenges it had faced while interacting with local culture.

Cuba's "New Man" and metal music

In my effort to understand metal in Cuba, I decided to meet with other scholars who were engaged in research with this music. One of the most productive meetings I had was with Dr. Liliana González, who worked as a researcher at the *Centro de Investigación y Desarrollo de la Música* ("Center for Research and Development of Music"). She had coordinated a showing of my documentary on metal music in Puerto Rico for faculty and students at the center. After the screening, I had the opportunity to interview Liliana in one of the meeting rooms at the institute.

Liliana's knowledge about music in Cuba is encyclopedic and covered many genres, from classical to metal music. She is one of the very few, if not the only, researchers in Cuba to detail the use of fanzines within the metal community during the 1980s and 1990s (González Moreno 2013). Upon sitting down for our conversation, she immediately urged me not to concentrate on the petty fights between bands. Instead, she advised me to speak to them about the bigger picture of metal in Cuba. Her comment made me feel at home, since this infighting between bands seemed a common practice everywhere I went. While setting up my cameras, I mentioned that our microphone had been confiscated at the airport, a detail that left her unimpressed. She merely expressed with mortification that this had become an all-too-common occurrence, one of those realities that had been amplified with the passage of time.

Liliana segued into speaking about the marginalization of rock and metal fans in Cuba. She explained the process as part of a larger historical sequence linked to the Cuban Revolution of 1959, when the guerrilla army led by Fidel Castro overthrew the US-backed dictatorship of Fulgencio Batista. The way Liliana explains it,

> During the sixties (rock aficionados) felt very marginalized, mainly because of the fundamental problem of language. Rock was in English and it was seen as an ideological threat. We were going through a difficult process in Cuba, a process of liberation. A foundational revolutionary process where there were fears about many things. Rock, in that sense, was affected. On the one hand, it employed English, and on the other, it had gestures and iconography related to clothing that clashed with the tenets of what was considered adequate behavior. The "New Man" [...] the image of the "New Man." All of these issues, which were unrelated to music, impacted that marginalization of rock in terms of it being a musical culture. Of course, those people that enjoyed and consumed rock were immersed in that dynamic.

Her comments on the rationale for marginalizing rock and metal music were very insightful as they referenced a political process that had been in place since the 1950s in Cuba. To eliminate the dictatorship that crippled the Island, revolutionaries had proposed the development of a different type of individual. The ideas of the Argentina-born revolutionary Ernesto "Che" Guevara would directly inform this process. After all, the concept of the revolutionary "New Man" was heavily based on his writings. For Guevara, this new form of being and engaging in the social arena would need to be developed from the ground up as a way of guaranteeing the efficacy and eventual success of the revolution (Anderson 2010). Social justice, education, and the eradication of racism were some of the tenets that would guide this revolutionary ideal. The "New Man" was expected to be "selfless and cooperative, obedient and hard working, gender-blind, incorruptible, non-materialistic, and anti-imperialist" (Hansing 2002: 41). Liliana expanded on this vision:

Understanding the relationship between the "New Man" and being a metal fan in Cuba is complicated. Both are areas of much research. For example, the ideal image of the "New Man" was, I would dare to say, military. It showed corporeal discipline, a certain hairstyle, a certain dress code, a search for rectitude and discipline in appearance. In the case of metal fans, their appearance was completely different. Long hair […] men with long hair. The sixties brought a strong marginalization of homosexuality to Cuba. There were a lot of features that were stereotypically homosexual, like long hair in men, clothes that made it unclear whether you were male or female. Metal, with its own stereotypes, had a lot of those features. They were marginalized because of it. They were censured for that image. The music had not been heard, and yet the image was not accepted within society's notion of what was good behavior or correct morality. I think those were things that marked them a lot.

Rock and metal music were entirely out of place in revolutionary Cuba for the reasons Liliana cites above. It is interesting to note that the reasons for this marginalization were driven more by political ideals than musical preferences. The widespread anxiety directed at rock and metal fans from a general public entrenched in stereotypes concerning homosexuality seemed to be a common motif, an issue often mentioned by the various individuals I interviewed throughout my visit.[1] Similarly, anxieties surrounding music performed in English, seen as a supposed ideological strategy deployed to "Americanize" the youth, echo concerns documented in other studies about rock and metal elsewhere in the Caribbean.[2] The reaction directed at this music seemed to have little to do with its sounds and more to do with what it meant to government officials. Still, it is hard (if not impossible) to control the youth's musical interest, and rock eventually found its place in Cuba. Metal would do the same later on. Liliana provided a snapshot of this process:

Nevertheless, rock was produced. Mostly in Spanish. It became one of the available alternatives and concessions when facing marginalization. To create rock in Spanish. The Beatles were banned. Rock was passed around via tape trading. It was a story that transcended the sixties, seventies, eighties, and nineties. During all those decades, rock became present in that way, in a very clandestine and underground manner. Using tapes that were listened to at parties. There are stories of "quinceañeros," which is a relevant phenomenon in Cuba, being celebrated with rock music. With live bands that visited houses and youths who danced to the music.

The concerns over rock music in Cuba would only be heightened by the emergence of metal music in the 1980s. The sounds were more extreme; the looks distanced themselves even more from what was expected of revolutionary Cuban youth, and listeners seemed to have developed a new attitude toward persecution. María Gattorno, the director of the Cuban Rock Agency (to which I will return to later in this chapter), mentioned her admiration for fans and their courage in facing these local challenges.

> Rock fans are very radical in their image. Most of them are mostly orthodox metal fans. They had bomb-proof courage. They did not care, don't you see? I always admired that. I said the same thing about the punks, who at the time were a small group tied to an aesthetic that had nothing to do with classic Cuban society. Still, they faced it with pride and dignity. Both the rock fans and the musicians. Musicians had it worse because it wasn't only the hair and pants; it was the guitar and the volume. That was too much for some people.

Although negative attitudes toward metal fans in Cuba may still be present in everyday interactions, it is evident that things have changed for them in the last two decades. The conceptualization of rock and metal fans as counterrevolutionaries has fortunately subsided. The tension between the "New Man" and the "Frikis"[3] (the local name given to rock and metal fans) seems to be mostly a thing of the past. Commenting about this apparent waning, one musician stated the following:

> Luckily this has changed a lot. Cuba has evolved a lot with the years. Today, rock fans are common youth. Very accepted. Most of the people that go to our concerts, in contrast with other countries, are university students. Students from [...] I don't know what you call them in other countries. We call them basic secondary, what happens before pre-university or university. Workers. Common people. Even families. It is not like before when the public was comprised of people who were sitting around and did not work. It has changed a lot in Cuba.

This change in attitude toward metal fans was directly linked to the tenacity of local metal fans, who would continue to make their music despite the reactions of those who made up their surroundings. These fans would find great support in the figure of María Gattorno, a government official who worked with young Cubans throughout the 1990s and who is, in hindsight, considered to be the mother[4] of metal music in Cuba. I had the chance to meet with her on several occasions and discuss her role in the development of Cuba's metal scene. As we will see, her work and interventions were a critical part in the survival of metal, both the music and the community, in Cuba.

Decolonizing spaces – El Patio de María as a point of origin

My first meeting with María Gattorno took place in a small room with three other employees of the Cuban Rock Agency. The meeting was short and interrupted many times by other individuals that needed María's input or approval regarding a plethora of issues. It was evident to me that María was a perpetually busy person and many people depended on her in the world of rock and metal. For a moment, I felt like I was speaking to a government official, which she in effect was, and that interviewing her would be a challenging task. After all, I was interested in her perspective as a supporter of metal and not as a government official. I spent some time talking to her about our research on metal in Puerto Rico and explaining the nature of my interest on Cuba's metal scene. In the midst of the many interruptions, María decided to invite me to her home so that we could talk there in detail and in a calmer setting.

The very next day I made my way to María's doorstep, anxious to talk with her about her work. Of course, I felt fortunate to have been invited to her home, as this seemed a more personal environment where we could talk about her life's work. María opened the door to her house and showed me around. Her house, although weathered by time, contained an impressive collection of Cuban art as well as an extensive library. It was evident that María was a scholarly individual who had extensive knowledge concerning Cuba's cultural landscape, a knowledge and landscape that extended beyond metal music. She brought out some croquettes, bread, and juice, which I felt lucky to share with her, as I was aware that access to this amount of food was, by no means, easy.

She sat on a large chair in her library and, without much preamble, began to talk about metal in Cuba. She must have been close to her seventies, but her mind was sharp, exhibiting an uncanny ability to recall detailed descriptions of metal bands in the country. Although I could go on and on about her vast knowledge of metal music, what struck me most about her was the humility with which she spoke of her work. María seemed almost reluctant to recognize her role in the development of Cuba's metal scene and would constantly remind me that she worked as part of a team of people; it was not just her doing the work, she constantly emphasized. This echoed the collectivist perspective I have already mentioned when describing decolonial metal music in Chapter 1. It was refreshing to meet with someone so significant to the local metal scene who was, in the same breath, so humble about her contributions.

As María explained, the epicenter that saw the emergence of Cuba's metal scene was a backyard patio located in a local culture house. Cuba's culture houses were spread across its various neighborhoods as a way to develop socializing activities for its residents. Their existence echoes the Cuban Revolution's position that

FIGURE 6.1: María Gattorno during one of our interviews at her home in Cuba. Photo provided by Nelson Varas-Díaz.

culture was, and still is, essential for the defense of the revolutionary ideals. One of these houses was located in the Revolution Plaza district, christened with the name *La Casa de Cultura: Roberto Branly* (the "Roberto Branly Culture House"). María was put in charge as the coordinator of cultural activities at the house, and during her tenure, she was approached by a handful of youths who asked to be granted some space to practice metal music (see Figure 6.1) (Manduley López 2013). According to María, these youths were practicing in public spaces (e.g., plazas) but faced great resistance from neighbors who perceived the music as foreign and anti-revolutionary. The use of the space in the culture house presented itself as a great way to avoid potential entanglements.

María allowed the youths to practice in the house's patio; soon, other bands started to see the patio as a safe space in Havana. It was not long before these practices evolved into full-fledged cultural events. María, seeing an opportunity, decided to schedule rock concerts every Saturday as part of the culture house's weekly "systematic activities" calendar. María recalled the way many reacted at the time, some going so far as to call her crazy, believing that her endorsement of metal music went against the auspices of Cuban cultural validity. In this context, metal music would seem completely out of place, some would even argue counterrevolutionary (Pacini Hernández and Garofalo 2004). Still, the patio would become their home, and metal musicians throughout Havana and other parts of Cuba would come to the patio to play and enjoy metal music. In light of María's support of the local metal bands, they would informally call the space *El Patio de María* ("María's Patio").

Once formally established, *El Patio de María* would become the place to be for metal fans. Juan Carlos Torrente, from the death metal band Combat Noise, would fondly describe the patio in one of our conversations:

> Well, *El Patio de María* was almost a mythical space. It was a space we came to know well and in which glorious moments were lived. *El Patio de María* was the Mecca for Cuban metal bands. All the bands wanted to go there and play. María Gattorno, who started as just another employee and would later become its director, gave us that space. *El Patio de María* was a culture house where popular and communal music concerts were held. Suddenly, María discovered a subterranean world of rock and metal bands that had nowhere to play. She gave us that space, which in the beginning was once a week. Later, it became every weekend. Then, it became something big and everyone wanted to play there. When we first got there, we had been to several concerts, but the patio was fascinating.

This fascination echoed throughout Havana. Young metalheads, who initially approached the patio with suspicion, began to attend regularly. Many of the most important metal bands in Cuba (e.g., Zeus, Metal Oscuro, Combat Noise) would take their very first steps there. In time, the patio's Saturday events would fill to the brim, the youth in attendance spilling onto the streets. María would have to constantly explain to the local police what was happening there, as moshing seemed like gratuitous violence to the untrained eye. Although the police never raided the patio, youths were in fact arrested on the streets outside of it. In an interview, Dr. Lilliana González Moreno provided a portrait that effectively explains how the patio became a space for the marginalized.

> All marginalized people felt they had a space there, a space where they were also protected. That doesn't mean there were no incidents. There were violent incidents, mostly because of misunderstandings which some people ascribe to cultural policies. I don't think it had to do much with cultural policies, but rather with the way some people use power and interpret a cultural policy, sometimes by people who have no political position. This included simple policemen who believed that this should be censored.

But the patio's reach did not end there, as I would soon find out. During the early 1990s, the patio's influence would go beyond its support of metal music and spill over into other matters of Cuban life, some cultural and others of far-reaching social and political importance. The patio would open its doors and actively house health personnel in a concerted effort meant to tackle the HIV epidemic, a health crisis that was starting to impact the youth in Havana. In a revealing example of music and culture's influence on matters beyond the artistic realm, international funds for HIV prevention projects would help provide the patio with a stage and an appropriate sound system. This may seem like an odd use of HIV prevention funds, but María helped describe the logic behind this effort:

> During the end of 1990 [...] early 91, a group of health specialists arrived at the patio. It was composed of specialists from the *Sanatorio de Santiago de las Vegas*, which was where they sent all individuals that were seropositive and who had AIDS in the city. This included specialists from the "National Center for Sexual Education" and the Health Department. They were doing a study to understand why HIV rates had skyrocketed among young people between 15 and 18 years of age [...] in that very young age range. They wanted to see why this was happening. [...] I thought it was very important that a large group of youth, like the one we systematically had, could be exposed to prevention work on the matter. It was very, very important.

In other words, investing in a stage and sound system guaranteed that more youth would be reached in this effort. It was evident that the patio had become more than just space for music fans. It was a place where alternate visions of music, society, and even health could manifest. To make this all the more interesting, we need to highlight María's positionality in this process; this was a cultural space led by a woman. Although metal music has been much criticized for being a space dominated by men, it was a woman who fostered its development in Cuba, a fact that has fortunately not gone unrecognized locally. In this scenario, metal musicians, and María herself, had engaged in the decolonization of gender stereotypes in metal music.

El Patio de María, however, seems to have garnered too much attention for its own good. Government officials would close its doors in 2003, with María finding herself suspiciously promoted to another position. The unfounded accusations painting metal fans as drug users seemed to be the main reason provided for closing the patio. Some interviewees mentioned that the patio was too close to the Revolutionary Plaza and the State Council and, therefore, was marked for elimination due to its proximity to these symbolically important places and structures. María described the process, confessing that she always became emotional when discussing the matter.

> What can I tell you? Talking about that always hurts, because it was a very sad thing for me. *El Patio de María* closes [...] and many excuses were given for it. They said

there were lots of drugs, too many problems, and too many "strange people," as they would label us. The patio could not house everyone, so the streets were full of people. Not just the two stages inside were full of people [...] but the street, the sidewalks, and the whole avenue.

María was emotionally impacted by the decision, but, true to her character, found in this process a silver lining.

I firmly believe that it was for the better. The closing of the patio was paradoxically great for the rock movement. Listen to what I am about to say. If we had stayed at the patio, we would have faded away. We had no means. [...] The material and physical conditions were going to be more difficult. If we had continued that way, it would have disappeared or turned into something even more dismal. They closed the patio! It disappeared. That hole was so large and important that it demanded the emergence of the "Maxim Rock." Without the closing of the patio, we would not have the "Cuban Rock Agency." Never – never.

In hindsight, María's words and attitude toward the situation would prove almost prophetic. Like a phoenix rising from the ashes, *El Patio de María* would mutate into something with arguably the same, if not a greater, reach in the realm of Cuban metal. That something would be known as the Maxim Rock.

The Cuban Rock Agency and the Maxim Theater

After the closing of *El Patio de María,* Cuba's metal scene found itself homeless. The place had become an iconic locale, intimately linked to how metal music was experienced on the Island, particularly in Havana. Metal fans would systematically petition the local government for a place in which to create and develop rock and metal music. Out of that concerted effort, the Cuban Rock Agency was born. Its role would be to organize rock and metal musicians under one roof and promote the development of the music in the name of the Cuban people's interest. The agency's central hub would be adjacent to the Maxim Rock, a refurbished movie theater that would serve as a concert hall for local metal bands (see Figure 6.2). Juan Carlos Torrente described the new reality as follows:

When the patio was closed, there was an impasse. There were many years in which concerts became more isolated, taking place in other locations. We suddenly didn't have a home to have concerts in. Then we got the "Maxim Rock." We got the Ministry of Culture to give us the "Maxim Rock." It was a movie theater that was destroyed. We got them to provide a budget for getting it back into shape. They turned it into a good space for metal concerts. We were also lucky, since they allowed us – by us I mean the metal movement, bands, promoters, and fanzine editors, those of us who met and demanded that space; they had the prudence to allow metal fans to work all jobs at the Maxim. These were people that we recommended.

After being directed by several persons, oftentimes unsuccessfully,[5] metal fans contacted María and actively asked her to head the Cuban Rock Agency and the Maxim Theater. Her presence would help link Cuban metal's previous organizational structure (*El Patio de María*) to the new government-supported entity (the Cuban Rock Agency). I had the opportunity to visit the agency and the Maxim Theater on several occasions while in Cuba. I was also able to attend a concert in which local bands Zeus and Combat Noise shared the bill. These are two of the most recognized bands in Cuba, particularly for their long trajectory that spans more than two decades. The three-story building lies in the middle of a residential area, and I was struck by the closeness of the venue to apartments and houses. The noise at night inevitably spills onto the streets, and it was evident that neighbors

FIGURE 6.2: Home of the Maxim Theater and the Cuban Rock Agency, Havana, Cuba. Photo provided by Nelson Varas-Díaz.

FIGURE 6.3: María Gattorno working with her crew during a concert at the Maxim Theater, Havana, Cuba. Photo provided by Nelson Varas-Díaz.

had become used to it. The building is modest and, like so many others in Havana, shows the wear and tear of time.

Upon entering the main lobby, there was a small window through which tickets were sold as well as a desk for a security guard. María was running around making sure everything went as smooth as possible (see Figure 6.3). She coordinated the movements of everyone involved, much like an orchestra director. She commanded the respect of others through a benevolent approach. It was evident that a community, and not mere employees, was running the place. The stage, sound, and light systems were of professional quality, and it was evident that the scene's members did all they could to take care of those hoping to make them last as long as possible. "Who knows how they would be replaced if they broke down?" said the person in charge of the sound. In Cuba, the reminders of scarcity are constant.

The importance of the Maxim Theater was not lost on me while walking through it. This was the only rock- and metal-specific agency/theater that is sponsored by any government in the Caribbean and, I would dare venture to state, Latin America. All the people working there are members of the local metal scene. It is truly a labor of love for all involved, and it shows. This seemed to me as a perfect example of the decolonization of cultural spaces. Metal musicians had carved out

137

their own space within the cultural structures of the Cuban government and done so through communal actions. Metal had gone from being a menace to revolutionary ideals to a legitimate cultural manifestation in Cuba. Of course, not all is perfect, and as I stepped outside to speak with kids in the street, some of their main criticism came to the surface; these included having to pay to enter the venue, a perceived unfair process of selecting bands to play there, and the conditions of the theater's roof, which was slowly falling apart (it would be remodeled in 2018 after I had visited). Still, all criticism aside, the importance of the Maxim should not be understated precisely because the space stands as a testament to the struggles faced by metal fans in Cuba and what they have achieved together.

Of course, not everyone would interpret the organizational structuring of metal music via the Cuban Rock Agency and the professionalization process as a positive and supportive strategy. Some would eye these with suspicion, going so far as to label these counterintuitive for metal musicians. How could metal music be critical toward its context if the government was subsidizing it? I would ask this question on several occasions to metal fans, only to receive ambiguous responses. This tension was also present in several of my conversations with local musicians. Lilliana González Moreno placed it in context and highlighted its economic implications:

> There are many perspectives surrounding this Cuban cultural policy and the creation of the "Cuban Rock Agency," the "Maxim Theater," and the idea to professionalize musicians. Many ideas [...] and they all can be discussed in many ways. I don't think it was a mechanism to control heavy metal. I really don't. I think it stemmed from a collective demand by the musicians, a strong visibility of the genre. I think the "Saiz Brothers Organization" had a lot to do with it, as an institution that gathers the aficionado movement in Cuba. And out of all of that – which includes the problem of socially parsing out the professionals from the nonprofessionals and how we assign value to their artistic output – all of that led to the creation of the "Cuban Rock Agency" and the professionalization movement, which has a lot of advantages. Because many musicians – who during the nineties had to work multiple jobs, unrelated to music – could now devote themselves fully to playing heavy metal. They are recognized in a field in which they were previously unseen.

After spending several days in Havana talking with musicians and those involved with the Cuban Rock Agency, I decided to move away from this focal center and engage in conversation with individuals in another province. I traveled to Pinar del Río to meet up with Tendencia and discuss with its members issues of race and ethnicity in Cuban metal music. Much like with other metal-related discussions in Cuba, the country's revolutionary past and present would make their way into reflections on race and ethnicity in this musical genre.

Race and ethnicity in Cuban metal

Early one morning, I took a cab to Pinar del Río. Pinar is the westernmost province in Cuba and is widely known for its tobacco production. It would take me around three hours to get to Pinar by taxi. Most Cubans do it via government buses that are quite unpunctual and always packed. Since I was taking my filming equipment with me, I decided to travel by cab, a choice that cost me around USD 150. The silver lining was that it provided me with the opportunity to see the countryside and converse with the driver.

The road to Pinar from Havana is long and straight. The beauty of the trip lies mostly in seeing the fields covered in sugar cane and tobacco. These went on and on for miles and were sometimes interrupted by pig farms and the occasional cow roaming the fields. Given my upbringing in Puerto Rico, I was struck by the use of land for agricultural purposes in Cuba although, in hindsight, I should not have been. Unlike Cuba, Puerto Rico imports most of what it consumes, and agriculture has been basically abandoned as a strategy to feed the local population. Cuba's situation is quite different, and you just needed to look at the countryside to notice that difference.

Once the cab reached the main bus station in Pinar, I paid the driver, invited him to have a cold beer, and, after all was said and done, off he went. A few moments later, Sergio Puentes the guitar player for Tendencia, showed up to pick me up. Sergio is a small guy, boasting a huge personality. We immediately struck up a conversation as we walked toward the car to load my equipment. Sergio took me to a house in which I rented a room for USD 10 per night. I left my equipment and went with him to walk the streets of Pinar along with other members of the band.

We walked through the main street of the town. It is a long two-way road divided by a small patch of grass. The few local shops available for local consumption are located on this street. The rest are quite far and geared primarily toward tourists. As we walked through the streets, it became quickly evident that people knew Sergio and, more importantly, they knew his band. Some shouts of "Tendencia!" could be heard from across the street as we walked by. I was quite amazed by this occurrence and asked him about it. He responded, "In Cuba, metal is part of local culture. […] We are just as important as the ballet." It was interesting to hear him say this, but, after my experience at the Cuban Rock Agency and the Maxim Theater, I was beginning to somewhat understand his perspective. We continued to walk through the streets, visited a local painter, and ended up having some coffee.

That night I would show my documentary on metal music in Puerto Rico at Pinar del Río. The showing took place at the local office of the "Hermanos Saiz" organization, which Sergio directed. This organization supports amateur artists from all fields within the arts. That night, while I set up my computer to project the documentary, Sergio pointed out that the audience was composed of metal musicians, metal fans, hip hop artists, poets, and plastic artists. He said, "It's the only way to survive. We need to support each other." I was amazed that metal had found its place among these other artistic exponents. Sergio was less concerned with my observation as this seemed to be an everyday reality for him. Just as the event was ready to start, Sergio pulled me aside and mentioned that word of our showing had gotten around, and I had to sign some documents before moving ahead. I handed him a copy of my passport and signed a document stating that the content of my documentary was not counterrevolutionary. Moments like this made me feel like I was inadvertently taking part in that Cold War-era mentality. I was once again reminded of the line I had crossed at the airport. With all documents signed and my ID copied, the showing of the documentary began. People seemed to enjoy it and the night closed with many great conversations with local metal fans.

The next few days were spent with the members of Tendencia. They invited me to hang out with them at their rehearsal space and talk about the history of the band as well as their musical vision regarding Cuban metal. The rehearsal space was a few blocks away from the house where I was staying, so that morning I had some breakfast at a local street café and headed over to the rehearsal space. Their space was in an abandoned open-air amphitheater. The theater itself looked completely shabby, showing signs of not being used for a long time; this included the public toilets, which had no running water. The situation in the amphitheater, which would easily house 500 people, was dire to say the least. Still, the gates opened and we walked into the venue. I was confused as to how this was going to take place since they had no instruments with them and I could not, for the life of me, see where you would store them in such a place.

Sergio walked me over to the stage and explained that they had converted the backstage space into a rehearsal room. Once you stepped into the backstage area, the precarious feel of the space changed drastically. Marshall amplifiers, a plethora of guitars, MIDI pedals, and a fully functional soundboard were part of the equipment they had in the rehearsal space. I was quite impressed with the setup, and I think my face showed it. They were quick to state that they felt fortunate to have received this equipment. Most of the equipment had been donated by Germany as part of a solidarity campaign entitled *Cuba Sí* ("Yes, Cuba"). What was interesting to me was the simultaneous abundance of equipment and complete precariousness within the band. Even with all this equipment, the band's work could be drawn to a halt if a guitar string broke. They had no place to buy new guitar strings, and they made it clear that they relied on what they could buy themselves when traveling abroad or on what friends who visited Cuba brought with them during those visits. The US-imposed blockade of Cuba continues to impact their capacity to have access to basic equipment and many other aspects of their daily lives (Haney 2005; Amnesty International 2009).

For the next couple of days, I would spend my time with the band at their rehearsal space, listening to their music and getting a sense of what they were trying to do. I felt fortunate to be there as they are one of the longest running bands in Cuba, having released their first demo in 1995. When I met them they had released three full-length albums throughout their career, entitled *Re-evolución* (2002), *Rebeldes* (2004), and *Confidencial* (2009), respectively (Manduley López 2015). Considering the limitations of their context, this was no small feat. Their sound can be described as thrash metal with the integration of Afro-Caribbean instrumentation. Their music prominently features *congas* and *timbales* as part of their rhythm section. What was most salient for me about the band is the label they use to describe their sound; they see themselves as a *mestizo metal* band. Mestizo is the local word used to describe individuals who are of mixed racial and ethnic heritage.[6] This entails that the band has willingly assumed a musical identity based on the integration of different races and ethnicities into their sound. More importantly, their choice of instrumentation seemed to highlight the centrality of their African identity, a phenomenon that is almost completely absent from the metal scenes in the Caribbean. In my conversations with María Gattorno, she had brought up the band's decision to use this label and engage in experimentation with local music. She mentioned the difficulties the band faced initially when doing so:

> From the very beginning, Tendencia experimented with the roots of Cuban music. Some liked it, some did not. There was some resistance at the beginning to assimilating them as rock musicians, particularly between other musicians. The fans accepted them naturally. They were a bit surprised because they integrated things, but did it so well. Opinions were divided among musicians. As always, life is stronger than everything else. When you are convinced about what you are doing and do it well, you can achieve things. They achieved that rare balance, which is to integrate and not juxtapose.

The band was well aware of the tensions they had caused among local metal musicians, particularly as it concerned their use of the mestizo label and their integration of local Cuban music into metal. Sergio was very vocal about this tension and the importance of the band's deployment of racial and ethnic elements in their music. One afternoon, while hanging out after a rehearsal, he described their use of the label *mestizo metal*:

Mestizo metal is a term we used because we did not want to be pushed into a box. Since we were always asked how we labeled ourselves [...] we decided upon mestizo metal in light of Cuba's mestizo heritage. Also, our music is a hybrid [...] a "culinary stew" of many things. Respect for the human race is important for us, and, therefore, we claim respect for the Latin race, our customs, music, ideas, and ways of living. That is what we sing about in our lyrics.

He went on to add:

We have fought a lot for Cuban culture, for our ancestors, the history of Cuban culture. We include instruments from African percussion. We have passages from Spanish music. That is where we all come from. [...] Spain, Africa, Cuba. We mix it with metal, without diminishing the heaviness. We make a hybrid, a mixture. It turns out like a stew where we mix everything. But that *ajiaco* (local word for stew) is mostly metal. Then we mix in all other elements of Cuban music, African music.

Alfredo knew that the integration of racial and ethnic components into their music possessed a political dimension. The decision was part of what he perceived as the band's critical positioning. In Spanish he specifically used the word *contestataria* (i.e., rebellious, seditious) to describe the band. He said the following:

I think we have embraced being Cubans and contributed to national culture from that premise. The idea of being socially critical, honest. We don't need to sing explicitly about the revolution. We make revolution criticizing the bad things that happen. We also make revolution when we rescue particular rhythms that people only used in *son* and *salsa*, and we use it in metal. It is our contribution, our grain of sand.

The use of the *mestizo metal* label as part of their musical identity is an important issue to consider for several reasons. First, it seems that the emergence of this label reflects a context in which racial issues are discussed as part of local national identities. More importantly for this discussion, it represents the acceptance and celebration of the varied racial and ethnic identities that characterize the region. Second, there is a decision on the part of local fans and the band members themselves to link their sound to a label that purposefully merges racial issues and metal music. In this sense, and through the use of Afro-Caribbean rhythms, a band like Tendencia celebrates their Black heritage as part of their musical and performative output. Both of these issues need to be understood within the larger context of racial and ethnic discussions in revolutionary Cuba.

Cuba's history with race and ethnic issues is somewhat different from that of other Caribbean countries, like Puerto Rico and the Dominican Republic, where the contributions of people from African descent tend to be systematically forgotten (Varas-Díaz and Mendoza 2015). People of African descent would be saliently present in the historical development of Cuba and be recognized as important individuals in the formation of the island nation. For example, as part of its fight for independence from Spain (1895), Cuban historical accounts recognize the importance Black men like General Antonio Maceo Grajales, second in command of Cuba's independence army against Spain, had in the island's fight for freedom (Zacaïr 2005). He is better known as the *Titán de Bronce* ("Bronze Titan"), a reference to his skin color. One of Cuba's most important leaders, who is still recognized today as a vital figure in its move toward independence, was a Black man. Although Spain would use Maceo's race as the focus of their fear-mongering efforts directed at scarring locals away from the idea of independence, Cubans would discursively alleviate this concern with the phrase "Cuba for the Cubans." The phrase aimed to highlight the belief that an independent Cuba would prevail beyond these racial tensions. Interestingly, Maceo's story would not be the last time race would appear as part of changes in the political landscape of the Island.

The Cuban Revolution of 1953–59 would bring the issue of racial relations yet again to the forefront. Fidel Castro was perceptively aware of the toll racial and social class divisions had taken on the Island. After all, local support for the revolution stemmed in part from people's mistrust of the presiding government. Fulgencio Batista was perceived as a stand-in for US control over the Island and, consequently, an extension of the former's segregationist policies. Under the revolutionary government, a change of perspective on politics and its accompanying ideological dominants would need to emerge. The "New Man" described earlier in this chapter had to be conceived as free from oppressive economic and political regimes. This meant eliminating any perceived differences among Cubans, including prevailing discourses around race and racism. Cultural practices like "Nova Trova" music would reflect this desire for a new social theater (Moore 2006). In fact, Fidel Castro would address this issue publicly in his speeches as Cuba's president. The new Cuba would need to surpass racism as an obstacle for its new worldview to take root. After all, in the eyes of the socialist perspective, the notion that all men were equal became central to the revolutionary idea. Although a post-racial Cuba would never be achieved (González 2015), one cannot deny that discussions about this matter took place publicly at a national level (Prevost 2012). Thus, it would be difficult to conceive of a band like Tendencia in a Caribbean political context other than that of Cuba. Metal bands focusing on racial and ethnic issues, like Tendencia, would be almost unheard of in Puerto Rico or the Dominican Republic.

Our discussions surrounding Tendencia's use of race and ethnicity as guiding principles for their music would go on for hours. We conversed about everything,

FIGURE 6.4: Member of the Cuban band Tendencia playing the *batá*. Photo provided by Nelson Varas-Díaz.

from the influences of Cuban *son* to the drumming patterns of black slaves on the Island. At one particular moment during our discussion, Israel González, the band's percussionist, asked us to step outside of the rehearsal room. He wanted to show us how he specifically incorporated African culture into his drumming patterns. He set up his drums in the middle of the standing space for the amphitheater, asked me to turn my camera on, and began to play. His ability to play the drums was uncanny. It was evident that years of musical education and practice had informed what he was doing. It is not surprising given that music is an integral part of the education of all children in Cuba. This particular setup he played was called the *batá* (see Figure 6.4). It is comprised of three separate drums of different sizes each. He went on to explain that the *Iyá*, the largest one, is referred to as the "mother drum"; the middle one was known as *Itótele* (the "father"); and the smallest one, *Okónkolo*, is seen as the "baby" drum. This type of drum arrangement is used in the Yoruba religion and in *Santería* practices to summon specific deities and saints. Each rhythmic pattern calls upon a particular saint; needless to say, variations abound. Israel also explained how each drum set was specially prepared via religious rituals for a particular musician. Therefore, I was not allowed to play it. He played the drums for

144

a few minutes, and everyone in attendance was simply captivated by his ability and the sounds he produced. Hearing Israel play, right then and there, made palpable Tendencia's active integration of local culture into metal music, a practice that was well thought out and that showed to me how deeply entrenched Cuban history, and by extension African culture, were in this band. Israel had managed to explain that connection in sound; no additional words were needed after that.

NOTES

1. In many of my conversations with participants throughout Latin America, the linkages between metal music and homosexuality were described as expressions of uninformed social prejudice. Still, it should be noted that recent metal scholarship has shed light on the links between this musical genre and nonnormative gender/sexual identities. Amber Clifford-Napoleone (2015) has written extensively on metal music's use of elements derived from queer culture. Queerness has manifested in metal's aesthetics (e.g., leather), lyrical context, and the self-identification of many of its main musicians as members of the LGBTQI community. Of course, this does not mean that homophobia is not present in metal music; far from it (Clifford-Napoleone 2016). It is a problem that must be addressed, and decolonial metal has the potential to do so in the Global South and beyond. What decolonial metal entails for reflections about metal music in Latin America is the realization that, without diminishing the discrimination suffered by rock and metal fans, we must now recognize that the linkages between metal music and queer culture have been there from the genre's inception, and the association of metal to homosexuality had an underlying level of truth to it, even when this truth became a tool used by society in its discriminatory practices.

2. Jeremy Wallach has pointed to the fact that the concerns over rock music's role in fostering Western cultural imperialism were mostly ill placed, as it "did not ultimately compel Third World masses to submit meekly to US hegemony" (Wallach 2020: 472).

3. "Friki" is a term used to describe rock and metal fans who constantly exhibit a music-centered dress code, regardless of context. Earrings, black t-shirts, jeans, and boots are mostly part of this dress code, which aims to inform the rest of society about the musical preference of a metal fan. During my fieldwork, I gathered conflicting information with regard to the term's meaning and emergence. For some participants, the concept had its roots in the word "freak." Other musicians, however, linked the word to the term "free kids" and the search for freedom that characterized rock in the 1960s.

4. The idea that María was the "mother" of the metal movement in Cuba was mentioned by many participants. It kept coming up again and again during my trips there. It always struck me as interesting that while metal scholarship in the Global North published on the experiences of sexism faced by women in metal scenes (Hill 2016), or how women navigated their femininity in these settings (Kummer 2016), Cuban metal fans and artists held María in such high standards. Maybe it was her stern yet nurturing character or her fierce attitude in

protecting these young musicians, but one thing was certain; her presence was everywhere in the metal scene. This does not mean that sexism was not present in Cuba's metal scene, but it seems like an important window into how gender dynamics were different in this historically transgressive and revolutionary context. I would also argue that María Gattorno's presence in the local metal scene was characterized by a decolonial positioning, as she surpassed traditional female gender roles associated with passivity and motherhood, and adopted an identity based on influence, respect, and power (even if yielded in a very affectionate manner). For more information on coloniality and gender, I suggest examining the work of María Lugones (2008), Gloria Anzaldúa (1987), and Rita Laura Segato (2010). Their work, although with explicit differences in terms of their positionalities and opinions on the role of the colonial process on gender dynamics, clearly stresses how coloniality used gender as an oppressive category/strategy towards women. Segato's work in particular is useful to understand María's decolonial positioning in the Cuban metal scene. She stresses the importance of *vínculos* (linkages) and community in challenging oppression in its many forms, be it patriarchy or coloniality. It seems to me that María embodied those principles in her everyday actions by challenging authority, exerting leadership, serving as a model for women in the scene, and standing alongside the marginalized.

5.   Miriela Fernández (2020) has published an important and detailed description of the tensions experienced during the Cuban Rock Agency's first decade of existence. Her work is one of the very few in the academic world to address this topic. It is useful for readers interested in the leadership transitions experienced there and the context of María Gattorno's return to the metal scene.

6.   It was interesting to see how the band used the concept of *Mestizo* to describe their music. This concept is usually used to describe individuals with mixed European and indigenous ancestry. Mulatto is another term used to describe racial mixing between people of European and Black African ancestry. Although their musical style was mostly described as linked to Afro-Caribbean rhythms, the band never used the term "mulatto." This seemed very important and strategic, as the term can have a highly stigmatizing undertone. The idea is closely linked to the mule, a cross between a horse and a donkey, which can rarely have offspring.

REFERENCES

Amnesty International (2009), *The US Embargo Against Cuba: Its Impact on Economic and Social Rights*, https://www.amnesty.org/download/Documents/44000/amr250072009en.pdf. Accessed August 25, 2020.

Anderson, Jon Lee (2010), *Che Guevara: A Revolutionary Life*, New York: Grover Press.

Anzaldúa, Gloria (1987), *Borderlands – La Frontera: The New Mestiza*, San Francisco, CA: Aunt Lute Books.

Clifford-Napoleone, Amber R. (2015), *Queerness in Heavy Metal Music: Metal Bent*, New York: Routledge.

Clifford-Napoleone, Amber R. (2016), "Metal, masculinity, and the queer subject," in F. Heesch and N. Scott (eds.), *Heavy Metal – Gender and Sexuality: Interdisciplinary Approaches*, New York: Routledge, pp. 39–51.

Fernández, Miriela (2020), "The metal scene in Havana, Cuba: An assessment of its cultural development from 2007 to 2017," in N. Varas-Díaz, D. Nevárez Araújo, and E. Rivera-Segarra (eds.), *Heavy Metal Music in Latin America*: *Perspectives from the Distorted South*, London: Lexington Press, pp. 133–59.

González, Ivet (2015), "Cuba requiere actualizar lucha contra nuevas formas de racismo," *Diálogo*, http://www.ipsnoticias.net/2015/02/cuba-requiere-actualizar-lucha-contra-nuevas-formas-de-racismo/. Accessed August 25, 2020.

González Moreno, Liliana de la C. (2013), "Colección digital Fanzines cubanos de rock: Descripción y valoración desde una perspectiva patrimonial," *Cuadernos Cidmuc*, 1, pp. 68–96.

Haney, Patrick Jude (2005), *The Cuban Embargo: The Domestic Politics of an American Foreign Policy*, Pittsburg, PA: University of Pittsburg Press.

Hansing, Katrin (2002), *Rasta, Race and Revolution: The Emergence and Development of the Rastafari Movement in Socialist Cuba*, Berlin: Lit Verlag.

Hill, Rosemary Lucy (2016), *Gender, Metal and the Media: Women Fans and the Gendered Experience of Music*, London: Palgrave Macmillan.

Kummer, Jenna (2016), "Powerslaves? Navigating femininity in heavy metal," in B. Gardenour Walter, G. Riches, D. Snell, and B. Bardine (eds.), *Heavy Metal Studies and Popular Culture*, London: Palgrave Macmillan, pp. 145–66.

Lugones, María (2008), "Colonialidad y género," *Tabula Rasa*, 9:July–December, pp. 73–101.

Manduley López, Humberto (2013), *Hierba Mala: Una Historia del Rock en Cuba*, Havana, Cuba: Nialanai Ediciones.

Manduley López, Humberto (2015), *Parche: Enciclopedia del Rock en Cuba*, Havana, Cuba: Nialanai Ediciones.

Moore, Robin D. (2006), *Music & Revolution: Cultural Change in Socialist Cuba*, CA: University of California Press.

Morales Domínguez, Esteban (2012), *Race in Cuba: Essays on the Revolution and Racial Inequality*, New York: Monthly Review Press.

Pacini Hernández, Deborah and Garofalo, Reebee (2004), "Between rock and a hard place: Negotiating rock in revolutionary Cuba, 1963–1980," in D. Pacini Hernández, H. Fernández L'Hoeste, and E. Zolov (eds.), *Rockin' Las Américas: The Global Politics of Rock in Latin/o America*, Pittsburg, PA: University of Pittsburg Press, pp. 43–66.

Segato, Rita (2018), *La Crítica de la Colonialidad en Ocho Ensayos: Y una Antropología por Demanda*, Buenos Aires: Prometeo Libros.

Segato, Rita Laura (2010), "Género y colonialidad," in A. Quijano and J. Mejía (eds.), *La Cuestión Decolonial*, Lima: Universidad Ricardo Palma.

Tendencia (2002), "*Re-evolución*," CD, n.l.: System Shock.

Tendencia (2004), "*Rebeldes*," CD, Havana: Independent.

Tendencia (2009), "*Confidencial*," CD, Habana: Santo Grial Records.

Varas-Díaz, Nelson and Mendoza, Sigrid (2015), "Ethnicity, politics and otherness in Caribbean heavy metal music: Experiences from Puerto Rico, Dominican Republic and Cuba," in T. M. Karjalainen and K. Kärki (eds.), *Modern Heavy Metal: Market, Practices and Culture*, Helsinki: Department of Management Studies, Aalto University, pp. 291–99.

Wallach, Jeremy (2020), "Global rock as postcolonial soundtrack," in A. Moore and P. Carr (eds.), *Bloomsbury Handbook for Rock Music Research*, New York: Bloomsbury, pp. 469–85.

Zacaïr, Philippe (2005), "Haiti on his mind: Antonio Maceo and Caribbeanness," *Caribbean Studies*, 33:1, pp. 47–78.

7

Navigating Racism, Classism, and Complex Airwaves – Dominican Republic

Exploring decolonial experiences within the metal scene in the Dominican Republic is a complex process deeply informed by the country's history. This is a setting still sharply marked by the experience of colonialism, particularly when it comes to discussions about race and the systemic devaluing of Black people. It is no surprise, then, that these ideas find their way into the local scene and, consequently, exert great influence on metal music. This becomes particularly apparent when one comes to understand the ways in which this musical genre has tried to avoid identification with local sounds and themes. In this setting, *extreme decolonial dialogues* carried out by the younger members of the scene have been characterized by communal exchanges and approaches that have allowed them to engage in reflections and actions that challenge the historical legacy of racism and classism, two of the more damaging consequences of the colonial experience in the Caribbean region.

"Chopo Metal" and racial tensions

The cameras were set, microphones were hot, and my team was ready for an important interview, which began with a simple question: Why does metal music in the Dominican Republic seem to avoid integrating local culture into its output? The informant looked somewhat uncomfortable. After a few seconds of silence, he answered: "It's musical racism." Silence filled the room for a brief moment while everyone processed those words. Before a follow-up question was stated, the manager jumped from behind an amplifier and shouted: "You can't say that! You can't say it that way." My team was asked to stop our recording devices while an impromptu chat was held. We could not hear what was being said, but it was clearly evident that the question had struck a chord. Right then and there I became aware of the importance of exploring issues of race in order to truly understand the Dominican metal scene.[1] I would not let this line of inquiry subside without a fight.

My question was not posed in a vacuum. I had started traveling to the Dominican Republic in 2013 to better understand metal music in the country. By then I had completed most of my research in Puerto Rico and Cuba. Therefore, I had been in direct contact with two metal scenes in which the integration of local culture into metal music was evident and salient (Varas-Díaz and Mendoza 2015). I was curious to examine whether this practice extended to the Dominican metal scene, whether the metal community in the country had carried out a similar cultural integration, and, if so, how it had manifested. After the event described earlier, I continued to ask local informants about this issue. I was surprised when my queries about this potential link between Dominican culture and metal music continued to yield long moments of silence and, at times, even some uncomfortable stares. "We really don't play *chopo* metal here," stated one of my informants in a street interview. The meaning and baggage of the word *chopo* will be considered below.

I had gotten to know some musicians in the local metal scene and began to hang out with them in bars where bands would play. One night, while listening to a covers band, I brought up the notion of integrating local instrumentation and rhythms into Dominican metal music; I was trying to find some examples. To help describe what I meant, and trying to get the discussion going, I mentioned examples like Tendencia in Cuba and Puya in Puerto Rico. One of my informants initially mentioned the bands Sinesthesia and Altum Mortem, who had incorporated the *tambora*, a local percussion instrument, into some of their songs. Although these bands were provided as examples of the integration of local culture into metal music, the informant rapidly stated that "these were used in particular songs" and that such instances did not define the respective sounds of those bands. He wanted me to understand clearly that the *tambora* was not a centerpiece of those bands' music. He also mentioned that no current bands were known for integrating local instrumentation or arrangements into their music. When I probed into the rationale behind this fact, he immediately stated that this was done to avoid having metal music be labeled as *chopo*. In all my years living in the Caribbean, which also included frequent visits to the Dominican Republic, I had never come across this term. I was intrigued and, judging by his facial gestures, felt that we were heading toward a sensitive conversation. The term had an evident derogatory connotation, something I could easily sense in his tone of voice.

Chopo is a local slang term derived from the English word "shopping." Its entry into colloquial usage is linked to the 1916 invasion of the Dominican Republic on the part of the United States (Castor and Garafola 1974; Ferguson 1998). Americans who settled on the country following the invasion would employ locals as "shopping boys" who helped them carry out everyday tasks, which included shopping for goods. Locals appropriated the word *chopo* as a way to refer to these individuals who served the Americans. In time, the term's meaning evolved; nowadays, it mostly refers to individuals whose style, taste, and habits fall outside of what is currently considered cool or trendy in Dominican society. The individuals I interviewed expanded the word's meaning to include concepts like "low class," "ridiculous," and "servants." They went on to describe how lovers of *reggaeton* music, for example, were all considered *chopos*.

It quickly became evident throughout the interviews that the use of *chopo* as an adjective to describe a sector of the population included many factors not limited to musical preferences. Its association to the "lower classes" (i.e., the poor) and servitude, I soon found, was intrinsically related to race. As is the case in most countries in the Caribbean, those individuals who find work in service jobs (particularly those who work within private households) are usually racially Black; they also tend to belong to the economically poor. Thus, *chopos* has become an umbrella term that signifies not just the lower classes and the service sector but also blackness. Thus, the negative characteristics attached to the word *chopos* are informed by an underlying thread of racism mostly directed at Dominicans of African descent. While during these conversations informants were quick to mention that "Whites can also be *chopos*," they always qualified this observation by adding that these "would be a minority." Therefore, in the end and after having consumed some local beers, these same informants would come to freely state that *chopos* were mostly racially Black individuals.

Several other fans and musicians had joined in the conversation after a while. They, too, shared the idea that integrating local instrumentation into metal would immediately open the door to discard this hybrid as *chopo* music. When examined in detail, the word revealed a cognitive and instrumental distancing of Dominican metal music from local racial issues, particularly those related to the country's African heritage. In order to comprehend Dominican metal music's aversion to integrating local racial and ethnic traits into metal music, one must come face to face with the way racial and ethnic relations are experienced in the Dominican Republic.

For those who enter the Dominican Republic with the ideological racial dominants of the North (US, Canada, Europe), that is, those stereotypes entrenched from years of racializing physical features, among other traits, most Dominicans would be seen as Black following those countries' standards of racial categorization. However, Dominicans see race in a much more complex and dynamic way. In fact, Dominicans have developed a complex process of racial categorization in which dark-skin individuals may not always be considered Black. For example, a term like *indio* (literally translated as Indian[2]) is used to describe individuals who are of African racial descent but whose skin color is on the lighter side of the spectrum, in what seems like an outright manifestation of colorism. In the local racial imaginary, which is heavily influenced by the region's colonial past and its racists practices, the term Black is almost exclusively reserved to describe Haitians from the neighboring country. Racial identification here becomes an exercise in nuance; Haitians' darker skin tone clearly links them to their African racial heritage, something Dominicans are quick to point out. Many Dominicans contrast their own lighter skin tone against Haitians' darker features and levy it as a mark of superiority. Although some dark-skinned Dominicans have no problem recognizing this African influence on their racial composition, they rarely categorize themselves as belonging to the same group as Haitians. Their shared African heritage is not always a welcome notion for many Dominicans.

The idea of Dominicans as a mostly White society is long-held, which gained a lot of traction during the dictatorship of Rafael Trujillo (1930–61) (Gates, Pollack, and Petterle 2011). As part of his plan to strategically position the country on the world stage, Dominican whiteness would be greatly highlighted via magazines and the press. In fact, Trujillo took this obsession further when he began to wear makeup as a way to lighten his skin tone (Gates, Pollack, and Petterle 2011). These actions nurtured the idea of Dominicans' whiteness within the country: so long as they were whiter than their neighboring Haitian counterparts, Dominicans would be in a better position, the logic went. This phenomenon is even present in the local school curricula taught to children (Pérez Saba 2009). Racial comparison has historically served to define politics and local identity in the Dominican Republic (Howard 1997).

The tension between Haitians and Dominicans must also be understood in light of the constant public debate over what is perceived as the uncontrolled immigration of Haitians into the Dominican Republic (Rosario and Ulloa 2006). I witnessed, on several occasions, the way in which Dominicans frequently mention Haiti's invasion of their territory in 1822 (Paulino 2006) in even the most trivial of conversations. This perception has not abated, with many Dominicans stating that a Haitian invasion, always in waiting, is a reality that must be constantly avoided. These discussions usually avoid mentioning that Haitians have been systematically killed in the Dominican Republic (Turits 2002) and that violence toward them is frequent and ever present (Paulino 2006; Simmons 2010), oftentimes under the auspices of the government itself. In summary, racial differences among Dominicans and Haitians, although sometimes invisible to the untrained eye, are a constant source of discussion in the country. These tensions make racism and xenophobia a constant problem and unavoidably make their way into music-related discussions.

With this in mind, it becomes easier to understand how the integration of racial and ethnic local influences into metal music can be perceived as a potential devaluation of the genre and a threat to the "purity of metal," as one informant described it. It must be noted that this discussion of racial issues is not limited to metal music; the topic encompasses many other facets of life in the Dominican Republic.

Still, it sheds light on the context within which Dominican metal musicians craft their music and how it influences that creative process. Needless to say, the entire dynamic made me curious as to how the local metal scene interpreted these racial tensions. Fortunately, after engaging in multiple conversations with a cadre of informants, the issue of social class and metal would firmly come to the surface.

Social class and Dominican metal music

As I delved deeper into the issues of race and ethnicity found in the Dominican metal scene as mentioned earlier, it became readily evident that examining its origins could shed some light on these tensions. I decided to concentrate some of my interviews with older members of the local scene on the origins of the metal scene. At the outset, two important events stood out as cornerstones for the formation of the local metal scene. The first was the *Olimpiadas del Rock* ("Rock Olympics"), a cluster of yearly talent shows where local musicians played original music and competed for prizes. One of these *Olimpiadas*, held in 1985, was won by the local metal band Cygnus. Locals described these events as evidence that, at some point, metal musicians had some level of access to local cultural circles in which their music was appreciated. This level of access, however, would be short lived; metal bands would later be summarily banned from the event due to local moral panics, something I will go into further detail later in this chapter. This backlash led metal fans to coalesce around an abandoned house where they would continue to hold their concerts, a place locals affectionately called the Metal House (see Figure 7.1). This impromptu venue would become embedded in the scene's collective memory as an important geographic space for metal musicians.

During deeper reflections on the scene's origins, and the aforementioned events in particular, local metal fans would, without hesitation, bring up the issue of social class. To a great extent, it was as if the wound never healed, and any mention of the matter would quickly open it. They divided the local scene's history into three time periods. The first period started during the early 1980s and held strong until the early 1990s (with bands like Empiphis, Hekaton, Nexuc, Cygnus, and Abaddon RD). A second generation joined the scene in the 1990s (with bands like Necro and Archaios). By 2002, a third period took root, remaining active until the end of the decade (with bands like Mithril and Merodac). Metal fans frequently described the first generation as "elitist." While they showed great respect for this generation, I could sense an underlying tone of emotional distance and disengagement whenever it was brought up. One informant mentioned that the first generation of metal was "classist," explaining it as an issue that boiled down to access.

FIGURE 7.1: Maik Abbadon playing at the Metal House, Dominican Republic. Image provided by Maik Abbadon.

When metal started in the eighties, it was extremely classist. Why? Because you could not listen to it on the radio. You could not read about it in the newspapers. These were the means of free access to information for people. You could not access it on the radio, on newspapers, or the television. How could you access metal? How did it reach you? You needed a family member living in another country. You had to visit another country or have a friend send it to you from another country. Those three options were not available to most Dominicans. That was reserved for an elite within the country.

Another informant mentioned how this access to economic resources made the local musicians different from the concertgoers. While musicians had economic resources to buy instruments and put on a show, their audience found themselves stuck in the role of spectators, something that was evident during local concerts.

During the eighties, concerts were put on with power generators and your own money. They did not have today's technology. People who attended, and mostly the musicians, were from the upper class. Those that were musicians in the scene were sons of people with money, people who studied abroad. They had money to buy instruments, which was difficult to do in our country. Socially and economically speaking, they were different from the public and the scene we have today.

Metal fans were not the only ones to mention this sense of elitism. Throughout my visits, some of my family members living in the country had become aware of my research and felt inclined to provide their input on how they perceived metal during the 1980s. Metal musicians were described as "well educated" and "respected." These conversations yielded more evidence that during this initial phase of the local scene, and probably for a long period of time, metal musicians garnered local respect. I sensed that this respect had little to do with their musical preferences, but rather with their education and social class. Informants mentioned that the sense of "class" and "entitlement" ascribed to the first generation of metal musicians had a racial undertone. Access to resources (i.e., records and instruments) was mostly available to racially White Dominicans. One informant described it as follows:

> You could say that it was a club. Being a metal fan in the eighties gave you some sort of distinction from others. You felt proud because it was something that not everyone could share. That lasted for a very long time. Only people who had a certain level of income could get the music, buy instruments, and make that type of music. That was for Whites, and not for the rest of the 98 percent of the country.

These conversations with local metal fans shed significant light on the initial composition of the local metal scene. Most importantly, it allowed me to understand why the integration of local culture and sounds to metal music was considered problematic. Social class and race had played an important role in the development of the scene, and the upper social class would rarely interact with the local cultural output of Black Dominicans. By extension, metal fans had reproduced traditional colonial discourses that devalued local culture and, in turn, promoted the racial categorization of their context. This had limited, at least during its initial phase, the presence of more Black Dominicans in the scene.

This often unspoken categorization within the local metal scene through the lens of "elitism" would not be their only problem. The local media would also do its part, blatantly harassing the movement's members, a reality that would spawn an important event in the scene's history. Below I will discuss how this persecution occurred, how the metal community reacted to it, and how this response influenced the racial and social class composition of the local scene.

Mediatic persecution in the Dominican Republic

During my conversations with local metal fans and musicians, many began to provide me with documents that they believed would help me understand the local scene's history. Many of them would bring clippings from local newspapers, urging me to read through them, as they captured the intense media persecution metal had faced in the country during the 1980s and 1990s. One informant mentioned that, although they "were able to enjoy the music with some level of isolation" within the country, they, nonetheless, experienced "some contagion with the international criticism of heavy metal." The moral panics over the music's perceived effects manifested in the United States had reached the Dominican Republic. Judging from the news reports I had access to, the local media's reaction had been intense, to say the least.

Local fans mentioned being "singled out in the media," be it in newspapers, magazines, or local television. One mentioned that, in a highly religious context, the country "usually mixed 'destruction' with 'lack of research'." Many interviewees described how they felt bombarded by these attacks on the genre and their emerging scene. One of them saw it as an attack on metal music's critical nature and its capacity to denounce the prejudices and harmful ideals of Dominican society.

> There was a form of blackmail [...] cheap and ugly publicity. I don't even know how to describe it. I would see it on television programs that are still active today in our country. It's shameful! Award-winning journalists that would say, "This is what we are talking about today. Let's talk badly about metal." With no research! This is a genre that has been attacked by particular interests, because heavy metal opens your mind. It makes you do your research. It makes you study. It makes you think that there is more than shaking your (ass). [...] Heavy metal gives you the opportunity to say, "There are things happening in this country that I can denounce with my music, even though it may be violent."

I was aghast at the content of the newspaper reports provided; I had not seen media attacks like these anywhere else in the Caribbean. One of the names that came up the most was that of journalist Huchi Lora. Therefore, I decided to contact him and have a conversation about his reporting on metal music. It took me several months to schedule an interview with the local news reporter. Initially, I thought this process would be easy. After all, I was just trying to corroborate research findings from my local informants. Still, it became evident during the process that Lora was a busy man who is very sought out in the country. Upon finally granting me the interview, he decided we should meet in a local restaurant in Santo Domingo. I scheduled my trip to the Dominican Republic, jumped in a cab, and headed for the restaurant.

I spoke to the driver about Lora to get a sense of how locals perceived him. He was very impressed that I was meeting with him. More importantly, he was surprised that I did not know much of his work. He described Lora as a "journalist of the people." He was a professional without "blemishes," rapidly adding "up to now" as a reminder that anything can change in the blink of an eye in the Dominican Republic. Still, the driver gave me a glowing review of his work and told me to "remember that Huchi Lora was a pioneer in journalism when the country was getting out from under Trujillo's dictatorship." He went on to explain how journalists like Lora had to travel with security as their lives were in danger in light of their work.

I arrived at the restaurant about fifteen minutes before our prearranged time. I had never met Lora, so I was unaware if he would be there or not. I told the hostess that I was meeting with him, and she immediately told me not to worry, as she would show him to the table when he arrived. Lora arrived about forty minutes later. A small man in his seventies, his presence was felt in the room. It was evident that a celebrity had arrived at the restaurant, as people were sneaking glances over to our table, with some even asking to take pictures with him. We proceeded to introduce ourselves and began to talk about metal music.

I explained to Lora the nature of my study and how I had come across multiple news articles critical of metal music in the Dominican Republic. I mentioned that he had written some of those news reports and that understanding his intentions was the motivation for our meeting. When I outlined what I wanted to discuss with him, he immediately stated that he would be "surprised to remember an article from so long ago." I placed my laptop computer on the table and showed him one of the articles in question. His face lit up and he immediately said, "I remember that article. That was in the late eighties." It turns out that Lora remembered the publication and the context that motivated it in great detail.

Lora had become interested in metal music during the 1980s, mostly due to his concern over the music and its accompanying images, a concern that was widespread among parents or family members of the time. He mentioned that his "nephew had rock magazines and some albums" and he was interested in what he called the "insistence of symbols like daggers and skulls." He was outright honest about the origins of his interest. Lora stressed on multiple occasions that his main concern was the alleged drug consumption associated with the music genre. He saw in the magazines and the music's imagery the potential to motivate drug use among the local youth. I asked him if he ever saw metal artists consuming drugs, but received no direct answer. I was surprised about this concern, since Lora, a musician himself, had been a participant in the world of salsa music, a realm in which drug use has been well documented, but this link between music and drugs did not seem to extend beyond metal music in Lora's views. He stated the following:

> In the case of rock, with so much insistence on blood, suicide, knives, and all those symbols [...] I equated that with drug consumption. I don't think anyone in a lucid, conscious, and tranquil state could be in on that. That had to be related to drug use, I thought.

Throughout our conversation it became readily evident that Lora was concerned about the use of music, and metal in particular, during the 1980s, as a front for the drug industry. His concern may not have been misplaced, as drugs consumed in North America frequently make their way there through the Caribbean. What was interesting to me was his insistence on metal music as the epicenter of this behavior. When asked to describe how he came to this conclusion, he stated that he had started "buying magazines and saw that those symbols had an industry behind it. They had offers for shirts with those symbols. Blood [...] a lot of insistence on the blood. [...] I saw it as an industry and was concerned." I asked him to define how both "industries" were linked, but Lora was unable to provide a clear response. He seemed to be shocked by the imagery more than anything else, having mentioned Ozzy Osbourne (after confusing him with Bon Jovi) and his "killing of a goat" as an example. The link between metal music and the local drug industry may have been an initial concern at some point for Lora, but the way his articles portrayed metal internationally and locally was more complex and nuanced than that.

An example of this nuance can be seen in an article Lora published in the September 18, 1988, edition of the local newspaper *El Nacional* (Lora 1988). The article became an instant source of influence for the discussion of metal in the Dominican Republic (see Figure 7.2). Although Lora highlights his concern over drug consumption and trafficking in the first paragraph, the article's content reflects how his apprehensions surpassed that initial concern. In it, he linked metal music to satanic cults, homosexuality, bisexuality, suicide, AIDS, crime, violence, anarchism, and murder. Some of these examples were supported with descriptions of criminal events that had taken place in the Dominican Republic, but which were, in fact, unrelated to metal music. It was a strategy at the service of regulating and, one could argue, colonizing a young population that was perceived as out of control. The article, when looked at objectively with the benefit of the elapsed time, is a collection of all the moral panics ascribed to metal music internationally, but compiled and presented with a local flair. That flair came in the shape of a specific mention of the local metal band Abaddon RD.[3]

FIGURE 7.2: News article on the perils of metal music written by Huchi Lora and published in *El Nacional*. Image provided by Edwin Demorizi.

When describing local metal bands of the time, Lora stated in our interview, "There were some groups here but they had little incidence." Still, as part of his writing he had placed his sights on the local metal band Abaddon RD. He described the band, as part of the ongoing link between metal music and Satanism, clarifying that although the band's name had a religious origin, it was mainly linked to the book of apocalypse and the figure of Satan himself. He went on to describe the local musicians as pawns in a scheme that was much larger than them. The fact that Abaddon RD had walked on stage carrying a coffin as part of their participation in the second Rock Olympics held in Santo Domingo only served to fuel the fire of discord between the metal band and the journalist. The content of the newspaper article soon found its way into TV programs and, suddenly, the Dominican Republic seemed obsessed with metal music in general. Abaddon RD, in particular, was at the center of it all. As Lora himself stated in our interview, "I was the one to mainly talk about this; others echoed the sentiment."

As part of my visits to the Dominican Republic, I had the opportunity to meet on many occasions with Maik Abbadon, vocalist and guitarist for the band bearing his name. He stressed how the mediatic persecution via newspapers and TV programs could be felt on the streets. He shared vivid memories of the many ways the media had persecuted metal in the Dominican Republic and minced no words when factoring in Lora's role in that process. He mentioned the following:

> Abaddon was a victim of those accusations. Since we were in the middle of it, we were the most accused. Specifically by a journalist called Huchi Lora. He wrote many articles in the paper for which he worked, *El Nacional* newspaper. He also worked on TV and spoke a lot of shit about us. The main accusation was that we were Satanist, drug users, and homosexuals.

Maik did not see the media's attention to metal music or his band in a vacuum. He was inquisitive about these events and placed them within his rich description of the country's history. The emergence of the metal scene during the late 1980s and early 1990s coincided with the rise of Joaquín Balaguer to the presidency. Balaguer's government was active in identifying and controlling what was perceived as deviant behavior. Metal fans, mainly due to the described media coverage, would be labeled as "delinquents." Maik explained how, as a young teenager, he was frequently stopped by the *cascos negros* ("black helmets"), a local name given to the police, merely for the metal attire he sported:

> At the time, Dr. Joaquín Balaguer was in power. He was Trujillo's right-hand man at one time. He had that dictator profile, although he was not one per se. He had that influence from his youth, after having worked with someone that was a hard-liner in the Dominican Republic. All the military and the police that worked in that government saw us as delinquents. To the extent that on one occasion I had an encounter with a patrol car, which stopped me for wearing a leather bracelet with spikes. They were small, which is what I could get my hands on. I was detained for carrying a lethal weapon. I thought it was illogical. Still [...] they would detain you and tell you, "Either hand it over or we're taking you to jail." As a young person, an adolescent [...] intimidated by those people who were called "the black helmets" because they used a black helmet and a gray uniform. [...] They always had a baton to hit whoever got in the way of their job. Not only me [...] it happened to many who were intimidated by the police, even while being good people. We were only interested in music.

Maik knew that many metal fans experienced these run-ins with the police. The idea of metal fans as delinquent youth had emerged in great part from the mediatic accounts. Although Lora had played an important role in this process, in truth, other media outlets had run with similar stories, putting out editorials describing the music as demonic and linked to animal sacrifices. Local news outlets would publish metal-related information regarding concert events and compare these gathering to cult meetings (Placencia 1991). Metal clothing was described as demonic, and this did not fare well in a highly religious country. Images of metal fans using black t-shirts adorned with devils and skull corpses and imprinted with the names of international bands were included in nationally distributed newspapers. In them, moshing was also criticized and described as a dance practiced by "possessed people." Echoing my previously described discussions with local fans and musicians, one report stated that metal fans in the Dominican Republic hated being called *chopos*. In summary, Lora's reputation and initial publication had served as a rallying call against metal in the country. In a religious country where the church, the media, and the police had a history of being instrumental to a repressive dictatorship, metal music fans became a targeted population that was perceived as a threat to the country's more traditional religious values. Still, this perception would change over time, and metal-loving youth would use the same media outlets that once persecuted them to change this.

The metal counternarrative hits the airwaves

As my travels to the Dominican Republic continued, I had the opportunity to talk with more local metal fans, this time focusing on how they had challenged the media's bombardment and the local moral panics that had spread as a result. One silver lining came up in every conversation I had with local metal fans and musicians: the *Avanzada Metallica* radio program. So, I set out to meet with the creators of the seemingly famous radio show.

Created in the early 2000s, the *Avanzada Metallica* was a multilevel platform that allowed people from all over the world, but especially Latin America and the Caribbean, to contact each other, talk about bands, and listen to metal music. Initially, the group hosted a traditional radio show, which later became a web-based experience through the use of internet radio and a webpage[4] with online chats and discussion boards. They also organized metal concerts and educated the public about Latin American, Caribbean, and international metal bands from different time periods. Initially, this platform was created somewhat inadvertently when the hosts played a heavy metal song as part of a local rock radio program. As one of its members put it, "The phone rang off the hook" with calls from people in the Dominican Republic requesting more metal music. That happy accident evolved into a radio program known as the *Avanzada Metallica*. The radio show slowly grew and the group was able to organize local and international shows. More importantly, the group developed an internet platform for exchange among music lovers, a development that gave the *Avanzada* great reach.

The *Avanzada Metallica* was created with two specific purposes in mind: to use the media to counter-attack the stigmatizing representations of metal being disseminated in the press and to create a platform that helped connect metal fans internationally, while still focusing on bands from Latin America and the Caribbean. Junior Maiden, one of its members and main organizer, pointed out how the *Avanzada Metallica*'s contact with Latin American and the Caribbean was one of its most important accomplishments:

> It was a radio show that started as something almost clandestine. It grew and they achieved their goal, which was to be on Dominican radio. I always compare it to Puerto Rico. When I met Erico (singer for Puerto Rican band Dantesco), he told me that we were blessed to have a metal radio show where local bands were showcased. That did not exist at the time in Puerto Rico. [...] The *Avanzada* has supported Latin American metal, and we try to show all of our metal brothers that metal isn't only consumed in the Dominican Republic and that many of us [metal fans] are also from the other Caribbean islands and Latin American countries, that we are united thanks to the internet, which allows us to share our good music.

Bárbara Rodríguez, one of *Avanzada Metallica*'s radio hosts, reiterated their intention of creating a metal community that included international bands, but whose main focus was on those from Latin America who sang in Spanish. She also recalled how the *Avanzada Metallica* helped her appreciate and learn all she knows about heavy metal bands from the Caribbean and Latin America. By listening to these bands, she learned to value metal bands that sang in Spanish, as she was accustomed to listening to bands sing exclusively in English:

> Spanish-speaking bands started to communicate with us via our webpage, e-mail [...] "I am from Venezuela, Colombia, Perú and I have a band. My name is X, can I send you my music? Will you play it?" We were thrilled. [...] I feel proud that many Latin American bands use their sociocultural context to write their music. Their music speaks about them. It allows you to know them a bit more even though you can't travel to that country. With our contact with Latin American bands, I started to appreciate more metal in my language. I usually listened to more music in English. Suddenly, because of the program, I began appreciating metal in my own language. There are bands that I love for that. I would not change them. That is what the connection between the *Avanzada* and the Latin American countries taught me [...] to appreciate metal in my language, Spanish.

In spite of the previously described stigmatizing representations of the local metal community, and worries that the *Avanzada Metallica* would be censured, it became a platform to contest the negative portrayal of metal fans. Now, the same media outlets that participated in stigmatizing metal were being used as an instrument to challenge those depictions. In a newspaper clip from 2003, the *Avanzada Metallica* organizers (Edwin Demorizi, Ruth Paredes, and José Maracallo) explicitly announced its purpose: the use of the media to counter-attack the stigmatization of metal fans in the Dominican Republic (Saba 2003). This idea would be stated in many other publications (see Figure 7.3). In order to do this, the *Avanzada Metallica's* program moved through several radio stations looking to widen their audience and impact more listeners. Junior Maiden recalled how the platform allowed access to metal music while also creating an educational and cultural space that began to construct a more positive view of metal fans, as well as debunk social prejudices:

> Another contribution that the *Avanzada Metallica* made to Dominican metal was [...] Now that we were in a traditional media outlet, the same one that had attacked us, by the way, we could finally demonstrate what metal really is. Break with some of the stereotypes held by people. [...] I said, "This is a great opportunity to change the face of heavy metal here." [...] We had the great opportunity to get to the heart of where the attacks were coming from. [...] We metal fans are not delinquents; we are professionals. One time, during a radio interview we asked how many of the metal fans present were professionals. "I'm an engineer, I'm a doctor," they said. Coincidentally, everyone in the radio booth was a professional, and everyone was like [...] wow.

It seemed important to me that this emphasis on portraying metal as a music enjoyed by professionals echoed the previously described links between the music and the upper social classes in the country. Although not all listeners would fall under this category in terms of education and professional experience, these interventions helped advance the *Avanzada Metallica*'s aim of addressing the stigmatizing portrayal of the metal community. The perception of metal fans as delinquents began to shift. For example, the metal shows organized by the group, which they called *descargas* ("discharges"), had security as part of the events and ensured that no violent situations would occur. This was seen as an educational initiative directed toward the local metal community and the general public. It was a way of publicly demonstrating that metal fans could mosh and headbang without causing damages to the spaces where the events took place. By having well-thought-out and organized events, the musicians and the audience began to conscientiously support and expect more from their shows.

FIGURE 7.3: More positive news article on the *Avanzada Metallica* published in *Listín Diario*. Image provided by Edwin Demorizi.

Local journalists attributed the increasingly positive perception of metal to the *Avanzada Metallica*'s efforts. An in-depth examination of newer newspaper articles evidenced a drastic shift away from the tone that characterized similar publications in the 1980s and 1990s. For example, in April 2011 the local newspaper *Listín Diario* published a full-page article entitled *El verdadero rostro de la música y el movimiento heavy metal* ("The true face of heavy metal music and its movement") (Gil 2011b). The article would shed light on metal's origins and sense of community, critically questioning the music's supposed relation to criminality. The same would happen later that year when the newspaper would print a one-page article praising the efforts of the *Avanzada Metallica* in fighting against social discrimination. The article was aptly titled *"A palos y opresión sigue avanzando 'La Avanzada'"* ("Despite attacks and oppression, the 'Avanzada' carries on") (Gil 2011a).

In less than a decade the members of the *Avanzada Metallica* had positioned themselves as a player in the media landscape, ushering in a balanced counternarrative of metal music and actively challenging the stigmatization of the genre in the Dominican Republic. Still, their most important achievement was yet to come. In a turn that would make any social movement proud, they would successfully change the racial and social class composition of the local metal scene in their country.

A new and different metal scene

The *Avanzada Metallica* had achieved what most people thought impossible: challenging existing media discourse toward metal music in the Dominican Republic. Although this was an important achievement, limiting the discussion to this sole contribution would be insufficient to accurately describe their impact. Their weekly presence on the radio airwaves, followed by their subsequent presence over the internet, would give access to the participation of new Dominicans to the metal scene, and this new generation would be different from those that composed metal scenes of years past.

As mentioned earlier, the first generation of the metal scene was described as one comprised of upper class people, those who had more access to metal-related information and music. Economic resources would dictate access to instruments as well as places to practice and play. Even the seemingly simple act of listening to metal would be difficult for people pushed to the periphery of these social circles. Decades later, the *Avanzada Metallica* radio show would disseminate metal to a larger group of people from various regions of the Dominican Republic. More fans from all types of socioeconomic and racial backgrounds would become aware of metal music and would eventually find ways to play in bands. The scene progressively became more diverse. Access to metal music via the radio, and later the internet, meant that people from poorer economic backgrounds could search online for more information on the bands they had initially heard through the radio show. José Maracallo from the *Avanzada Metallica* explained the following with regard to the diversification of the local metal scene.

My experience in the *Avanzada* helped me reflect on the three generations that local metal has had. The first generation came from a higher social class. They had access to the money needed to buy their instruments, which were expensive, and also access to education. Because, let's be clear about this, metal, to me, is synonymous with having an open mind. In order to have that, you need access to education. During the second generation, the country's economy was beginning to grow, and this was when the scene began to expand and include people from lower classes, but there still was a more dominant economic class. You can even see it in the color of the skin. There were more White people that would listen to metal than darker ones. So what happened when the *Avanzada Metallica* began? We started receiving calls from people in *barrios* as well as the capital. *Los Mina, Alcarrizos* [...] whose population is composed of people with scarce resources. Those kids started to listen to the music and became protagonists of the local metal community. They wanted to form their bands, they brought us mp3s, and we would play them until they became popular. That's when the third generation of the Dominican metal scene began, which, in my opinion, has been the most successful. Evidence of this can be seen in the packed concerts that were organized and also in the integration of females to the scene, who were only two or three before this.

The social transformation of the Dominican Republic went hand in hand with the *Avanzada Metallica*'s strategy to take the music to all corners of the country. Access to the internet, particularly for home use, played a vital role in diversifying the scene. Richard Joa from the *Avanzada Metallica* described this process and explained how access to information would eliminate the elitism that had characterized the first generation of the local metal scene.

Around 95–97, the internet reaches homes in our country. The telephone companies start to bring the internet to homes. Logically, with the internet you have access to the information. Music-related material is still scarce, but at least you have information about different bands. Their members and things like that. That was very difficult to get in previous years, unless you bought magazines. The internet had reached the country. The people start to use it [...] they abandon that zeal they had about their music materials. It was being disseminated, so you would share it more. In 2002, when the *Avanzada Metallica* started, we really took the music to the masses. [...] A lot of people had internet and, thanks to that, metal in our country was easy to access. Then you could not feel too proud about being a metal fan [...] that elitism disappeared. As soon as sharing started [...] elitism disappeared.

These verbalizations regarding the *Avanzada Metallica*'s role in diversifying the local metal scene were part of some of the very last interviews I carried out in the Dominican Republic. I believe they perfectly place in historic perspective the important role the radio program had in challenging existing notions of metal music in the country, while also making metal more racially reflective of its setting. Although concerns over playing *chopo* metal still lingered in many of my conversations with local metal fans, it was evidently clear that the notion of metal as a white, upper class phenomenon in the country had been challenged and modified.

Before leaving the Dominican Republic in one of my last visits, I spoke to a young man who had formed a new metal band. He lived in the *barrios* once reached by the *Avanzada Metallica*. At one point in our conversation he stated that the radio program had taken the music "beyond the bridge," in reference to the Juan Bosch Bridge, which crosses the Ozama River and symbolically divides Santo Domingo into discreet economic sectors. It was evident that communal actions like the one described in this chapter would help challenge a larger legacy of racism and classism, which had found its way into the small metal scene. To some it was just a radio show, but to others it encompassed a decolonial act within the metal music itself. As the young musician went on to explain what metal meant to him, I could not escape the feeling that it had transformed a life that would have otherwise remained on the other side of that racial and social divide.

NOTES

1. The exploration of race in metal studies has been mostly present in scholarship developed in the Global North. It has been championed by scholars who are themselves part of racial and ethnic minority groups and/or who have engaged in extensive ethnography in geographies far from their countries of origin. This call for "recoloring the metal map," as Esther Clinton and Jeremy Wallach (2015) have coined it, has been answered via insightful research by people like Kevin Fellezs (2015, 2016b, 2016a, 2018) and Laina Dawes (2013), for example, who have addressed the experiences of Blacks and Latinos in metal music. Further explorations of the role of race in Latin American metal music are pressingly needed. These are particularly important in light of the high levels of racism present in the region, which is something seldom discussed and which can sometimes become reflected in metal scenes.

2. As is the case in the United States, Canada, and various European countries with the word "Indian," the word *indio* has had widespread usage in Latin America as a way to speak of native peoples, regardless of region, identity, ethnicity, culture, and language. Latin American countries have generally used *Hindú* to refer to individuals attached, originating, or belonging to India and its varied ethnicities. A turn has begun in Latin American over the last few decades, similar to the one occurring in the Global North, to promote the adoption of accurate terminology when referring to native or indigenous populations; this includes the use of the actual tribe or group name. Nonetheless, many in the region continue to use

the term *indio*, ignoring the calls for a more inclusive nomenclature. The mention of Dominicans' use of the word *indio* above highlights this prevailing colloquial usage.

3. Abaddon RD is one of the Dominican Republic's most popular bands. With the exception of some minor periods of silence, the band has been active since the rise of the local heavy metal scene in the 1980s.

4. As of January 1, 2019, their webpage can still be accessed through the following link: http://www.avanzadametallica.net/am/.

REFERENCES

Castor, Suzy and Garafola, Lynn (1974), "The American occupation of Haiti (1915–34) and the Dominican Republic (1916–24)," *The Massachusetts Review*, 15:1, pp. 253–75.

Clinton, Esther and Wallach, Jeremy (2015), "Recoloring the metal map: Metal and race in global perspective," in T.-M. Karjalainen and K. Kärki (eds.), *Modern Heavy Metal: Markets, Practices and Cultures*, Helsinki: Department of Management Studies, Aalto University, pp. 274–82, http://iipc.utu.fi/MHM/Clinton.pdf. Accessed December 8, 2019.

Dawes, Laina (2013), *What Are You Doing Here?: A Black Woman's Life and Liberation in Heavy Metal*, Brooklyn, NY: Bazillion Points.

Fellezs, Kevin (2015), "Talk shit, get shot: Body count, Black masculinity, and metal music culture," in T.-M. Karjalainen and K. Kärki (eds.), *Modern Heavy Metal: Markets, Practices and Cultures*, Helsinki: Aalto University Press, pp. 283–90.

Fellezs, Kevin (2016a), "Five djentlemen and a girl walk into a metal bar: Thoughts on a 'metal after metal' metal studies," *Metal Music Studies*, 2:3, pp. 325–39. doi: 10.1386/mms.2.3.325.

Fellezs, Kevin (2016b), "Voracious souls: Race and place in the formation of the San Francisco bay area thrash scene," in A. Brown, K. Spracklen, K. Kahn-Harris, and N. Scott (eds.), *Global Metal Music and Culture: Current Directions in Metal Studies*, New York: Routledge, pp. 89–105. doi: 10.4324/9781315742816.

Fellezs, Kevin (2018), "Edge of insanity," *Journal of Popular Music Studies*, 30:1 & 2, pp. 109–26. doi: 10.1525/jpms.2018.000009.

Ferguson, James (1998), "Independence and the Cold War," in *The Story of the Caribbean People*, Jamaica: Randle Publishers, pp. 262–303.

Gates, Henry Louis, Pollack, Ricardo, and Petterle, Diene (2011), *PBS: Black in Latin America*, Kingston: PBS.

Gil, Anhays (2011a), "A palos y opresión sigue avanzando 'La Avanzada'," *Listín Diario*, May 26, p. 10c.

Gil, Anhays (2011b), "El verdadero rostro de la música y el movimiento Heavy Metal," *Listín Diario*, April 7, p. 6c.

Howard, David (1997), *Coloring the Nation: Race and Ethnicity in the Dominican Republic*, Oxford: University of Oxford.

Lora, Huchi (1988), "Utilizan el rock para promover culto satánico," *El Nacional*, September 18, p. 16a.

Paulino, Edward (2006), "Anti-Haitianism, historical memory, and the potential for genocidal violence in the Dominican Republic," *Genocide Studies and Prevention*, 3:December, pp. 265–88.

Pérez Saba, Leovigildo (2009), *Dominant Racial and Cultural Ideologies in Dominican Elementary Education*, Montreal: McGill University.

Placencia, Luchy (1991), "Diablos, calaveras, cráneos y cadáveres adornan fiesta de jóvenes dominicanos," *El Nacional*, May 7, p. 11.

Placencia, Luchy (n.d.), "El comportamiento de 'jevitos' responde y contesta la agresividad de la sociedad," *Hoy*, n.pag.

Rosario, Reina and Ulloa, Jorge (2006), "Algunos aspectos socioculturales de la inmigración haitiana hacia la República Dominicana," *Ciencia y Sociedad*, 31:1, pp. 64–124.

Saba, Samir (2003), "'Avanzada Metallica' en la capital," *Listín Diario*, June 30.

Simmons, David (2010), "Structural violence as social practice: Haitian agricultural orkers, Anti-Haitianism, and health in the Dominican Republic," *Human Organization*, 69:1, pp. 10–18. doi: 10.17730/humo.69.1.8271r0j17372k765.

Turits, Richard Lee (2002), "A world destroyed, a nation imposed: The 1937 Haitian massacre in the Dominican Republic," *Hispanic American Historical Review*, 82:3, pp. 589–635. doi: 10.1215/00182168-82-3-589.

Varas-Díaz, Nelson and Mendoza, Sigrid (2015), "Ethnicity, politics and otherness in Caribbean heavy metal music: Experiences from Puerto Rico, Dominican Republic and Cuba," in T. M. Karjalainen and K. Kärki (eds.), *Modern Heavy Metal: Market, Practices and Culture*, Helsinki: Department of Management Studies, Aalto University, pp. 291–99.

8

Restoring Memory/Surviving Violence – Colombia

Metal music has a role in fostering critical memory as a way to challenge efforts to erase specific aspects of local history in Latin America. To highlight this decolonial aspect of metal music, I focus on historical events that are not part of a distant colonial past but which are, in effect, recent occurrences intimately linked to extreme forms of violence. Colombia is a perfect example of this decolonial aspect, serving to highlight how everyday acts of violence can be traced to experiences of coloniality with countries in the Global North and between local communities within the same country. In this instance, metal music has engaged in specific acts (both symbolic and practical) meant to foster remembrance of these violent events with the hope of showing the country the importance of not falling into the trap of eternal repetition. Furthermore, Colombia's brand of decolonial metal engages in a discussion about the ways in which violence still remains present today. Finally, and in a more controversial vein, Colombia's decolonial metal seeks to promote a type of metal music capable of effecting change through direct action, gearing these efforts toward achieving social justice. In trying to grasp the complexity of this particular model, one must understand the country's context, as it is impossible to comprehend metal music in Colombia without first examining the history of violence in this setting.

No one left untouched

"This chocolate is from the region of Boyacá," the young man stated with a proud smile on his face as he brought my cup of hot cocoa to the table. His shop was unassuming and would not catch your eye in the midst of downtown Bogotá, where the streets are filled with the simultaneous hustle of tourists, local businesspersons, and street vendors. Still, the underlying story about his business was strikingly poignant and serves as a brief summary of Colombia's recent history. "Our chocolate is special because the cacao is grown by farmers who previously worked with coca. In the year 2000, our seven supplying families stopped using their fields for coca leaves and began to plant cacao as a way to help the country distance itself from the wars we suffered." I was immediately drawn to his mention of the specific seven families engaged in this process. "Was your family involved in the cultivation of coca?" I asked, in the least abrasive tone I could think of at the moment. He looked down at his feet and said, "Yes, but those times have changed." The few seconds of what I interpreted as shame were replaced with a smile as he looked directly into my eyes and explained, "This is the new legacy our grandfathers and fathers have left us. A way out of the world of violence and drugs." I thanked him for his openness and expressed my admiration for his new business endeavor. While I drank the hot beverage, I could not help but think that, in different ways, no one in Colombia had been untouched by the consequences of violence and the drug trade; no one.

Colombia's armed conflict is now more than 60 years old and dates back to the period known locally as *La Violencia* ("The Violence"), which took place between 1946 and 1966. Clashes between the Liberal and Conservative political parties turned violent, giving way to an outright civil war. The stories of violent encounters between those political factions are gruesome. Although those events seem like a distant past to many in Colombia, they are referenced as the onset of a continuous exposure to violence as part of their everyday life. When one speaks about violence to local people in Colombia today, it is more likely that they will resort to telling you a more recent story. That story is one about guerrilla groups with leftist ideologies that sprung up during the 1960s to challenge the power of a State who many saw as disconnected from the plights of the poor. While several can claim historic importance, inarguably the most notable guerrilla of them all was the *Fuerzas Armadas Revolucionarias de Colombia* ("Revolutionary Armed Forces of Colombia"), better known as FARC for its acronym in Spanish. To fight the guerrilla, the State armed non-military locals who were given free rein to engage in illegal activities so as to create the perception that the official army was not involved in some of the most gruesome aspects of the conflict. These paramilitaries, or *paracos* as they are contemptuously called, would turn into a right-wing arm of the government through which the latter indirectly engage in illicit activities, including the murder of guerrilla members and farmers. Even though these *paracos* were funded by the local government and, it must be stated, the government of the United States, they would quickly balloon into a bigger problem, for little could be done to control their actions in the open fields of Colombia. As if this scenario were not complex enough, other gangs who had gathered strength during the 1960s became a force to be reckoned with during the 1980s in light of the trafficking of cocaine. The drug trade in Colombia became such a lucrative business during the 1980s that the guerrillas, the paramilitaries, and their respective activities became intertwined, although in very different ways, with the illegal business (Yaffe 2011; McFarland Sánchez-Moreno 2018). In summary, the violence Colombia has seen in the past 60 years is perceived by many as a spillover of the acts of the guerrilla, the government, the paramilitaries, and the drug cartels. The population of Colombia is continually trapped in the middle of this armed conflict. Thus, violence seems like an everyday occurrence for many in the country.

Explaining the root causes of the Colombian armed conflict represents a mammoth task. Scholars have recognized that it is not a one-dimensional phenomenon but, rather, a complex process resulting from the convergence of and interaction between economic reasons (i.e., inequality, greed), institutional factors (i.e., inefficient police presence, the precarious situation of the State, political disenfranchisement), and cultural factors in a society that has normalized violence as a problem-solving strategy (Yaffe 2011). These events should also be contextualized in a much larger global dynamic, where the more ample stage is the so-called "war on drugs." Colombia, as one of the major producers of coca leaf in the hemisphere, has been a target, and sometimes willing actor, of antidrug policies emerging from the United States. "Plan Colombia" would be the best example of the prevailing strategy. The policy, signed into law by the United States in 2000, aimed to end the armed conflict and its catalyst, coca production in Colombia, by funding the local army and other paramilitary groups. The billion-dollar project, however, resulted in a very different and perhaps unexpected set of consequences. Authors have argued that this "war on drugs," led by the United States and severely impacting Colombia, is a "continuity of imperialism between the end of the Cold War and the war on terror" (Corva 2008: 178). This strategy, one designed to exert control over populations and countries, filled the vacuum left after the waning of global communism and the end of the red scare. The US involvement in Colombia, although projected as a drug control strategy, has been described as an imposition of biopolitical systems of control, which mainly target disadvantaged populations; such a view sheds light on the socioeconomic problems that plague the country, turning those affected into targets for the paramilitaries (Stokes 2003). It has also allowed for external control over the local government, primarily via economic regulations. For example, the US-Colombia drug policy has been mostly characterized by the one-sided actions of the former party in this relation, highlighting the neocolonial dynamics of the "exchange" (Bagley 1988b, 1988a). Thus, the US involvement in Colombia should not be seen as an act of benevolence but, more accurately, as a strategy whose goal is the control of regional actors as well as the protection of the US interests in Latin America.

Even though people on the ground might argue about the many factors that fostered the armed conflict in Colombia, one thing is for sure: its consequences are widespread and undeniable. Take, for example, the long-lasting effects of sexual violence. Sexual violence against women has been systematically used throughout the armed conflict as a process of intimidation and degradation. This fact, however, is rarely discussed. Research has shown that women have had to learn to live side-by-side with their aggressors, an already difficult situation compounded by the lack of organized registries of these sexually violent acts (Wilches 2010). The armed conflict has also created lingering effects on children. The latter are constantly forced to drop out of schools and end their education early (Rodríguez and Sánchez 2012). As if these examples were not enough, studies have also documented the enormous toll of the armed conflict on the mental health of the Colombian people, with high levels of anxiety-related psychopathology (Bell et al. 2012). The conflict has also had environmental consequences, which have in turn impacted local communities. As part of "Plan Colombia," many sectors of the country were sprayed with defoliants in an effort to eradicate the coca plantations. Studies have shown that those pesticides impacted the regular food crops needed by farmers to survive (Messina and Delamater 2006). This fumigation, in turn, fostered community displacement (Oslender 2016) and has also disproportionately impacted indigenous and Afro-Colombian peoples (Rincón-Ruiz and Kallis 2013).

Finally, the armed conflict has also had severe effects on the country's economy. Researchers have estimated that Colombia would be almost 20 percent richer if it had not gone through the process of armed conflict (Álvarez and Rettberg 2008). Concerns over violence have driven industry out of the country (Camacho and Rodríguez 2013). In places where the armed conflict continues, research has documented an increase in the production of coca (Díaz and Sánchez 2004). The illegal drug industry has strengthened the reach of the guerrilla groups and paramilitaries while continuing to weaken the State (Cornell 2007). In summary, the effects of the armed conflict have impacted all aspects of Colombian society. This includes its culture and, more to the point for the purposes of this chapter, its music.

Violent context, violent sounds, violent themes

When I arrived at the small community theater in the middle of Bogotá, the place was empty. A group of university students were screening one of my documentaries on metal music in Latin America as part of a small film festival. The screening room had a cheap projector, and a large white bedsheet hung from the ceiling to serve as a screen. The room was small and full of plastic chairs on top of wooden steps, which looked like they could fall at any given moment. Half an hour later, and to my complete surprise, the place was packed with metal fans. Half way through the film, I stepped out of the screening room, where I bumped into a woman who was smoking. She was in her late thirties and sat with me to talk about the film.

173

"You know that topic of violence you describe in the film? That is nothing," she said with a smirk on her face. "We have gone through much worse. The violence in Colombia was not a traditional dictatorship, like people describe in those countries, but we have had our own sort of dictatorship." She was referring to the control that the armed conflict has had on the country's population, and which she described as "still present today."

Our conversation turned to metal music almost seamlessly. She mentioned that people had little understanding of the impact of growing up in a city where the paramilitaries would play soccer with the severed heads of the farmers they had killed. "Those things scar you. They never leave you." She attributed Colombia's love of the extreme subgenres of metal to this experience. "This is why I relate to grindcore and death metal. Those sounds and lyrics speak to me about what I lived through as a child [...] and survived!" Almost simultaneously, a young man who seemed to overhear our conversation opened his backpack and handed me a CD. "Professor, this is my band's album and I want you to have a copy." I thanked him for the gift. As he handed me the CD, he turned it around to show me the song titles. "Each song is related to one massacre carried out by the paramilitaries in Colombia. We just can't seem to find other things to write about," he said in a very somber tone. "See what I was telling you?," said the woman who was chatting with me. We continued to talk for a while about local metal music and this link with contextual violence.

These impromptu conversations with metal fans in Bogotá made it clear to me that the topic of violence was a persistent issue of discussion, which they saw as a constitutive experience in their lives. This exposure influenced their preference for certain subgenres of metal. It was evident that the contextual experience of Colombians had made its way into their music, and I wanted to use my time there to explore this connection. "You have to go to Medellín," she said. "This is where it all started for us." Two days later, I took a 40-minute flight to the city.

Medellín is 418 kilometers from Bogotá. It is embedded in the mountain ranges, enmeshed with vegetation, and is mesmerizingly beautiful. It is difficult not to fall in love with the city almost immediately. Still, a local stroll through the city rapidly shows you the high levels of inequality between the rich and the poor. It can take your breath away because of its beauty and, simultaneously, leave you gasping at the knowledge of the injustices it hides. I was there to talk to Colombia's seminal extreme metal band, Masacre, and its founding member Alex Okendo.

I met Alex in his tattoo shop. He was courteous, but I initially perceived him as distant and somewhat disinterested in my presence. He had the attitude of a metal musician who had been asked the same interview questions thousands of times, and I, in all honesty, could not blame him. Albums, tours, stories from the road, these things are the usual content of fan-based magazines and local news outlets. He has been a part of the local metal scene for 30 years, and these topics can become boring very quickly after constant repetition. As soon as we sat down to chat, I told him that I did not want to talk about these matters. I wanted to discuss "the social context that gave birth to Masacre." His eyes lit up, he became more relaxed, laughed, and thanked me for discussing something different. We both smiled and went ahead with our interview.

It was as if the floodgates had opened, and the topic of violence once again dominated the conversation. He was eager to discuss how the band's sound was directly associated to its violent context. As kids during the 1980s, the band had no comparison to other subgenres of metal, so the metal fans in Medellín called their style *Ultra Metal*. The sound was raw, recordings were suboptimal, and instruments were played with very little dexterity. Still, it was an outlet amid the violence they experienced in their daily lives.

> We (Masacre) emerged in the eighties. The first extreme band of Colombia was Para-bellum. It was dissonance, discord, and a stunned sound. Violent, like the moment Colombia was living though. It was rebellion against music, our Catholic society, and right-wingers. We were trying to go against religion, politics, society, and love. We did not know about music. We had no recording facilities. There was no internet! We had no information! That noise formed those first chords of violence that gave way to Medellín's *Ultra Metal*. We even gave it a name. Medellín is the cradle.

This rebellious spirit echoed the daily experiences they lived on the streets. "Violence in Colombia has always been present," he mentioned stoically. "Everything you can imagine in terms of violence, we have lived it." For Alex, the actors in this armed conflict were one and the same. In his description of the events, there was little differentiation between the guerrilla, the paramilitaries, the narcos, and the government. They were all in bed with each other in some way, shape, or form. Although he mentioned that the guerrillas "had respectable ideals at some point," he was keen to explain that those ideals had been "lost along the way." His position echoed that of recent research that has documented how, at one point during the conflict, the interactions between these actors were all related to the narco culture; the consequences of these interactions severely affected the population at large (McFarland Sánchez-Moreno 2018). "The Colombian people are in the middle of this war," Alex stated. "If one of them (guerrilla, paramilitaries, or the army) arrives at your house, you have to say 'I am with you' or you die. So then, people are in the middle of this problem with little chance to get ahead." The situation seemed dire for Colombians, particularly those in the countryside, and Alex showed very little hope for a transformation in this process in the near future.

Masacre's music, for an outsider, evidenced this scarce sense of hope for the country's future.[1] Songs like "Brutales Masacres" ("Brutal Massacres") and "Ola de Violencia" ("Wave of Violence") describe the killings of individuals and communities (Masacre 1991). Alex mentioned the pain he felt when thinking about the killings of innocent people in the country as inspiration to write those songs. As part of the conversation, he would explain the gory details of these murders, including the use of the "Colombian necktie," where an individual's neck would be slashed and his tongue exposed through the open wound. He also mentioned local tales about wild crocodiles that would feed only on human flesh (provided by the *paracos*) and mass murders in public spaces. The song "Cortejo Fúnebre" ("Funeral Procession") addresses the violent murder of politicians like Luis Carlos Galán, who at one point carried the people's hope for a better country, free of violence (Masacre 1991). "Justicia Ramera" ("Harlot Justice") addresses how the justice system in Colombia works for the very few, can be bought, and always tips in favor of those who have money (Masacre 1991). "That is why the song has two voices in its chorus. One screams 'justice!' and the other responds 'harlot'!" Alex stressed before we discussed another song, which is always included in the band's concerts, and which, I believe, best reflects one of the worst problems faced by Colombian society.

The song "Éxodo" ("Exodus") addresses the plight of displaced communities in Colombia (Masacre 2001). These are individuals and populations who have been forced out of their lands by the actors in the armed conflict, mostly paramilitaries, in order for the latter to use their fields for the cultivation of the coca leaf (Ibanez 2014). Colombia has frequently ranked high in the number of internally displaced people as a consequence of the armed conflict (Shultz et al. 2014). In 2013, the estimate of those displaced was 5.7 million, which was the largest number of displaced people in the world at the time. Colombia had 17 percent of the internally displaced people in the world during 2013, and most were women and children (70 percent). These individuals rarely return to their homes after being displaced. After 50 years of war it is estimated that 1 out of 10 people in Colombia have left their lands (Wilches 2010). Alex was fully aware of this dire situation and explained his decision to sing about it.

"Éxodo" is not about Colombians that went to Venezuela, or vice versa. It is that our country is being displaced. There are people who live in neighborhoods that are a focus of interest for subversive groups that want to recruit you into their army. People leave their homes to prevent them from recruiting their children. That is a social phenomenon in the city. It happens in the mountains too. The guerrillas have stolen children and women. If they resist, they are banished. They use their land to grow coca, and if they don't give in, they kill them. It is a tenacious, incredible war. I don't know how a country can endure so much. We have killed each other.

This last statement struck me as odd. It seemed like Alex was holding Colombians solely responsible for the violence experienced in the country. I wanted to explore this issue further and asked him if he "saw any foreign influence in the manifestation of this violence." "Of course!," Alex responded vehemently. "Everyone in Latin America is more of a producer (of drugs) than a consumer. Consumers are in the North and Europe. But to get the drugs out of here, they have to go over governments and laws. That is why these violent groups are created and governments are bought. Everything has a price." With this answer, Alex exhibited a keen awareness of the social and contextual forces that shaped the armed conflict in Colombia and how colonial dynamics between the Global North and the Global South have impacted his country.

Violence, memory, and metal music

It was evident from my conversation with Alex that Masacre's music, filled with the words and sounds of violence they described, had a profound purpose. Alex stressed on many occasions the need to use metal music as a way to preserve the country's memory. This notion seemed important to me, particularly considering that many people I spoke with during my visits preferred to forget the traumatic events they had lived through. It felt like people had experienced such trauma, that many thought it best to forget. Memory seemed to be an important agenda underlying Masacre's music. Alex's efforts to preserve the memory of these events had not gone unnoticed.

In 2018, the local government awarded him with the "Juan Corral Award" for his contributions to Colombian society. I was astonished when I found out that he had received this award; after all, it seemed unusual for politicians to highlight a band that was so critical of its context, particularly one whose images and sounds were so intimately associated with violence. Alex was quick to contextualize the accolade, mentioning that the band's fans, who began following them in the 1980s, had by now "become politicians, professors, doctors, and they know what we were talking about. They know Masacre is a cultural phenomenon. Our lyrics, which are a form of social and political protest, have never changed. We have won our place in society because it is honest work. It was positive for the youth. Instead of seducing them with money, we gave them music. That is why politicians were impressed." And, indeed, they were impressed, as evidenced by the proud smile of the local politician Santiago Jaramillo Botero upon bestowing Alex with the award. The moment, which was caught on video for posterity, seems kind of surreal, as a country that wants to surpass its violent history gave an award to one of the most "violent"-sounding bands in Latin American.

Alex, who spoke about the event with great humility, highlighted once again the important role metal music played in preserving the memory of what has happened in Colombia. "A society without memory repeats its misfortunes. If the youth do not understand what has happened in Colombia, it may happen again. We hope to have a moment of peace and that is why we emphasize our social and political history." He had an important sense of responsibility toward future generations, and metal music was his vehicle to materialize that vision. I sensed he became somewhat emotional when speaking about his son. "We inherited from our parents a violent country. I have given my son an even more violent country. Therefore, you have to keep the memory alive so as to not have future generations fall into the same misfortunes."

A new generation's memories

Masacre's influence on Colombian heavy metal music and its role in promoting the importance of historical memory can be seen everywhere one looks within the local scene. Its influence is not limited to government recognitions or awards; this influence is also felt in the lives of young people. I will highlight two examples – the bands Corpus Calvary and Tears of Misery, both hailing from Bogotá – which I think are important for several reasons.

Corpus Calvary is an up and coming metal band from Bogotá formed in 2018. When I met the band's guitarist, Juan David Vargas, they had released only one album. Their sound is quite raw, very reminiscent of traditional death metal. The band's thematic choices are of particular interest, especially when one considers their album *Masacres con Criterio Social (Socially-Sanctioned Massacres)* (Corpus Calvary 2018). In it, each song tells the story of a specific massacre carried out by the paramilitaries. Songs like "El Aro" and "El Salado" explain in graphic detail how villagers were murdered, raped, and tortured once paramilitaries reached their lands. The song "El Salado" tells the story of that particularly horrendous massacre from the first-person perspective of a woman. She describes how the *paracos* arrive and rape her, accusing her of being part of the guerrilla. The song eventually gives way to a chronicle of the murder of 60 people at a public plaza. The specificity of the lyrics in the song is of utmost importance here, as it turns the song into a history lesson. Details that few people want to or actually remember (like the community it took place in, those responsible, the number of dead, and the reasons for the killings) take center stage for the listener, who is urged to never forget. Of note is the fact that the narrative is presented from the perspective of a female, a viewpoint largely ignored by the local establishment when describing the effects of violence on particular populations (Wilches 2010).

The band extends the same treatment to the massacre at *El Aro*. This time the band concentrates on what they call "terrorismo de Estado" ("State-sponsored terrorism") to highlight the active and complicit role of the government in this and other massacres. The lyrics focus on how the bodies of farmers were burned by the army in order to hide the crimes. The last line in the song states, "Bones that still wander in our memory. Never to be forgotten!" The importance of memory, and metal's role in this process, is prominent in this song. It seems significant that these songs, by a group of very young musicians, highlight the atrocities perpetrated in these communal massacres. This practice is not very different from the work of scholars or journalists who have also described these in detail in order to avoid these memories falling into the obscurity of Colombia's collective amnesia (McFarland Sánchez-Moreno 2018).

Tears of Misery, the second example, aim to highlight the important role of memory in Colombia. Formed in the year 2000, the band has released a demo recording, an EP, and a full-length album. Although their output has not been as consistent as that of other local bands, the importance of their role in promoting the work of memory has more to do with their stage presence. Oscar Bayona, one of the band's guitarists, wears a red piece of cloth, which he ties below his left knee (see Figure 8.1). This otherwise insignificant piece of clothing gains great meaning when one finds out that Bayona uses it as a reminder to audiences about the number of people who have lost limbs during the armed conflict. Although this might seem like a small gesture in the midst of so much death, the symbolism weighs heavily on both the band and the audience, and for good reason. Estimates show that more than 100,000 landmines are presently buried in Colombia, covering approximately 40 percent of its territory (Lopera and Milisavljevic 2007). Most of them are used to protect coca crops or halt the incursion of the army into guerrilla- and paramilitary-controlled lands. Between 1990 and 2009, Colombia registered 4289 landmine-related accidents; 34 percent of those affected were civilians (Gallego 2009). This story had personal meaning for Oscar, given that he lost a cousin in the armed conflict. Because of this connection, Oscar used this visual strategy to remind the audience of the ongoing challenges faced by everyday Colombians, even after the armed conflict had officially ended. For him this was an educational strategy, much in line with the role I ascribe to *extreme decolonial dialogues* in Chapter 1 of this book. Regarding this strategy, he stated:

FIGURE 8.1: Guitarist for the band Tears of Misery (Oscar Bayona) wearing a red piece of cloth below his left knee. Image provided by Sebastián Rodríguez.

I do it to remember those that were mutilated. I put it on my leg because it is the most common injury they face. It is a visual way to discuss those incidents. You are walking, inadvertently step on a mine, and simply lose a limb. That is why the leg is a key point. Not everyone understands why I do it. They can be confused. I have to explain the logic behind it. With these symbols, you reach people and make them aware of what is happening. These are harsh things to discuss, and what better way to do it than with symbols? It is an act of resistance.

Violence, metal, and social change

Fostering memory serves as one of the most important acts of resistance found in decolonial metal music. Acts of resistance, however, are varied and sometimes very complex. As I have previously explained, they can encompass anything from writing a song about a historical event to wearing a red bandana on stage to shed light on a social issue. On some occasions, these acts of resistance become even more tangible, using metal music as inspiration. The next example I will provide will surely prove controversial to some readers, as it involves the intricate relation between metal music and a member of the FARC, Colombia's most notorious guerrilla. Nonetheless, I must present it here because I believe it is an important example that helps highlight the varied ways in which metal music is used to foster resistance to social oppression in an individual's context. I do this with the knowledge that others, looking from the outside and living in different scenarios, may interpret this example as problematic.

After my documentary had screened in Bogotá, the organizers asked me to field some questions from the crowd. During the interaction, I addressed issues regarding technical aspects of the film; the discussion was going smoothly. After a while, one man sitting in the back of the room, whom I identified as being in his early forties, raised his hand and was given the microphone. "Why do you think people continue to state that metal is not political?," he asked and the energy in the room drastically change. Most of those in attendance looked back at him as if he had uttered an inappropriate question. Some cracked smiles while redirecting their gaze at me, eager to see how I would tackle this question. It was evidently a previously touched upon topic of discussion among them. Sensing the tension in the room, I grabbed the microphone and went on to discuss how this conceptualization of metal music as apolitical was mostly developed in the Global North, specifically in the United States and Europe, and how I believed it applied differently in the Global South, particularly in Latin America. I, then, provided some examples of how this was manifested in Colombian metal through its explorations of violence and political unrest via song lyrics. Those discussions were political even though some people felt the need to distance themselves from such reflections and the potential subsequent actions that could come from those reflections. The man seemed pleased with my answer and sat back down. Little did I know that his question foreshadowed a deeper conversation he and I would end up having in the following days, a conversation that brought Colombian metal music and politics together in a way I could not have expected.

A few days later, while walking though the street of Medellín, I received a text message from an unknown number asking to speak with me about local metal music. With suspicion I continued the conversation for a while until the caller identified himself. "I am the man who asked you about metal and politics in Bogotá." I immediately remembered the person and continued to chat. After a while, and as if he was expressing something he needed to get off his chest, he simply wrote: "I am a former member of the FARC, and metal has been an integral part of my life. Would you be interested in talking about this?" The revelation, and his linking of guerrilla involvement with metal music, left me aghast. I was still a bit suspicious about the communication and asked the person for his real name. "Johan Andrés Niño Calderón," he answered immediately. "Look me up on the internet by my guerrilla name, René Nariño." Once provided, I did a quick search and found multiple news reports about his time in prison as a result of his FARC activity. One day later, he flew from Cali to Medellín and we were having our first in-depth conversation.

At first, Andrés struck me as a very open person, unambiguous in his ways. He was eager to talk about his experience with the FARC, the rationale behind it, and the group's relation to metal music. I asked if he wished to be interviewed anonymously, to which he replied in the negative. His story, or at least the official media-constructed version of it, was all over the newspapers; now, it seemed to me that he wanted to tell his side through the lens of metal music. We sat down in a local restaurant and began to chat.

Andrés came from a political family. His grandparents were communists, and his parents were part of the leftist *Partido Unión Patriótica*. Several of his family members were persecuted and murdered for their political activity, which forced the remaining family members to move from Santander to Bogotá during the early 1990s. Andrés and his family were part of the *desplazados* ("displaced"), something that has characterized Colombia's history. His cousins introduced him to metal music by exchanging vinyl records, specifically from bands like Iron Maiden and Metallica. After having more children in Bogotá, his parents left politics. Nevertheless, he continued to learn about the topic as part of his college education. While living in the city, metal music complemented his college experience and, as he explained, "fostered in me the seed of critical thinking." His formal education in the field of political science strengthened his ideological convictions, which were supported by the fact that other members of his family were, at the time, part of the FARC. His awareness of social class and oppression continued to grow in light of his first job, a stint in the textile industry, where he witnessed social oppression first-hand. Through his college contacts, he became increasingly involved with the FARC and would eventually accept a training session in Bogotá's mountainside. After one of his training sessions, he decided to stay and join the Antonio Mariño Front; Mariño was in charge of activities in Bogotá and Dinamarca (see Figure 8.2). His proximity to the city of Bogotá allowed him to engage in FARC activities in the mountainside, activities that included attacks on

182

FIGURE 8.2: René Nariño with the FARC in the Colombian countryside. Image provided by René Nariño.

the military, this while also continuing to interact with and recruit college students in the city.

At the time of our interview, Andrés was aware that public opinion in Colombia was quite negative against the FARC. Although more recent written accounts have shed a more favorable light on the group (Villar and Cottle 2011), I perceived the same negative opinions while talking with other people in Medellín and Bogotá. Still, his vision of the organization remained intricately linked to social justice issues. He described the entity as an "insurgent organization made up mostly of people from the countryside. At one point 90 percent were people from the countryside who wanted to transform the power structure in Colombia." He stressed, time and again, that the organization emerged, in part, due to the abandonment of the poor by the local government and the inequities this process had caused. He stated:

> The emergence of the FARC is a breaking point in Colombian reality. It has to do with a dissatisfaction linked to the inequality suffered in the countryside. The peasants arm themselves and the FARC rises. This group of 48 farmers then expands and receives support from the Communist Party in ideological and logistical matters. But it has to do with the apathy of the State and the social elite to address

183

issues of democracy and the abandonment of the countryside. Their demands were simple: a school, a road. Instead, they received bullets. Thus, the armed conflict arises. While the FARC grew, so did its demands to create a different economic model for the country.

In 2011, the process of *las capturas* ("the captures") took place; Andrés became one of the imprisoned. His 6-year internment in the Colombian prison system was simply described as *fuerte*, which could be translated as "hard, difficult," but it would lack the emotional tone I think he aimed to convey. "My friends received long sentences. Thirteen, seventeen, sixty years! They were trying to make an example out of us." Judging by the amount of press I found about his capture and release, he was not exaggerating. "When they caught me, you would have though they caught the local Bin Laden! It was all over the place." Once in prison, he engaged in several hunger strikes to denounce the conditions of the system. Some attention would be garnered by these acts, but these would do little to help his situation. He described the prison system in Colombia as one focused on "vengeance" and not on "restorative justice." The word "degradation" was mentioned again and again in our conversations. Living in inhumane conditions, eating alongside rats, and being physically abused were only some of the experiences he mentioned. Andrés was clear about the role of prisons in Colombia and how these became a manifestation of the oppression in his society. At one point he stated, "80 percent of those in prison are from the lower classes, put there for petty crimes like stealing. They need to steal to achieve the dreams they see on the TV screens." As if this were not problematic enough, Andrés saw in this system a "machine of degradation." "It is humans degrading other humans," he stated as his face took on a pale tone. In the midst of all this degradation, metal music became an oasis, the one thing that would lift his mind and heart in the midst of the suffering he was witnessing.

He began to explain his connection to metal music in general terms. "Those first notes mark you. It has to be that way because I can't find another way to explain why I can't stop listening to it." He went on to describe how he used metal music to survive in the prison by forging "friendships related to metal."

> I had friends in the metal community on the outside. In some way, they contacted people on the inside and let them know I was into metal music. One of them was a prison guard. When he found out, we began to have conversations about metal. Later, we spoke about politics. He was aware of the reasons for my involvement with the FARC and seemed sympathetic. At night, he would come and take me out of my cell, and we would listen to metal music together. That guard, the "metal guy," was one of the very few who did not abuse prisoners.

FIGURE 8.3: René Nariño in a Colombian prison wearing a metal shirt. Image provided by René Nariño.

Andrés also remembered how his friends on the outside would send him shirts from his favorite metal bands. "Getting those shirts was incredible. People on the inside knew I was a metalhead because of them. It was a very emotional thing" (see Figure 8.3). His friends would also get him access to a cellphone within the prison. They would call him from metal concerts and allow him to listen in to the live music. "Of course, you couldn't really hear anything, but those were good experiences with the metal community." Out of all the signs of support his metal friends showed him, one would stand out above all others. They organized three festivals (in 2011, 2012, 2013), aptly named the "Terrorizer Metal Fests," in order to show him support and gather funds for his needs in prison. One of the flyers clearly stated that the fee for entrance is a "fraternal bonus for freedom" (see Figure 8.4). The festivals would be named after his moniker in the metal scene, Necro Terrorizer. Andrés was keen on explaining that his friends were open about the logic behind the festivals. "They were done to help 'our friend who has been captured'." I understand Andrés made this clarification as a way to emphasize that his friends in the metal community knew about his political activity and were in agreement with it at some level.

Andrés was released from prison in 2017 after the FARC and the government agreed and signed off on a peace treaty. As part of the treaty, the FARC surren-dered their weapons and became a political party allowed to participate in local politics. Andrés would become dissatisfied with the internal goings-on of the party. He mentioned in one of our conversations that he "could understand the militar-istic regimen during warfare," but could not see the utility of such "authoritarian styles" once the group became a political party. Thus, he ended his involvement with the FARC and its political party. I asked him if he had also abandoned the overall worldview and goals of the FARC, to which he immediately replied in the negative. "The inequality in our country is still there, so no. Mistakes were made but the ideas were the correct ones." He quoted a report from the National Center for Historic Memory stating that out of the estimated 215,664 deaths attributed to the conflict, 16 percent were guerrilla related, while 48 percent were attributed to the paramilitaries and the government (Romero 2018). He was fully aware of the negative acts committed by the FARC, but seemed invested in the idea of achieving social justice by any means necessary. Even events like kidnappings and the incur-sion into contraband taxation were conceived as needed in order to subvert the power of the local elites in Colombia. Having seen some of the inequality in the country first-hand, I felt a sense of connection to what he was explaining.

Still, as I mentioned above, and as was echoed by other members of the metal scene, people subsequently lumped the crimes committed by the government, the paramilitaries, and the guerillas together. Each actor is rarely, in my experience, compartmentalized when talking about the "violence experienced in Colombia." Violence is attributed to them all equally. That said, Andrés would disagree with this idea vehemently:

> Placing the FARC, the government, and the paramilitaries on the same scale means ignoring the history of inequality that was experienced in Colombia. The FARC was a reaction from poor peasants and the disadvantaged popular sector of Colombian society in response to inequalities. In contrast, in order to protect the privileges of the country's elite, the government engaged in violence against the FARC. There

FIGURE 8.4: Flyer for a metal concert in Colombia held in 2011 where donations for the imprisoned FARC member René Nariño were collected. Image provided by René Nariño.

was no open dialogue. Their response was State violence. When the State realizes that it cannot end the FARC, they create paramilitary groups to engage in the dirty war it could officially not. The paramilitaries were the ones murdering children, raping women, and beheading communities.

An important question remained. Now that Andrés was no longer with the FARC, but was so keenly aware of the social injustices still present in Colombia, how would he engage in some form of social activism? It was evident to me from our conversation that this was still an important aspect of his life and that the ideas he once defended through his guerrilla involvement were still with him, even if these were now put into action in different ways. This is where metal music would play its most important role, and Andrés was eager to explain.

Now living in Cali, Andrés worked with former guerrilla members in a process of *reincorporación* ("reincorporation") through which individuals are coached in order to facilitate their return to society. He was very vocal about the importance of this process and how the Colombian government had failed to deliver on many of the promises it had made to ensure its effectiveness. He stressed that the "government's lack of action creates the conditions for their reintegration into the guerrilla movement." Still, even with all the bureaucratic challenges, Andrés seemed very committed to this venture. He is also part of a group named *Metalmorfosis Social*. The concept is a play on words on the idea of social metamorphosis, alluding to social change, but adding the extra "l" to make it reference metal music. The group uses metal music as a strategy to foster and reflect on social change in Colombia. The day after we met, they were marching against the murder of social activists in the country, a problem that has garnered international attention. It was clear to me that his involvement in politics, and the role he sees metal playing in it, accompanied Andrés on a daily basis.

During one of our conversations, I perceived that his metal music–inspired activist group had given him a different strategy for social action, now distant from the FARC. Still, when I asked him if "metal had allowed him to leave the FARC in the past," he rapidly answered with a firm "no." He understood metal as a tool that had accompanied him in every stage of his life, including during his time in the FARC:

> During that whole process, metal accompanied me. Since I was a kid, when they violently took us out of Santander, I already listened to the distorted chords played in the villages. […] Before prison, metal was always there. I sat down with friends who were very critical and listened to metal music and talked about the political reality of the country. Metal complemented the ideological and critical feelings that I had at that time. Friends organized the "Gritos de Paz" ("Screams for Peace") festivals

to address the internal conflict in Colombia. When I was in the mountains, I had metal mp3s that were brought to me from the city. I used to hang the mp3 player up in my tent and play metal music. At night, I listened to metal amid the silence of the camp. I talked with friends in the mountains about metal music with social themes. Metal was always present. Then in jail, when you think you are broken in your convictions, metal is always there. Friends who visited me told me that other metalheads had seen me in the news and sent me hugs and strength.

It was evident that metal had played a vitally important role in Andrés's life. It gave him a critical outlook on social issues, which, coupled with his family's influence and his displacement experience, fostered his involvement in the guerrilla movement. Metal also carried him though the ordeals of the Colombian prison system. Finally, metal continued to be a catalyst for his involvement in social justice issues, presently through the *Metalmorfosis Social* collective. Although the guerrilla days were behind him now, those concerns over social justice were still very much present. It was clear that metal music had inspired a critical perspective toward his context to begin with, accompanied him during his armed activism, helped him survive prison, and, now, inspired his social justice–oriented work.

Although the use of metal music for social change described by Andrés might seem out of the ordinary to some people, it is an important example of the use of metal as a decolonial tactic and, more importantly, as an example of *extreme decolonial acts*. The extremity of his actions, in this case armed warfare, would seem to many in Colombia as the antithesis to those traditional means of social change more widely accepted in society. This would make it difficult for some people to see the decolonial implications of his actions and the role of metal in inspiring them.

The examples provided in this chapter, based on the Colombian context, evidence the important role of metal music in critically fostering memory as an approach to familiarize new generations with the horrors of the armed conflict in the hopes of having them not repeat these again. Songs, body demarcations, and social activism, all influenced by metal music, work today in Colombia as strategies geared toward social change. They help metal fans develop an understanding of the dynamics of coloniality by addressing the effects of the conflict on disadvantaged communities (the poor, farmers) and by exploring the complicit role of local and foreign governments in supporting the manifestations of violence. In other words, Colombian metal thrives in its decolonial tactics by fighting fire with fire. One can only hope that the fire will eventually subside, but for now, it seems to be the only effective means of effecting change.

NOTE

1. Author Pedro Manuel Lagos Chacón (2020) has carried out an exhaustive and detailed analysis of the lyrics for Masacre's first demos and albums. His findings evidence how the pervasive violence of the Colombian context influences the main themes addressed in their songs: death, war, and pain.

REFERENCES

Álvarez, Stephanie and Rettberg, Angelika (2008), "Cuantificando los efectos económicos del conflicto: Una exploración de los costos y los estudios sobre los costos del conflicto armando colombiano," *Colombia Internacional*, 67, pp. 14–37. doi: 10.7440/colombiaint67.2008.01.

Bagley, Bruce M. (1988a), "Colombia and the war on drugs," *Foreign Affairs*, 67:1, pp. 70–92.

Bagley, Bruce M. (1988b), "The new hundred years war? US national security and the war on drugs in Latin America," *Journal of International Studies and World Affairs*, 30:1, pp. 161–82.

Bell, Vaughan, Méndez, Fernanda, Martínez, Carmen, Palma, Pedro Pablo, and Bosch, Marc (2012), "Characteristics of the Colombian armed conflict and the mental health of civilians living in active conflict zones," *Conflict and Health*, 6:1, pp. 1–8. doi: 10.1186/1752-1505-6-10.

Camacho, Adriana and Rodríguez, Catherine (2013), "Firm exit and armed conflict in Colombia," *Journal of Conflict Resolution*, 57:1, pp. 89–116. doi: 10.1177/0022002712464848.

Cornell, Svante E. (2007), "Narcotics and armed conflict: Interaction and implications," *Studies in Conflict and Terrorism*, 30:3, pp. 207–27. doi: 10.1080/10576100601148449.

Corpus Calvary (2018), *Masacres con Criterio Social*, CD, Bogotá: Independent.

Corva, Dominic (2008), "Neoliberal globalization and the war on drugs: Transnationalizing illiberal governance in the Americas," *Political Geography*, 27:2, pp. 176–93. doi: 10.1016/j.polgeo.2007.07.008.

Díaz, Ana María and Sánchez, Fabio (2004), "Geografía de los cultivos ilícitos y conflicto armando en Colombia," *Crisis States Programme: Development Research Center*, 5807.

Gallego, Pablo Esteban Parra (2009), "IEDs: A major threat for a struggling society," *The Journal of ERW and Mine Action*, 13:3, http://www.jmu.edu/cisr/journal/13.3/specialreport/gallego/gallego.shtml. Accessed June 1, 2019.

Ibanez, Ana María (2014), "Forced displacement in Colombia: Magnitude and causes," *The Economics of Peace and Security Journal*, 4:1, pp. 48–54. doi: 10.15355/epsj.4.1.48.

Lagos Chacón, Pedro Manuel (2020), "The role of death metal in the Colombian Armed Conflict: The case of the band Masacre," in N. Varas-Díaz, D. Nevárez Araújo, and E. Rivera-Segarra (eds.), *Heavy Metal Music in Latin America: Perspectives from the Distorted South*, London: Lexington Press, pp. 81–105.

Lopera, Olga and Milisavljevic, Nada (2007), "Prediction of the effects of soil and target properties on the antipersonnel landmine detection performance of ground-penetrating radar: A

Colombian case study," *Journal of Applied Geophysics*, 63:1, pp. 13–23. doi: 10.1016/j.jappgeo.2007.02.002.

Masacre (1991), *Requiem*, Vinyl, Medellín: Osmose Productions.

Masacre (2001), *Muerte Verdadera Muerte*, CD, Medellín: Decade Records.

McFarland Sánchez-Moreno, Maria (2018), *There Are No Dead Here: A Story of Murder and Denial in Colombia*, New York: Bold Type Books.

Messina, J. P. and Delamater, P. L. (2006), "Defoliation and the war on drugs in Putumayo, Colombia," *International Journal of Remote Sensing*, 27:1, pp. 121–28. doi: 10.1080/01431160500293708.

Oslender, Ulrich (2016), "The banality of displacement: Discourse and thoughtlessness in the internal refugee crisis in Colombia," *Political Geography*, 50:May, pp. 10–19. doi: 10.1016/j.polgeo.2015.08.001.

Rincón-Ruiz, Alexander and Kallis, Giorgos (2013), "Caught in the middle, Colombia's war on drugs and its effects on forest and people," *Geoforum*, 46, pp. 60–78. doi: 10.1016/j.geoforum.2012.12.009.

Rodríguez, Catherine and Sánchez, Fabio (2012), "Armed conflict exposure, human capital investments, and child labor: Evidence from Colombia," *Defense and Peace Economics*, 23:2, pp. 161–84. doi: 10.1080/10242694.2011.597239.

Romero, César (2018), "262,197 muertos dejó el conflicto armado," Colombia: Centro Nacional de Memoria Histórica, http://www.centrodememoriahistorica.gov.co/noticias/noticias-cmh/262-197-muertos-dejo-el-conflicto-armado. Accessed February 5, 2019.

Shultz, James M., Shultz, James M., Garfin, Dana Rose, Espinel, Zelde, Araya, Ricardo, Oquendo, Maria A., Wainberg, Milton L., Chaskel, Roberto, Gaviria, Silvia L., Ordóñez, Anna E., Espinola, Maria, Wilson, Fiona E., Muñoz García, Natalia, Gómez Ceballos, Ángela Milena, Garcia-Barcena, Yanira, Verdeli, Helen, and Neria, Yuval (2014), "Internally displaced 'victims of armed conflict' in Colombia: The trajectory and trauma signature of forced migration," *Current Psychiatry Reports*, 16:475, pp. 1–16. doi: 10.1007/s11920-014-0475-7.

Stokes, Doug (2003), "Why the end of the Cold War doesn't matter: The US war of terror in Colombia," *Review of International Studies*, 29:4, pp. 569–85, 464. doi: 10.1017/S0260210503005692.

Villar, Oliver and Cottle, Drew (2011), *Cocaine, Death Squads, and the War on Terror: U.S. Imperialism and Class Struggle in Colombia*, New York: Monthly Review Press.

Wilches, Ivonne (2010), "Lo que hemos aprendido sobre la atención a mujeres víctimas de violencia sexual en el conflicto armado colombiano," *Revista de Estudios Sociales*, 36, pp. 86–94, http://www.codhes.org. Accessed January 21, 2021.

Yaffe, Lilian (2011), "Conflicto armado en Colombia: Análisis de las causas económicas, sociales e institucionales de la oposición violenta," *Revista CS*, 8, pp. 187–208. doi: 10.18046/recs.i8.1133.

9

Education for the Chosen Few – Guatemala

In various locations throughout Latin American, metal music has become a tool at the service of education. Guatemala serves as the perfect example of this quality; metal fans there have engaged in work that aims to strengthen the crumbling education system. Given that education in Guatemala is widely perceived as a strategy capable of combatting discrimination toward indigenous populations – discrimination that goes back to colonial times and remains active today – metal's pedagogical tendencies there intimately intertwine with decolonial agendas. Metal and metal pedagogy are also involved in a larger reflection about the role of public education in settings where neoliberal agendas have promoted the privatization of the public education system. Although my ethnographic work in Guatemala was initially interested in the effects of war and violence on metal music, exposure to this nation and its people quickly changed the focus of my research agenda, moving the work toward the topic of education. Before describing in detail the ways in which metal and education are linked in this Central American country, it is necessary that we understand the political dimensions of education in this setting.

The politics of education in Guatemala

The kids in the school were playing with two piñatas that had been brought by a handful of metal fans, a gift celebrating the occasion of their visit. They blindfolded the kids and each one took turns at hitting the piñata with a broomstick. After a couple of them had made their best efforts, one of them, an older girl of 11 years of age, moved into position and after one attempt finally hit the piñata with great success. The piñata broke instantly, candy falling all over the dirt floor. The kids dove to the ground in a frenzy that would make anyone not in the know think that they had found gold. Getting dirtier by the minute, their shirts, pants, and the girls' autochthonous skirts seemed now unrecognizable. After the turmoil, they equally divided the candy among themselves, making sure the smallest ones got their fair share. They sat down to eat as if the world around them had ceased to exist, but, of course, it didn't. The rural school, which had only one classroom, was crumbling around them, having no books to speak of and only one teacher for the entire school. The setting was a stark reminder of the dire situation education presently experiences in Guatemala's rural towns, a situation aggravated by the willing disregard of the central government when it comes to funding schools. Some of the people I came across would argue that this entrenched disregard is, in fact, a silent strategy, a quiet, yet concerted effort to maintain oppressive control over Mayan populations in the region.

The role of education in Guatemala cannot be understood without considering its present political context, which has been heavily marked by a civil war fought between the government and leftist groups mostly comprised of peasants. The war itself began in 1960, after the toppling of the democratically elected President Jacobo Arbenz by a military coup backed by the United States' Central Intelligence Agency; a common refrain in the region, to say the least. Arbenz's presidency was mostly linked with land reforms, policies that were intended to benefit the poor in Guatemala. During the conflict that followed, 200,000 people were murdered or disappeared, most of them from indigenous communities. In terms of sheer volume, Mayans arguably suffered the most (they comprised 83 percent of the casualties according to some tallies). When it comes to the killings themselves, reports place the vast majority of the responsibility on the military, who are said to have been responsible for 93 percent of these killings (Poppema 2009).

The peace accords signed in 1996 brought a symbolic end to the war. An important component of the accords was the emphasis on education. In them, the school system was reinterpreted as a way to learn about the past, avoid the pitfalls that had helped bring the country to war, and take the next step forward. Education was seen as a way to dismantle the racism and discrimination that had, in many ways, fostered the economic inequality that gave way to the civil war. Indigenous populations became heavily involved in the peace process and fought for their right to access education.

Actions geared toward strengthening the education system were needed; after all, the system had been so heavily affected during the civil war that dropout rates skyrocketed. The peace accords report documented evidence of children who had been forced out of their schools due to the violence (Bellino 2015). Therefore, reincorporating children into a revamped education system could serve as a catalyst to a different society that was aware of its past, could respect indigenous populations, and would be willing to fight discrimination while providing better opportunities for its people. Some pedagogical proposals included in the peace accords were: the use of the students' own language in bilingual schools, the strengthening of Mayan culture, the promotion of women's access to school, and the active investment of funds on the part of the government in the entire process (Helmberger 2006). Unfortunately, much research has documented that those agreements ended up being systematically ignored; their implementation was never fully realized (Poppema 2009). Therefore, schools in Guatemala today suffer from a lack of funding and fall short of delivering the promises contained in the peace accords.

The challenges for education mentioned above (access, language, and discrimination reduction) were, and continue to be, of great significance for indigenous people in Guatemala. Take, for example, the issue of language; a large segment of the population in Guatemala is Mayan (43 percent); within this segment alone, one can count up to 20 different spoken Mayan language variations (Helmberger 2006). Bilingual education is seen as crucial to keep the history of those communities alive. Furthermore, schools play an important role in the process of transitional justice. Schools can serve as spaces where vast numbers of the population can effectively carry on the process of bearing witness to the events of the past, something essential for the continued healing of a nation once formal peace commissions are gone (Cole 2007).

The process of "teaching about the past" is not unproblematic in Guatemala. Research has documented how the historical teaching of the civil war varies between different schools. Upper class urban schools teach a version of the conflict in which all actors are equally responsible for the violence, while in rural schools, which experienced the conflict directly, the discussion is more embedded in reflections about the community's history, including meditations on their "identity as a community in struggle" (Bellino 2015: 70). The politics of social class mediate how the civil war is remembered and who is held responsible for it.

As if this problem were not enough, after the peace accords, neoliberal policies toward the school system were implemented and the country's investment on education continued to decline. Schools funded by the World Bank were more interested in developing new workers for the economy than in promoting the role of education in the peace accords. These externally funded schools have been criticized for not having good infrastructure, not providing a space to voice alternative positions, not paying teachers a livable wage, and placing a heavier-than-usual burden on parents. The use of Mayan languages in the education process of these schools seemed to be an afterthought (Poppema 2009). This scenario greatly contrasts with community-run Mayan schools, which, far from being part of a neoliberal model for producing professionals, critique the traditional education model and place value on the importance of work, community, respecting nature, developing a sense of responsibility, and learning from elders (Heckt 1999).

The battles over the symbolic and practical implications of education in Guatemala are not only related to the peace accords of 1996. They also respond to outright manifestations of coloniality from abroad. The United States has historically become involved in the modification of school curricula as an indirect (some might argue, direct) strategy to exert control over the region, including Guatemala. One example of this strategy can be seen with the incursion of Christian schools, particularly those with curricula developed in the United States through which the latter's ideals get introduced to the Guatemalan population. This venture found allies in the local elites for it echoes their interest in maintaining control over the general population. Christian education has harbored and promoted neoliberal ideas regarding the economy and the criminalization of communism (Rose and Brouwer 1990). While these battles over education continue to happen, people from indigenous backgrounds in Guatemala continue to earn less money than their counterparts, have lower levels of education, are mostly self-employed, and are less likely to work in the public sector (Psacharopoulos 1993). There is also an earnings gap between indigenous and nonindigenous people in Guatemala (Patrinos 1997). This is attributed, in great part, to longstanding manifestations of discrimination in the country.

The challenges faced by education in Guatemala, and the hopes placed on its transformation via the peace accords, have echoed the need for a different type of pedagogy in the region, one that tackles the economic disparity and classist and racial oppression of marginalized populations, using local approaches and respecting local needs. These perspectives resonate with what some scholars have called "decolonial pedagogy," a concept used to describe an educational strategy that aims to foster a deep understanding of how mechanism of oppressions function in Latin American societies and how these intimately intersect with the experience of coloniality (Ocaña, Arias and Pedrozo Conedo 2018). Heavily based on the ideas of Brazilian educator Paulo Freire, who conceptualized education as a liberating act (Freire 2000), decolonial approaches to pedagogy push for the adoption of educational models that promote a critical approach to history, which highlights the understanding of Latin American experiences and ideas, surpassing universalist (read Eurocentric) approaches (James Díaz 2010). It also advocates for the recognition of indigenous populations and the knowledge they bring to the education process (Ocaña et al. 2018). Finally, it understands that in order to achieve this through schools, the education system needs to change. These concerns are not only mentioned in the peace accords in Guatemala, but are also present in other educational approaches, as is the case of the Zapatista schools in México.

It is against this politicized backdrop, influenced by philosophies of education, war, and peace, that metal fans have decided to become engaged with the school system. This particular case of metal music usage and visibility, as manifested in Guatemala and unseen by me in any other Latin American setting, makes the country an extraordinary case study to understand metal music though its actions, thus moving the study of metal beyond considerations of sound, genre, style, and the other dominants that have been considered thus far.

Metal goes to school

I had decided to visit Guatemala upon hearing through a colleague about the voluntary work of a group of metal fans at schools in the country's rural areas. After several months of planning, I was able to connect with the group while filming a documentary about metal in Latin America. Although I had multiple conversations with the group's leader before heading there, nothing could have prepared me for what I was about to experience. I had been to Guatemala on at least five different occasions, but this particular group would show me a side of the country very few people have experienced.

The town of Sumpango is about 48 kilometers west of the country's capital. Traffic in Guatemala is incredibly congested and, on any given day, the trip could take between two to three hours. I tried hiring a driver to take me to the town, but none would accept my offer. You could tell from seeing their faces that this was not a place they felt comfortable taking tourists, and although I tried my best to blend in, my skin tone and accent gave me away as a foreigner. Gerardo Pérez Acual, the group's leader, had to get one of his friends to drive me there. That morning, his friend picked me up in the capital and we headed to Sumpango. He looked extremely tired and explained to me that both he and Gerardo worked in the city, selling produce in the largest marketplace in town. They would start working at 10:00 p.m. supplying vendors with items like potatoes and fish. After a long night's work, they would drive back to Sumpango the following morning and repeat the same routine every day. On top of all of this work, Gerardo somehow found time to engage in volunteer work with children. His work ethic intrigued me; it was truly admirable.

Upon arriving to Sumpango, one could immediately see how it was different from the capital city. It is a small town embedded on a hillside. All the buildings look similar to the untrained eye. Most of them have unfinished details in their façades and none is above two stories tall (something that made me think of Cinthia Santibáñez and her longing for the horizon back in Chile). It feels like no one possesses the necessary resources to finish their self-built houses. The roads are small, tight, and built out of a mix of cement, cobblestones, and dirt. The town gave me the sensation of being a place where renovations seldom occur, and when they do happen, they do very little to improve the overall precarious situation. Small shops are prevalent throughout the streets and people walk everywhere. Most women wear their traditional indigenous skirts, a sight found only at tourist sites when one visits the capital city. As we passed the informal entrance of the town, the driver said out loud that he would "never leave Sumpango," as the place was "quiet at night" and he could get quality rest away from the busy lifestyle in the city. That calm he experienced was not for everyone. Before dropping me off, he said, "You are here because people are expecting you. If not, they would not let you in." And with that ominous warning, I stepped out of the car and into the town.

I soon saw Gerardo, who was there to meet me, along with other members of his group. He greeted me warmly while simultaneously looking at my bags, which were full of camera equipment. He immediately grabbed some of them and placed them in a carport, which was being used as a warehouse. He locked the gate and we began to walk the streets of the town. As we chatted, I immediately noticed the townspeople looking at Gerardo and his group. They stuck out like a sore thumb. Dressed in black, with long hair, they were a distant cry from what most people in Guatemala, or Sumpango for that matter, look like. I am sure my presence did not help deter local attention. As we walked, Gerardo began to describe the place as a "small town amid the mountains." He stated that a small-town mentality pervaded there, and therefore, his group was always "fighting against the system." In such closed quarters, everyone knew everyone "and that makes the fight even more direct." He mentioned that a lot of people in the town saw them as criminals because of the widespread religious influence in the country, a factor that was even more intense in Sumpango. "If we talk about religion and politics, the pressure is intense. There are four or five churches in every block!" He stressed that they were seen as criminals for being into heavy metal music. Even though they engaged in community work, he stressed: "Politicians don't want to be involved in what we do. The pressure in this town is constant. A metal fan cannot go unnoticed."

Gerardo and his group were in the public eye, not only for how they dressed and the music they listened to, but also because of what they did with their spare time. The group, known as the Internal Circle, had decided that the metal community needed to become actively involved in the social problems that plagued their wider community. Initially, they had gathered food for victims of Hurricane Mitch; however, they immediately felt that those contributions were reactive and of limited lasting impact. One member of the group described this process:

> When Hurricane Mitch hit, many people were left without food and medicine. The news said help was not coming and that the government was incapacitated. That inspired us to help people. We gathered clothing and food. When we got there, we noticed the conditions of the schools: no books, seats, or blackboards. When we saw that, we decided to focus more on education. Education is a way to challenge the system that surrounds us. If we don't have access to it, nothing here will change.

In light of this experience, the group decided to focus their work on local schools in Sumpango and other adjacent communities. In general, the group's collaboration with the schools aimed to improve the conditions of the latter's infrastructure while simultaneously helping students complete their education. At the time of my visit, their work had been ongoing for a decade straight. In those 10 years, they had established ongoing collaborations with fifteen schools in the area and impacted more than 1200 children per year.

The process of intervening with the schools was quite remarkable and methodical. The Internal Circle holds an annual metal concert in Sumpango with local bands. In order to attend, people need to pay for their ticket. But that is not all: as part of the admission, they also have to donate three new notebooks. Gerardo frequently mentioned in our conversations that "you can pay for entry, but if you don't have those three notebooks, there is no way you are coming in." The materials are then taken to the schools and, alongside other activities, offered to the children as incentives to engage in their schoolwork and avoid desertion. The group also uses the funds from the concert to provide a fresh coat of paint to the schools they visit. Although this might seem like a simple act, in the context of rural Guatemala, this actually represents quite a large and significant gesture, as I will describe in detail later. As Gerardo and I sat down to lunch with the group, I inquired about their concern over education and children. He mentioned the following:

> We look at this from a historical and social context. In Guatemala, education, which should be the most important issue, blatantly receives the least amount of funding. We have schools without roofs or desks! The system encourages this lack of education because it is convenient. Uneducated people vote for the worst president. Thanks to metal music, one learns about history, becomes informed, and seeks alternative sources of knowledge. Therefore, education is key in order to transform the system. That takes time. If it has taken us 500 years to become what we are today, then we cannot think that these problems will be resolved in 5 years. We may not see the results ourselves.

There were multiple themes that came up during this particular conversation that struck me as important. First, Gerardo was keenly aware of the political dimensions of education in Guatemala after the civil war. The defunding of schools was used to control populations in rural areas, particularly those of Mayan descent. Although a commitment to education was a key component in the peace accords of 1996, Gerardo was swift to reveal those proceedings as mere "smoke screens." "They sign peace accords to get funds from the United Nations and other countries. It all fades away. It is a great hypocrisy." The abandonment of schools in rural areas was a mechanism at the service of the social oppression of indigenous populations. The Internal Circle minced no words when it came to this, bringing it up frequently with me. Also, Gerardo referenced a 500-year timeframe when describing the community's current situation. This number is important, as it is a direct reference to the long-lasting effects of fifteenth-century colonialism under Spain. It is widely known that when someone in Latin America mentions those "500 years," they are referring to the colonial experience. Gerardo saw the ongoing oppression of indigenous populations as an extension of this colonial mentality. Therefore, they see their work, the active involvement with the education of Mayan children, as a challenge to the effects of coloniality. In fact, this would not be the only time this perspective was mentioned by a group member.

The group's work with education had garnered the attention of the local people. "What were these Satanists doing in the schools?" was a frequent question discussed in Sumpango, according to Gerardo. As if this suspicion were not problematic enough, the group also had ongoing tensions with other metal fans. Their concerts in town had become the most important event of the year for local metal music. The crowds began growing in size and traveled from other provinces to attend the events. Promoters eventually saw this as a problem. Still, the Internal Circle would establish a strong foothold in their town. They controlled all the concerts and these were done to benefit the rural schools. This was seen by some as a lost opportunity to capitalize and make money. The group seemed unfazed by these concerns. They controlled the metal circuit in Sumpango, they were aware of it, and they continued to labor for the benefit of local schools. "We lost a lot of people along the way who only saw these metal concerts as a potential way to make money," Gerardo explained. The group's interest, however, lied elsewhere.

The Internal Circle had garnered the support of local bands that would become identified with the movement. One of them was the band Hacha ("Hatchet") from Chiquimula, who consistently played in the concerts held in Sumpango. I had the opportunity to interview the band's drummer, Luis Morataya, during one of my visits. While discussing their affiliation and collaboration with the Internal Circle's voluntary work, he explained that he himself saw in this town the ongoing effects of the armed conflict. "Although other places were more impacted than Sumpango, the war was horrible everywhere. We aim to reflect what people feel about that process and this connects us to Sumpango."

They were fully aware of the war's effects on indigenous people and their education. They described the town as having a capacity for "social critique" amid the "crumbling of society." This critical awareness was mainly linked to the presence and the activities of the Internal Circle in particular and metal music in general. "What they do is an act of resistance, because it aims to change our social paradigm," he mentioned while we drank some refreshments under an exposed roof at one of the Internal Circle member's house. "They haven't given up in 10 years. Some people see that and value them." For Luis, the group positioned "metal as an act of resistance that went against the current." "This is what they are leaving behind for future generations," he stated with a proud smile. "The most freeing act one can experience is education. That is their objective. I go with them to the schools. When a kid has a book and can read it, he is free! He won't have to work the cornfields for one dollar per day. Education is the best tool of resistance that we the poor have." Although these might have been lofty ambitions for what education could actually do for these children, the feeling and energy are quite contagious. He harbored the hope that at least for some it would pan out that way.

As the hot sun shone down on us, I meditated on the message of this conversation and all those other conversations that echoed how the Internal Circle had garnered the support of other metal fans and musicians. It was also evidently clear that the Internal Circle and the metal bands associated to it saw the current exploitation of indigenous groups as a continuation of fifteenth-century colonialism. This linkage between the colonial past and the oppressive present is still hard to accept for many people in Latin America. This was not the case for the metal fans I interviewed in Sumpango. Therefore, their interventions in schools seemed to me like clear acts of decoloniality. All that was left for me to do was bear witness; I wanted, more than anything, to see these acts first-hand.

Leave your cameras behind

The group was getting ready to visit one of the schools in Sumpango. It was the first time they would visit this particular school in the village, and one could tell that tensions were high. They had little idea of how they would be received. The student body was larger than those they had encountered at the other schools they usually visited, a logistical challenge that entailed purchasing materials for 450 children. In Sumpango, this is a major undertaking as there are not many stores in which these materials, specifically new notebooks, can be purchased. To make matters more complicated, this school was in a part of town that they described as "more dangerous" than others. This fact was made evident when the group asked me to leave behind my cameras, as these would garner unwanted attention. I agreed, and left them at Gerardo's house, which interestingly enough, did not have any locks on the doors. Anyone could come in at any given time and take them. Gerardo noticed my concern and told me not to worry, as "no one in town would dare enter the house of a *metalero* [metalhead]." He smiled while saying it. I left my equipment in his living room and left with the group, mildly at ease after his jovial reassurance.

The first thing the group did that day was rent a small bus and begin to drive through the streets of Sumpango. It is not an easy feat to purchase 450 notebooks in one day. The group went through several small stores acquiring all of the notebooks they could find. The shop owners were extremely happy with their presence as they could sell their entire inventory in one day. After several hours of walking and going through the stores, the group had their notebooks, and we headed for the school.

In order to get to the school, we drove through several corn plantations. This highlighted for me how the schools impacted by the group were embedded in the most rural parts of Sumpango. This particular school was at the entrance to the village, right next door to their only water source, where people would come to gather the precious liquid for cooking and cleaning. The school would be hard to identify to outsiders, as it had no formal signs or markers. Other than some murals with childlike drawings stressing the importance of education and respect for each other, the walls surrounding the school made it seem like a military compound. The walls were at least nine feet high, made out of concrete, and lacked windows. The heavy metal gates opened and out came the principal, who glimpsed at the group of metal fans in astonishment. After a few minutes of conversations between him and Gerardo, we were allowed access into the school.

Once inside the school walls, one could see the classrooms, an inner patio, and a food stand with two women making tortillas for the children. While the kids were in class, the silence that pervaded allowed one to hear the sounds of construction; they were building new restrooms for the school. Since all of the kids would be brought to the inner patio for the event, the principal and some of the older students began to raise a makeshift roof to cover them from the sun. The tarp was made of old bags used in the fields to gather corn, which were sewn together as best they could. They had many holes, so the sun came through despite their best efforts to avoid it. Under this makeshift cover, the Internal Circle grabbed a microphone and introduced themselves to the crowd.

You could tell by the reactions of the teachers that this was their first time in that particular school. They looked simultaneously suspicious and concerned. Who could blame them? The group's aesthetics, their black metal shirts and boots, were completely alien to the school and the village. Since these settings also receive very little support from the government or the communities, it must be surprising when volunteers show up to help. The kids seemed more interested in their long hair than anything else. Children would grab me by the arm to touch my tattoos and see if they would rub off. To their amazement, they would not. It was evident that our presence there was a class on diversity and the presence of the other, their other.

What happened next served as a perfect mix of entertainment and education. After Gerardo spoke to the children about the Internal Circle and how much they loved metal music, he introduced a street performer. The latter made the kids laugh with some juggling and physical comedy skits, setting them at ease with this new group of strangers. After that, Gerardo introduced a magician. The young man captivated his audience with card games and tricks that made coins appear out of thin air. The kids were mesmerized. Then, amid what seemed like simple entertainment, the education process began to slowly but steadily emerge.

Sophíe Lorraine Villegas Zea, the only female in the Internal Circle, accompanied us at the school that day, brought out her acoustic guitar, and began to play a song for the children. She had them under a spell, and they were completely enthralled with her playing. The song had a catchy chorus and the kids sang along to it: *ser mejor* (to be better). The lyrics addressed the need to be better people, respect others, end violence in the village, and follow your dreams. After a couple of songs, she held up her guitar and began to teach the children the names of the different parts of the instrument (see Figure 9.1). She spoke to the children for a few minutes, asking them what they wanted to be when they grew up and commenting on the importance of staying in school to achieve those goals. This pattern of mixing entertainment and education continued for almost two hours. The kids were in awe of their visitors and the unrelenting sunshine did not seem to faze them. "Some of them have never seen a guitar," she would tell me later during the day.

After the show and chat were over, Gerardo made the kids form lines and the group began to give all of them new notebooks (see Figure 9.2). The children's

FIGURE 9.1: Sophíe Lorraine Villegas Zea, members of the Internal Circle, explaining the parts of the guitar. Photo provided by Nelson Varas-Díaz.

FIGURE 9.2: Members of the Internal Circle handing out school materials. Photo provided by Nelson Varas-Díaz.

faces lit up when receiving their notebooks. Immediately, they ran back to their classrooms to show their teachers their new materials. The group also brought cases of used books for the school, which the kids took to the principal's office as if these were newfound treasures. Before ending the event, Gerardo took to the microphone one more time to speak about respecting one another and the importance of peace in the community. Finally, he told the entire crowd, though I think his message was mostly directed toward the adults there, that the government would "always stifle our development." He ended by saying that they needed to "bring communities together to move forward." The crowd applauded and, just like that, the event was over. The gates swung open and the kids began their daily walk back home. Right behind them, the Internal Circle emerged from the school. Some kids stayed behind and asked me to take their pictures with Gerardo (see Figure 9.3).

As we got back into the truck, spirits were high among the group. They knew they were doing something that was important for the schools. Gerardo pulled me aside and said, "One may think this is insignificant, but for them it

FIGURE 9.3: Gerardo Pérez Acual, leader of the Internal Circle, interacting with children in a Guatemalan school. Photo provided by Nelson Varas-Díaz.

is enormous. It is seeing another world. Understanding that there is more in the world than they know." Even more important, it seemed to me at the time, Gerardo stressed how this was needed to "incentivize mutual respect in order to live in peace." For an outsider, this emphasis on peace in the community might have seemed like an ambiguous statement, but those that have lived through the civil war knew what he was talking about and what he was trying to avoid for the next generation.

Just before we left, some of the kids began to search for more school materials in the truck. As this happened, one of the Internal Circle members looked at me and told me, "Remember that the government has abandoned these schools and supplies don't get here for months. Classes begin in January and they don't get supplies until April. They never come. This is what we live with." We got in the truck and headed back to town. Even though I was deeply troubled by the conditions of the school, and simultaneously amazed with what I had seen the group do for the children, nothing could have prepared me for the conditions of the next school we would visit.

The school at the end of the dirt road

A couple of days after visiting this first school in Sumpango, I came back to the town to continue my interviews with the Internal Circle. On that day, they would visit a smaller school in the village of Guachipilín. The group was particularly enthusiastic about this visit, as this was the very first school they had adopted as part of their volunteer work. The school was deeper in the mountain region, and we needed a pick-up truck to get there. We all jumped in the back of the truck and headed out of the town. After a couple of minutes driving down the main asphalt road, the driver made a hard right turn and we were off road. The trek slowed down significantly as the road was full of holes and uneven stretches of land that needed to be navigated with caution.

While the truck made its way through the remote countryside region, one of the volunteers began to talk about the school and the students. It felt like he was preparing me for what I was about to see. He said, "This is Mayan population. They are descendent from the Mayas. The government has no interest in them, understanding the situation they are going through. This country has many resources, but since colonial times the region has been exploited. They don't want people to understand that and leave behind the ignorance in which they are drowning." I nodded to let him know I understood. In one short conversation, he was able to link the school's current situation and its abandonment by the government as a continuation of colonial politics in Guatemala. Ignorance was the goal, and the neglect of the schools was the government's strategy.

After half an hour on the dirt road, we reached the school. The structure itself was on the side of a mountain. I could not see it from the road, but could hear the children's voices through the trees. As soon as one member of the group started making their way up the mountainside, the children began to scream, "*¡llegaron los metaleros!*" ("The metalheads have arrived!"). The small school went into a frenzy. The children remembered them from prior visits and were expecting a treat. "*¡Trajeron dos piñatas!*" ("They brought two piñatas!") one of the kids screamed out loud. Everyone greeted the school's principal and the kids, while a sense of old friendships reacquainted filled the air. The kids had made a small sign with crayons that read "*Bienvenidos Internal Circle*" ("Welcome Internal Circle").

In this more intimate setting, with fewer students and a shared history of previous visits, a different type of interaction took place. The connections with the kids felt more profound and better planned out. Children played with the *piñatas* and were treated to pieces of cake. While they ate, one of the volunteers spoke to them about issues like self-esteem, interacting with others without violence, having clear dreams and goals, and the importance of academic success in order to achieve those goals. I initially thought these topics were going over the kids' heads, who seemed more excited about the piñatas and the cake. Still, when it came time to hand out the new notebooks, the volunteers turned the task into a small memory exercise. They would ask questions related to the content of the small talks, and those kids who provided correct answers received their notebooks first. Afterward, everyone got a notebook and was advised to participate more during the next visit. After the notebooks were handed out, the boys played soccer, while the girls went aside with Sophie to speak about what they politely called "girl issues." They really seemed to enjoy their time with her and asked many questions about her clothes, her academic preparation, and what she did in the town. She reminded me that, before meeting her, some of the kids had never interacted with a woman that did not work at home or in the fields. Sophie was using her metal attire and experience to decolonize gender, a strategy that women in metal have used elsewhere in Latin America (Varas-Díaz et al. 2017).

After spending some time with the kids, Gerardo and I sat to have a conversation with the school principal. He was very happy to have them there and it showed, but as soon as Gerardo asked him about the school, his facial expression changed. "We lost another one today Gerardo," he said with an air of defeat about him. One of the students, upon turning 15, had been taken out of school and sent to the cornfields to work. Without finishing his education, his chances of ever leaving those fields were slim to none. The conversation felt futile and the group's efforts like a drop of water in an endless sea. I could not blame them.

A look around the school spoke of the great uphill battle the principal was facing, even with the support of the Internal Circle. The school had two classrooms, one of which was simply unusable due to its conditions. The other one had more students than seats, so some would sit on the floor during class. The principal politely smiled when I asked him about his job. "I have all the jobs," he said. "I teach all the classes to all the children. I clean. I cook. You name it, I do it." That is when I realized that this was just one man with 15 children of ages ranging from five to thirteen in one classroom. The task seemed impossible. "I have to teach math to a 5-year-old and a 13-year-old at the same time!" The complexity of that process seemed monumental, but also appalling.

Gerardo noticed that the conversation was rapidly turning bleak. In an attempt to lighten the mood, he explained that they "try to give students alternatives and incentivize them. It is the only way to change society." But even he knew this was an uphill battle. "There were 25 students here initially and we have lost some of them," he said. Still, they continued to come to the school to "lift their spirits." The principal recalled the first time the group visited the school and the kids' less-than-favorable reactions to their metal aesthetics. After many visits, the children's perspectives had changed, of course. "Look where we are now!" he said. They had come a long way in helping the school and, at the same time, helping reduce prejudice toward metal fans in Sumpango. Gerardo observed that metal would "always sing 'against something'," but he needed something more from metal. "Where is the action?" he would ask in our conversation, before answering his own question. "This is action through metal music! It is a protest against what is happening. To us, this means being with the children."

Metal as decolonial education

Upon returning to the town of Sumpango in the back of the pick-up truck, I reflected on the many things that were happening to and because of the Internal Circle, all of which were related to metal music. Gerardo and his team were doing an incredible job with the local schools, but their work meant more than that. There were other instances of educational practices going on around them, some of which I think they were unaware of. Two of them stood out for me. First, the Internal Circle was educating the townspeople on issues of tolerance and diversity through their actions. Secondly, they were changing how metal bands integrated social issues into their music and how these metal artists saw metal music as an educational tool. Let us explore both of these issues individually.

Even though some townspeople still looked at them with suspicion, others valued what the Internal Circle was doing for the children. Gerardo was aware that the group's actions shed light on the inefficiencies of the local government and the church, who spoke a lot about social justice and education after the armed conflict, but did little to address it. He stated, "They are ashamed that we do their job at a lower cost and with our own resources." This call to action in light of the lack of concrete efforts by these institutions had garnered them the respect of some people in the town. In turning their efforts toward education, they were educating the people in Sumpango about the need to address social inequality among indigenous populations and, simultaneously, showing them a different side of metal fans.

Metal was a key element in fostering this "call to action" approach for Gerardo and for many others working with the Internal Circle. He stressed, "As fans we believe metal is the energy that lifts us up. It is knowledge. We want people to coexist in this town." He also saw this as a strategy for people to have control of their lives and not have politicians come and "take power away from them." The "freedom to think for oneself," as he described it, was important in this process. Since this was motivated by metal music, Gerardo argued, "Metal needed to be defended. It is that idea that we carry with us." The group expected more from metal music than just entertainment. Metal had educated them, and they would use it to educate others. Metal bands around them took notice.

I had the opportunity to speak about the educational role of metal with local bands who had played in the concerts hosted by the Internal Circle. One of them was the band the Maximones from San Pedro Sacatepéquez.[1] When interviewing guitarist Robin Orozco, we discussed the educational role of metal in his life. He stressed how metal's "social character" had influenced him as a young man. "That message caught my attention. I want other people to see bands with a social message, much like I did. Bands with lyrics that tell truths people don't want to hear. At the time, we had no internet and the radio was government controlled. We are now the counter-news; the ugly news. People only want to listen to beautiful things, but this is quite an ugly world." This process of becoming a socially committed metal band with educational aspirations for its listeners had a cost. He reminded me: "In the local scene we are not too popular. It is not something people like to hear. We play there because we want to leave a certain content with the audience."

Luis, from the band Hacha, echoed this sentiment in one of our conversations. He stressed that becoming a socially conscious metal band was not a planned process, but that meeting those affected by the armed conflict "brought one closer to the people." He also interpreted metal as an educational strategy, but stressed that through it, people learned together as opposed to learning via a top-down approach (echoes of Freire again). He stated, "There is an educational component to most things. There is education in art. It is not about teaching people, but rather about learning together. Our lyrics have evolved since interacting with the Internal Circle."

The idea of "learning together" brought forth by Luis seems important in order to understand how metal music can become a decolonial force in Latin America. In its own way, it reminded me of the emphasis placed by Freire (2000) on dialogue as a key strategy for education, that is, in opposition to traditional top-down approaches. This is part of the *extreme decolonial dialogues* I outline in Chapter 1. In fact, as I left Sumpango I could not stop thinking about how the Internal Circle was engaged in a sort of decolonial pedagogy of their own. For example: (1) they saw education as a way to understand oppression in their setting, (2) they engaged the entire community in supporting schools, (3) they conveyed messages of hope and peace in the face of oppression and violence, (4) they transformed the infrastructure of schools, and (5) they concentrated on impacting indigenous communities that are still being ignored via the traditional education system. As if this were not enough, they had impacted local metal bands that now adhered to this pedagogical approach to foster critical thinking within the metal scene. It seemed to me that they had engaged in a decolonial pedagogy. This mentality, in turn, had spilled over into the metal scene, which, in essence, was another learning setting they had impacted. I think it is no exaggeration to say that Gerardo and his group were not only changing the lives of young kids in the rural schools, but were also transforming how their community reacted to metal fans and how metal musicians interpreted their role in Guatemalan society. In essence they were engaging in the type of pedagogy Freire wishes us to adopt in the face of strife and oppression. I am reminded of Freire's words, when he writes, "No pedagogy which is truly liberating can remain distant from the oppressed by treating them as unfortunates and by presenting for their emulation models from among the oppressors. The oppressed must be their own example in the struggle for their redemption" (Freire 2000: 54). Thus, Gerardo and the Internal Circle have come to represent the praxis, Freire's teachings made action. Here is a pedagogy of learning together, of the abandoned, of the forgotten, of the oppressed. In capturing metal's work in Guatemala, I hope not only to shed light into this peculiar instance of metal in action, decolonial metal at that, but to reveal the possibilities of metal in action, as decolonial practice, as educational practice, and as community-building practice.

NOTE

1. Mario Efraín Castañeda Maldonado (2020) has written about The Maximones from an academic perspective, focusing on how the band transforms the local deity Maximón as part of their musical production. His work highlights how the band uses pre-Hispanic elements as a form of cultural resistance. It is one of the very few scholarly publications on metal music in the context of Guatemala.

REFERENCES

Bellino, Michelle J. (2015), "So that we do not fall again: History education and citizenship in 'postwar' Guatemala," *Comparative Education Review*, 60:1, pp. 58–79. doi: 10.1086/684361.

Castañeda Maldonado, Mario Efraín (2020), "The transfiguration of the deity *Maximón* as a practice of resistance in metal from San Pedro Sacatepéquez, San Marcos, Guatemala," in N. Varas-Díaz, D. Nevárez Araújo, and E. Rivera-Segarra (eds.), *Heavy Metal Music in Latin America: Perspectives from the Distorted South*, London: Lexington Press, pp. 219–37.

Cole, Elizabeth A. (2007), "Transitional justice and the reform of history education," *International Journal of Transitional Justice*, 1:1, pp. 115–37. doi: 10.1093/ijtj/ijm003.

Freire, Paulo (2000), *Pedagogy of the Oppressed*, 30th anniv. ed., New York: Bloomsbury Academics.

Heckt, Meike (1999), "Mayan education in Guatemala: A pedagogical model and its political context," *International Review of Education*, 45:3–4, pp. 321–37.

Helmberger, Janet L. (2006), "Language and ethnicity: Multiple literacies in context, language education in Guatemala," *Bilingual Research Journal*, 30:1, pp. 65–86. doi: 10.1080/15235882.2006.10162866.

James Díaz, Cristhian (2010), "Hacia una pedagogía en clave decolonial: Entre aperturas, búsquedas y posibilidades," *Tabula Rasa*, 13, pp. 217–33.

Ocaña, Alexander Ortiz, Arias López, María Isabel, and Pedrozo Conedo, Zaira Esther (2018), "Hacia una pedagogía decolonial en/desde el sur global," *Revista Nuestra América*, 6, pp. 195–222.

Ocaña, Alexander Ortiz, Arias, María Isabel, and Pedrozo Conedo, Zaira Esther (2018), *Decolonialidad de la Educación: Emergencia/Urgencia de Una Pedagogía Decolonial*, Santa Marka, Magdalena: Editorial Unimagdalena.

Patrinos, Harry Anthony (1997), "Differences in education and earnings across ethnic groups in Guatemala," *Quarterly Review of Economics and Finance*, 37:4, pp. 809–21.

Poppema, Margriet (2009), "Guatemala, the peace accords and education: A post-conflict struggle for equal opportunities, cultural recognition and participation in education," *Globalisation, Societies and Education*, 7:4, pp. 383–408. doi: 10.1080/14767720903412218.

Psacharopoulos, George (1993), "Ethnicity, education, and earnings in Bolivia and Guatemala," *Comparative Education Review*, 37:1, pp. 9–20. doi: 10.1086/447161.

Rose, Susan D. and Brouwer, Steve (1990), "The export of fundamentalist Americanism: US evangelical education in Guatemala," *Latin American Perspectives*, 17:4, pp. 42–56.

Varas-Díaz, Nelson, Rivera, Eliut, González, Osvaldo, Mendoza, Sigrid, and Morales, Eric (2017), "Heavy metal as a vehicle for critical culture in Latin America and the Caribbean: Challenging traditional female gender roles through music," in *Connecting Metal and Culture: Unity in Disparity*, London: Intellect.

10

An Elusive Word: *Aguante* as a Decolonial Reflection – Argentina

As mentioned in the initial chapter of this book, e*xtreme decolonial dialogues* can foster communal and celebratory reflections among its listeners, reflections that allow its participants to critically examine the oppressive practices taking place in their surroundings and grant them the space to challenge and change these practices in a collective manner, all in the hopes of fostering better conditions in the future. This salient characteristic of decolonial metal music can best be witnessed in Argentina. However, this time my travels there took on a different inflection. Contrary to the predominant focus I adopted in many of the other countries I visited, my latest trip to Argentina would not focus on a particular historical event within that nation's metal scene. After all, Argentina has been the center of a plethora of excellent research, primarily on its robust and long-lasting metal scene and in light of its historical significance for Latin American (Calvo 2016b, 2017, 2018; Scaricaciottoli 2016; Provéndola 2017; Panzini 2018). This time around, my visit would be taken up with the inherent need to understand a singular word that often gets thrown around between the participants of that metal scene, a word otherwise absent in the rest of Latin America. That word is *aguante,* and as we will see, pinpointing, defining, and understanding it entails a monumental task. However, any serious interest in Argentina's scene must grapple and come face to face with this term.

Aguante can be heard everywhere and anywhere within the local metal scene in Argentina. People use it as a verb (i.e., *¡aguante hermano!*) and a noun (i.e., *esa banda tiene aguante*). Argentinians use it to show respect for a friend, rally support for a band, and even as an all-encompassing sendoff capable of ending any casual conversation in good terms. During my visits there, I would also witness the term being used in a heartfelt conversation between metal fans as a coded substitute for the more upfront "I'm here for you" (i.e., *te hago el aguante*). The word has so many uses and meanings, and is so particular and pervasive to Argentinian metal, that it merited multiple ethnographic trips on my part to the country in an exhaustive effort to try to understand it in all its nuance.

211

One of my very first incursions into the understanding of the term came in the form of Pablo Alejandro Trangone, the lead singer for the local metal band Arraigo. We spent nearly an entire year having phone conversations and internet exchanges trying to plan my initial visit. After agreeing on a workable schedule, I found myself some months later walking through *Avenida Corrientes* with him on our way to some local pizza shop. While we walked, Pablo was attentively listening to my ideas about how the concept of *aguante* could be interpreted. From the outside, that is, from a foreigner's point of view, the idea of *aguante* seemed to be an expression of collectiveness. Although I knew that there were other levels of complexity embedded in its use, the most evident way for me to describe it at the time was as an expression of social support. As we walked, I explained my rationale; all the while, Pablo remained silent.

We reached the restaurant, which at the time was packed, and he proceeded to explain that the joint was one of the oldest in the city. One sat at the table and could not avoid rubbing shoulders with other *porteños;* the place was that small. Everyone seemed to be ordering red wine, *pizza de molde,* and *empanadas.* As our conversation continued, Pablo appeared more interested in listening to my interpretation of *aguante* than on being interviewed. After a while, we placed our order; he looked at me straight in the eyes and, finally, broke his silence.

"If you are so interested in the meaning of words," he said, leaving a brief pause as if to create suspense, "why not start at the beginning?" I was somewhat confused by his question. Was it rhetorical or hypothetical? I think he noticed my puzzlement and elaborated by asking, "What is heavy about heavy metal music?" We looked at each other for a few seconds in silence. I think we both felt, or at least I did, that the upcoming conversation would be profound and challenging. "You first," I told Pablo, this was all the encouragement he needed. The rest of the evening became a night-long conversation about the role of metal in Latin America. For Pablo, that role was inextricably linked to political reflections about social oppression in the region. Metal music had a purpose beyond entertainment; this much was clear to him. The music was a storytelling medium at the service of posing, as Pablo put it, "new questions to old answers." In this particular conversation, that "new question" seemed to be clear: What if we problematize the very meaning of *aguante?* What if *aguante* was more than just a show of support? What if *aguante*, like a lot of Argentinian metal music, had an underlying political agenda? One meeting would not be enough to cover all of this ground. And, so, Pablo and I agreed to meet on several occasions throughout my trips to Argentina. We frequently discussed this singular issue, the nuanced meaning of this vitally important word and its uses in the local metal scene.

212

Aguante *as social support*

The word *aguante* did not originate from within Argentina's metal scene, even though its constant use within that space might make it seem that way to anyone who interacts with its music fans. The idea itself first rose to frequent usage within the circle of soccer clubs and its fans, a phenomenon quite prevalent in Argentina and part of the everyday fabric of the country. *Fútbol* (what the English-speaking world calls soccer) in Argentina is an industry unto itself and has served as a catalyst for the development of group identities that sometimes rival in importance the very notion of nationhood. For some, identifying as fans of a particular soccer club or team has become just as important as being Argentinian. The emotional aspect of "belonging" tied to sports is that strong. The word *aguante* is used to show one's commitment to a soccer club and encompasses a collection of actions and behaviors expressed to show that support (Moreira 2008, 2010). It is seen as an issue of honor that is attained and sustained through the act of wearing a specific team's paraphernalia, attending games, and going to a particular bar. These, however, present just a handful of the practices deployed at any given time. In fact, violence and hooliganism can be and have been just as prominent as these other acts. Various social scientists have approached the idea of *aguante* in Argentinian soccer culture in an attempt to describe its use and particularities. For example, researchers have documented how the idea of *aguante* has specific corporeal manifestations during a game (i.e., use of team colors, rags, jumping up and down during the game, chanting) (Zambaglione 2010). They have also explored how these practices are frequently linked to perceptions of masculinity and power (Alabarces 2015; Alabarces and Garriga Zucal 2008), though female participation has also received scholarly attention (Alabarces 2006). Although several of these practices have frequently ended in violent encounters between team supporters and police forces, research on the internal dynamics of the process of *aguante* has explored its more nuanced uses in meaning-making through studies devoted to the unspoken rules regulating these sports outings (Alabarces, Garriga Zucal, and Moreira 2008; Garriga Zucal 2016). For the purposes of my reflection in this chapter, it should suffice to say that *aguante* has its origins outside of metal culture and that, in the specific context of soccer culture, the word is clearly linked to practices of social support.

Although the migration of the term *aguante* from soccer culture into other areas of Argentinian life has been documented, such as in the case of rock music as a call for social resistance (Hamed 2003), metal-focused scholarship has yet to unpack this term extensively (Calvo 2016a[1]). It is odd that the word has been so frequently used in the metal scene and yet it seems to have escaped a detailed academic gaze within and outside the country, at least judging from the lack of published literature. Still, it was evident from my travels to Argentina that scholars who engage in metal-focused research have understood this linkage between the world of soccer and rock and, by extension, metal music. For example, Manuela Calvo, a prominent metal researcher who has devoted her work to Argentinian metal, explained these linkages during an interview:

> The word *aguante* can be understood in two ways. It can be both a theoretical concept or a term proper. As a theoretical concept it was used by music sociologists to describe the social dimensions of *chabón* rock. That is, rock music made during the nineties, which started to have different characteristics from those found in the rock of previous decades. It had to do with its connection to soccer events, with the way crowds behaved at soccer events. Concerts were being held in stadiums, so people started chanting like they would do for the soccer teams. You would motivate the band just like you would the soccer teams. They would use flags, which in Argentina are called *trapos*. Jump up and down, very similar to a pogo dance. The intensity of motivating a fan base [...] Theorist conceptualized that as the *aguante*, a characteristic of local rock. Many of them include metal bands as part of that local movement.

The emergence of the concept of *aguante* within metal music seemed clear enough. However, its actual usage within the local metal scene seemed as varied as the people who would discuss the idea with me. Amid all its many definitions and uses explained during interviews with local musicians, fans, and metal scholars, a transitional pattern seemed to emerge. Initially, the idea was linked to the concept of community, a notion that has proven to be dominant within the study of metal music (Hill 2014; Riches and Spracklen 2014; Venkatesh et al. 2014; Rivera-Segarra et al. 2015; Varas-Díaz et al. 2015, 2016a, 2016b; Snaza and Netherton 2016). Social support shown through the day-to-day consumption of metal music and its practices drove those definitions. Manuela Calvo echoed this idea when explaining that the term was mostly linked to "the communion between the band and the audience. Communion between all of those agents." As she mentioned in our conversation, *aguante* became shorthand to saying, "We are all in this together."

This use of *aguante* as a signal of social support and commonality seemed to be the most frequently used. In fact, I could see it displayed in everyday interactions with metal scene members. Conversations with local metal musicians shed light on the use of the term and how it is seen as a way to show support to local bands. Gustavo Zavala, bass player of the local band Tren Loco (Minore 2010), described the term as a form of motivation. He explained it was like saying, "Strength. Resistance. To endure. It is to motivate someone: 'Let's go [...] we can do it. Don't give up. Don't fall down. Strength. Strength to the neighborhood.

Strength'. For us that is *aguante*." This collectivized strength would be transmitted to up-and-coming artists within the local metals scene as a way to show them support. Gustavo stated that you would say *aguante* to a new band to show respect and encouragement. "When you feel love for something, you express it that way," he stated. The band's lead singer, Carlos Cabral, echoed this conceptualization of *aguante* as a common support for the movement. "*Aguante* for the new bands," he stated, as he smiled in what I interpreted as a feeling of profound pride rooted in his band's role in promoting and cementing the scene with his band since 1982. Although the definition of *aguante* as social support would be the most prevalent throughout my interviews, it was not the only one. Other people within the local scene saw it as a political term.

Aguante *as politics*

As my interviews with local scene members continued, and more profound relationships were established, the complexities of the word continued to expand. My interactions with the members of Tren Loco became the epitome of this diversity in meaning. Although they had initially described *aguante* as a process of social support within the metal scene, with time the idea became more socially and historically embedded within the Latin American context and, by extension, more political in nature. Carlos Cabral described his band as one "committed to social causes and the working class." He mentioned feeling proud of his band for being able to serve as "communicators of things that people can't say in other ways." He perceived that people identified with the band because they were "the voice of people who want to say something. They find in our music what they want to say." What they wanted to say had a clear-cut political message. Gustavo Zavala linked that message to the colonial struggles faced throughout Latin America. He stated the following when describing the political nature of *aguante*:

> The upper class [...] conservatives [...] want to keep their privileges while the working class fights for its life. We feel that *aguante* to endure in the face of those permanent disasters, which manifested during the twentieth century in the form of coups. Many of them fostered by the CIA and those systems that want to interfere with other countries. Rock is a refuge. And I think music, and metal in particular, has a lot of strength and helps you overcome those moments.

Although this use of *aguante* was broader than simple social support and might seem to some as a mere abstract reflection, the members of Tren Loco felt it had very clear and practical day-to-day implications for metal fans. Specifically, these implications included the need to be connected to the region's history through education and its role in developing and maintaining social consciousness of what was prevalent throughout Latin America. At some point in one of our interviews, Carlos Cabral, as if to clear up any misconceptions about the implications of *aguante,* raised his voice and asked a rhetorical question, to which he provided his own answer. "How is that *aguante* that we have? What do they call *aguante*? It is to learn, study, and be socially committed to what we are doing. A lot of people look to the side and don't want to see what you are seeing." This perspective on *aguante* as something more than social support within the metal scene was not restricted to my conversations with members of Tren Loco. Argentinian scholarly researchers doing work on metal in the country expressed a similar idea.

One member of the local metal scene, who also happens to engage in metal scholarship, provided descriptions of *aguante* that were more political in nature, usage, and implications. Emiliano Scaricaciottoli is a founding member of the Interdisciplinary Research Group on Argentinian Heavy Metal (GIIHMA for its acronym in Spanish) and has researched metal music in the country and published several books on the subject (Scaricaciottoli 2016, 2018; Scaricaciottoli et al. 2020). The group is known in academic circles for being highly critical of traditional academia, preferring to understand metal music through its links to the Argentinian working class.

The first time I met Emiliano was in his apartment, where we sat to discuss metal music and the meaning of the word *aguante.* It was clearly evident that his definition of the word differed vastly from that of other interviewees who had decided to highlight issues of community formation and social support. For Emiliano, *aguante* was basically a political phenomenon. He recognized that there was "a lot of work in the social sciences about the culture of *aguante*." He mentioned, in a very sarcastic tone, that the idea had "allegedly" come from soccer. He also described this as one of the byproducts of the "soccerization of Argentinian culture." Although he recognized that most people believed the word crossed the cultural divide from soccer and arrived into heavy metal music, he was clear to point out that the GIIHMA "think it is not like that." The group understood that the idea, as well as its underlying cultural practices (including support), "comes from militant politics and heavy metal appropriates it. There is a strong militant attitude in Argentinian heavy metal. There is a militant attitude."

This militant attitude in the process of *aguante* was not limited to following bands, showing support for the scene, or feeling part of the metal community. It was more than a feeling one might experience while sharing something that one loves, like music. It was, in fact, an action expressed through both aesthetic and bodily practices in the streets. In his definition, *aguante* felt to me like a link between thinking critically about one's society or culture and acting on it. Thus, this understanding of one's oppressive historical context and the decision to act upon it pushed metal fans in Argentina to think about *aguante* as part of the realm of the political. Emiliano provided one example during one of our interviews:

> *Aguante* in Argentinian metal culture is the resistance to the processes of invisibilization that operate in hegemonic culture. It is a politics of intervention, not just in the cultural sphere, but in the social sphere. Consequently, it would be difficult to find somebody wearing a Madonna t-shirt during a protest. Instead, you will find people with t-shirts from Hermética, V8, Almafuerte, Malón, and Tren Loco. T-shirts from bands whose messages, lyrics, and aesthetic proposals include intervention. Intervention on the streets! It's not an aesthetic of complaint [...] but rather an aesthetic of intervention. There is a sensibility that heavy metal captures and learns from, which is later present in social protests. That is something very unique. Very unique.

The conversations over the political dimensions of *aguante* continued to emerge during my ethnographic observations and interviews, which brings me back to Pablo, the lead singer of Arraigo. During one of the most salient discussions on the matter, Pablo, with whom I had met earlier in one of my very first trips, expressed his understanding of the use of *aguante* as a way to express solidarity and support. The term had been frequently used in such a manner in front of me, but Pablo was quick to point out its limitations. For example, he stressed that when metal fans expressed the idea of "I will provide you with *aguante*," they usually emphasized notions like "I will not fail you. I will accompany you. I will be happy for what you are doing. Let's celebrate together what you were doing." But he was skeptical of the term's use in issues of social support, as he saw in it a verbal manifestation of care with little to no social or political action to back it up. He seemed concerned that the support that emanated from *aguante* could be merely symbolic, a verbal gesture with nothing more behind it. Pablo described the limitation eloquently:

> The question is what happens if you can't endure? On many occasions in my life I could not endure and what happened is maybe really simple and visible. When I could not endure, I held fast to others. My weight was spread across a broader base, a more ample base of affection, a more ample base of capabilities. Basically, a broader base of *aguantes*. When we say, "Don't confuse *aguante* with resistance,"[2] we are saying "don't be alone in that endurance." We believe that in that resistance we will find our political collective, and in that collective is where we ask ourselves: What conditions were you born into? From there, let's see what we can do and what we can accomplish.

Don't confuse aguante *with resistance*

My conversations with local metal fans, musicians, and scholars on the definition and use of *aguante* continued to take interesting turns. From basic notions of social support to its political use, the term seemed to shift in meaning and use within the metal scene. My conversations with Pablo and Emiliano had added another layer of complexity, now focused on the term's limitations. For Pablo, for example, the conceptualization of *aguante* as social support was clearly not enough, and the integration of social consciousness into its definition was also insufficient to foster its use as a political act within the metal scene. For him, the term needed to be surpassed, or at least modified heavily, in order to make scene members reflect on the social and political dimensions that impacted their country and the Latin American region. It was not enough to show *aguante* to your friends and scene members in order to change things. That feeling, or idea, needed to have practical implications in order to understand the role of oppression in one's social context and then be able to challenge it effectively. Pablo described this process in one of our interviews:

> If there is something to be said about Argentinian metal, and I would dare say Latin American metal, it is that it gave a voice to those of us who lived on the borders. When I speak of borders, I mean socioeconomic borders. I mean the borders of normalcy. I believe we found a voice and a place to show ourselves and be seen. [...] From there, however we can, we can start having a dialogue about things that are not being seen. These include political systems, poverty, discrimination, bodies that normalcy expelled, different sexualities. I talk about all those things that even today very few people want to see, because they make the equation more complex. They diversify the ways of being in the world, within systems and institutions that make us think that there's only one way of being in the world. That is the center. Those of us who live on the border of that center, sometimes as an obligation, sometimes as an option, see in heavy metal a scream to make us visible. That is where we are.

These concerns over socioeconomic issues, poverty, discrimination, and the incarnation of difference through particular bodies and sexualities indicated to me that, for Pablo, the role of metal music was linked to making people become aware of these mechanisms of oppression. The description echoed his initial question during our very first meeting: What is heavy about metal music? For Pablo, and it seemed to many other metal musicians in Argentina as well, this entailed questioning the very social structures that held oppressive practices in place. His main concern seemed to be the explanation of social problems caused by structural mechanisms of oppression from an individualistic perspective. The problems were structural, that is, fostered by the region's colonial past and present, particularly when it came to its neoliberal practices, and yet, most explanations seemed to blame the very people who suffer for their problems. Pablo was concerned that these conceptualizations of social problems in the region rarely addressed these levels of oppression and chose to criminalize individuals for not being able to manage them adequately. Regarding this particular topic, he stated the following:

> There is a strange shadow lurking through Latin America. A shortsighted perspective on social problems, which confuses the symptoms with its causes. It confuses the consequences with its causes. It does not want us to ask these questions. It holds stupid celebrations at the end of the day. It highlights one life story, among a thousand others that can't make it, and then uses it as an example to say, "You can make it under any conditions." But the reality is that people can't make it under these conditions. This shadow will ask us to strike down all the people that can't make it into this system. Going back to what we were discussing [...] what is metal if not that scream that makes visible all the people that will be struck down in Latin America during the coming years? What is metal, if it's not that? If it's not that [...] then it's nothing.

My conversations on the topic of *aguante* had shown me one thing; it was difficult to pin down a specific definition that applied to all situations in which it was used. It was used as a polysemic word whose meaning, depending on the situation, would range from basic expressions for the love of metal music, support for scene members, the need for more political reflection, and even political action in the streets. Even in this sea of possible definitions and practices, the moments when the term took political inflections seemed important to me in order to understand metal's potential role in decolonial practices. Emiliano and Pablo's interventions on the idea of *aguante* as a political act seemed crucial as they stripped the word of its more frequent use focusing on social support and linked it to the social issues and problems taking place specifically in Argentina and Latin America in general. These problems were never described solely from an individualistic perspective (i.e., lack of personal drive, vagrancy) but were always conceptualized as socio-structural issues that fostered social oppression and erased diverse experiences (i.e., those of indigenous peoples, racial/ethnic minorities, LGBTQI communities, and women). This understanding was important as it allowed members of the scene to discuss coloniality as the root cause of these problems and the problematic solutions proposed by many governments through neoliberal policies (i.e., selling land) and austerity (i.e., eliminating pension plans).

Now that the use of *aguante* was clearly positioned within the realm of politics, with metal musicians and fans using it as such, I became interested in examining how this issue was addressed via music. In the following section, I will use the band Arraigo as a case study for this integration of metal and politics in the process of *aguante* and, more specifically, the decolonial implications of this integration.

Aguante *as decolonial resistance*

"And that is how those who are born poor, die poor. Don't confuse *aguante* with resistance." The preceding is a segment found in Arraigo's song entitled "Cadenas y Antifaces" (Chains and Masks). The first line is particularly direct and poignant in that it aims to reflect on how the patterns of oppression that foster economic inequality in Latin America seem to be ever present. The second line feels like a stark warning on the need to resist. This distinction between *aguante* and resistance is important for the song; in essence, the song is a call for action, a need to move beyond talking (or singing) about social oppression and toward acting against it. My conversations with Pablo evidenced his critique of the use of *aguante* as a concept of mere social support. It was evident that he expected more from it, and from metal music itself, a belief he would communicate to the band's audiences. This awareness of the role of social oppression in Argentina, and the rest of Latin America, would address coloniality directly.

Arraigo addresses the subject of coloniality as a historical source of social oppression in their album *Fronteras y Horizontes* (Arraigo 2012). The song "Vidala para que Sigas" is of particular interest for the way it addresses one of the many problems promoted by the colonial experience, particularly the collaboration of locals in the exploitation of the colonized, that is, colonial exploitation from the outside, but aided by those on the inside. The song begins with a powerful lyrical passage that declares, "There's a gringo who buys us, there's a creole who sells us." The phrase echoes the writing of Argentinian politician and philosopher Arturo Jauretche.[3] The message is a particularly strong one, finding inspiration in the colonial literature, which described the process of foreign oppression through colonization. It captures how some sectors of the local population would end up accepting this experience as positive and even collaborate with the colonial entity to perpetuate existing patterns of oppression (Fanon 1965, 1967; Memmi 1965). This concern over the exploitation of locals by foreign powers, and the lack of trust toward other local people, needs to be understood with Argentina's political history in mind, a history that includes multiple instances of foreign involvement.

The lack of trust mentioned above arises from the harsh experiences faced by local people during the dictatorship (1973–83), the latter taking root after Isabel Perón's government was overthrown by a military junta (*Junta Militar* in Spanish). As part of this process, a systematic crackdown on the part of the military dictatorship aimed to wipe out left-leaning protestors who were perceived as a threat. This effort consisted of the use of widespread systematic arrests, torture, and disappearances. The process impacted both people actively engaged in politics and a multitude of uninvolved bystanders. Its effects would also be felt by future generations as the children of arrested pregnant women would be ripped away from the latter and given to military leaders to raise as their own (Cepeda 2013). The *Madres de la Plaza de Mayo* ("Mothers of the Plaza de Mayo") movement would bring international attention to the disappearance of these children (Egan 1984; Borland 2006). Later, the *Abuelas de la Plaza de Mayo* ("Grandmothers of the Plaza de Mayo") movement would engage in a monumental effort to find their grandsons and granddaughters, a process that remains active to this day in Argentina. The history of Argentinian dictatorship is closely linked to the United States' involvement throughout Latin America during the same period, this as part of Operation Condor and its aim of holding off the spread of communism in the region (McSherry 2002). Declassified documents have continued to evidence the United States' knowledge of the events occurring during this period and its involvement in the process (Board 2016; Deyoung 2016). The entrenched practices of torture and disappearance, which were carried out by Argentinians themselves, have fostered a tradition of mistrust toward governments that exists to this day among many in the country. Issues of impunity continue to be widely discussed, primarily because many of the responsible parties were never brought to justice (Pizarro and Wittebroodt 2002). As if this situation were not complex enough, harmful neoliberal policies were implemented in Argentina during this process, with economic support from the International Monetary Fund, all in an effort to directly benefit local oligarchs and transnational corporations (Cooney 2007). The effects of these decisions on Argentina's seemingly constant economic crises are ongoing (Teubal 2004).

Arraigo's album is full of other references to the colonial tensions experienced in Latin America. For example, the band mentions the devaluing of local culture by foreign powers in a song like "Zamba pa los Huérfanos." In it, the *gringos* (the word used to describe US nationals) are described as rapists. *Zamba*, a local music and dance style, is anthropomorphized, given the identity of a raped woman ("*Zamba fusite la hembra de un gringo violador*" – Zamba you were the woman of a rapist *gringo*). The effects of colonialism are not limited to culture, but are extended to the lives of poor children in the song "Cría de Crías." The song vividly describes kids living in poverty, arguing that the lack of resistance exhibited in this process is a direct product of the systematic privation of knowledge, particularly as it concerns the historical events and choices that placed them in their impoverished situation.

Arraigo explains the colonial problem, but their aim is not limited to simply stating the facts. Their music is a direct invitation to reflect on potential solutions. For example, the song "Nehuen" summons men to "wake up," for "weak men can't love anyone." This call for strength in the face of adversity is sustained throughout the album by way of recurring metaphors, with the central metaphor being that of a tree. The tree is utilized as a symbolic resting place for those engaged in the long-term struggle against injustice (see Figure 10.1). This metaphorical location serves as a refuge, providing shade to those engaged in critical reflections and social justice struggles during the long journey.

FIGURE 10.1: Artwork for the album *Fronteras y Horizontes* (2012) by the Argentinian band Arraigo. Image provided by Leonardo Pazos.

The narrative of the tree weaves its way through the majority of the album, making it a thematic concept album. The song "Vidala pa que Sigas," included in its entirety in Box 10.1, features the most salient example of that metaphor. In it, the tree is described as "full of hope" and part of a collective path where new generations will also find rest. Here, the band calls for the planting of more seeds (potential future trees) as many more of these places of refuge will be needed. This process is echoed in the song "En el Nombre del Padre" ("In the Name of the Father"), where the band states that "he who plants the seed will not always get to see the tree grow." This idea captures the perpetual struggles that are often part of decolonial and social justice agendas. Finally, the band admits their awareness that some people will "block the sun from that seed and tear the head from its body" (in the song "Cadenas y Antifaces") in an effort to block these decolonial efforts. In summary, the album captures the complexities entailed in reflections about, and actions against, coloniality in Latin America, all the while also shedding light on what the band sees as metal music's role in this process. Pablo Trangone explained the role of metal in challenging the historical mechanisms of oppression in Argentina and Latin America during several of our conversations. Regarding this challenge, he mentioned the following:

> We sing about social classes that ask questions that no one wants to answer. [...] We believe that our genre (metal) should address those questions. It should connect its origins, at least its Latin American origins. It's not about entertaining people. We state that in our concerts. "We are not here to entertain." We are here to propose new questions; to heal each other in this encounter. [...] We need Latin American expressions and questions for Latin American problems. Metal usually lives in the shadow of what it was. We bring it here both geographically and historically. As a musical genre, we need to have new questions for the usual answers.

Arraigo's reflection in the album *Fronteras y Horizontes* is a significant contribution to decolonial thinking in Latin American metal music. It adds an important level of complexity to the reflection on coloniality, effectively capturing the process of historical collaboration between both foreign and local powers. In this context, coloniality is willingly internalized by the local and used as yet another mechanism of oppression. Instead, this interaction, they argue, should serve as the starting point toward a critical questioning that ends with the implementation of decolonial strategies. Even though that reflection can seem nihilistic, Arraigo concentrates its energies on issues that promote hope for the next generation, with the confidence that future Argentinians and Latin Americans will understand and challenge the effects of coloniality.

Box 10.1 "Vidala para que Sigas," Fronteras y Horizontes, composed by Arraigo (Argentina) – 2012.

Hay un gringo que nos compra,
hay un criollo que nos vende.
Piedra libre pa' mis cumpas,
detrás la sombra, la muerte.

There's a *gringo* who buys us,
there's a creole who sells us.
I absolve my friends from the death
that lies behind the shadows in this game
of life.

Tengo un árbol de esperanzas,
que no me suelta la mano.
Yo voy sembrando un camino,
pa' que florezcan los changos.

I have a tree full of hope,
which won't let go of me.
I sow a path as I go,
so that the young may bloom.

Pena que sin saber donde,
viaja con el hombre que solía ser.
Porque la muerte es mentira,
y es la vida misma mi herida.

What sorrows grow
from accompanying the man I used to be.
Because death is a lie,
and life itself is my wound.

Noches y noches los caminos,
y en tu mirada tristemente,
siempre los mismos caminos,
ante la mirada de nadie.

Night after night, new roads,
but before your eyes, sadly,
always the same ones,
lost before empty stares.

No tengo miedo a morir y me planto a la vida.
Las heridas no se curan con tanto vino encima.
Voy contagiando esta pena que causa alegría.
Héroes fueron paridos en mi juventud suicida,
para estar despierto.

I meet life head on because I don't fear dying.
Wounds can never heal if we're drunk on too much wine.
I spread a sorrow that gives rise to contentment.
Heroes spawned from my reckless youth,
so that I could remain awake.

Noches y noches los caminos,	Night after night, new roads,
y en tu mirada tristemente,	but before your eyes, sadly,
siempre los mismos caminos,	always the same ones,
ante la mirada de nadie.	lost before empty stares.
No tengo miedo a morir y me planto a la vida.	I meet life head on because I don't fear dying.
Las heridas no se curan con tanto vino encima.	Wounds can never heal if we're drunk on too much wine.
Darse cuenta cuando algo es mas que todo.	Recognize when something is greater than everything.
Sigo y sigo empujando.	I forge ahead.
Vidaleando pa' que sigas.	Singing my folk song so you can carry on.
Hay un gringo que nos compra,	There's a *gringo* who buys us,
hay un criollo que nos vende,	there's a creole who sells us.
Piedra libre pa' mis cumpas,	I absolve my friends from the death
detrás la sombra la muerte.	that lies behind the shadows in this game of life.
Un corazón de tacuara,	Bend, but never break.
espera no nos cansemos.	Hold on, let's not give in.
Quien no se aferra a la vida,	Those that don't cling on to life,
no sabe lo que es el miedo.	never know fear.
Tengo un árbol de esperanza,	I have a tree full of hope,
que no me suelta la mano.	which won't let go of me.
Yo voy sembrando un camino,	I sow a path as I go,
pa' que florezcan los changos.	so that the young may bloom.

Aguante *as a manifestation of hope in metal music*

On April 5, 2019, I attended an Arraigo concert in Buenos Aires. The event was held in a local club called *The Roxy,* where metal bands frequently perform. The concert took place in much the same way as others I have attended throughout Latin America. About two hundred people were in attendance and the place looked quite packed, although the band would later mention that they were hoping for a larger audience that night. Still, several aspects of the concert seemed to set it apart from my other live musical experiences in the region. A sense of hope toward the future, expressed by the band in multiple ways, and experienced by the audience members, set the event apart. I felt this sense of hope on several occasions throughout the event, in great measure because the place was full of young people.

After being at the venue for a while, I engaged in a conversation with a friend of the band who was helping them sell merchandise. She explained that the band was selling t-shirts in order to gather funds for their future recording process. The shirts caught my eye as they were very different from traditional metal shirts. They included the faces of Argentinian figures, including Atahualpa Yupanqui (singer), Roberto Goyeneche (tango singer), Osvaldo Pugliese (tango musician), and Arturo Jauretche (writer and politician) (see Figure 10.2). It was evident to me that the shirts were there to make you think about these individuals' positive contributions to the country. They were used as a strategy to raise awareness of the history of Argentina and Latin America. Clearly some fans were unaware of who these individuals were and would need to do their research on them to understand their presence in a metal band's shirt. Just as I was reflecting on Arraigo's pedagogical strategy, Pablo's voice came through the amplifiers stating: "How very expensive is the milk today. How very expensive." The band launched into a song about the importance of children in building a new society.

There was a sense of hope in Arraigo's work and it manifested throughout their show. Their stage backdrop displayed images of their latest album entitled *Nosotrosacayahora* (Arraigo 2017), a play on words on the phrase "us, here and now" (see Figure 10.3). The cover shows the face of a child on top of images of Latin American places. The image is also sometimes altered to show the map of Latin America. The album is a call for metal music to become embedded in the region, consider its origins, and reflect on the historical challenges that have characterized it. One of the songs ("Traen la Pregunta" – "They Bring the Question") states this message outright, describing the forgotten and oppressed communities in the Latin American region. "They come with what they could muster in light of what has been done to them," state the lyrics, as they describe people who "pose the question, that no one wants to answer." These people are described as "confused and somewhat bored with what metal talks about." Hearing that phrase ring throughout the concert hall became a revelation. It dawned on me then and there that the phrase describes Arraigo in a nutshell. This band was addressing oppression and coloniality in Latin America because they themselves are tired of metal music's complacency in the face of these topics. For the most part, they would seem to argue, metal in general has been content with offering a critique that is too general and does not account for the specific situations faced in the region. In response

FIGURE 10.2: Arraigo t-shirts with faces of Argentinian figures, including Atahualpa Yupanqui (singer – top left), Arturo Jauretche (writer and politician – top right), Roberto Goyeneche (tango singer – bottom left), and Osvaldo Pugliese (tango musician – bottom right). Image provided by Leonardo Pazos.

to this complacency, Pablo sees his band as a chance to break the mold and offer a new way of engagement. As he explained during one of our interactions:

> That is Arraigo's proposal. We are not here to just resist. We will advance. I have no doubt that within this genre, along with many other musicians with whom we interact daily, there will be a movement in Latin America that will restore resistance and move us toward those other questions.

FIGURE 10.3: Artwork for the album *Nosotrosacayahora* (2017) by the Argentinian band Arraigo. Image provided by Leonardo Pazos.

I felt optimism floating in the air during that concert, something that mingled with a deep critical reflection. Through its songs, Arraigo would tell their listeners that "anybody can do anything at any given time" (in the song "Mambolindoquilombo"), instilling hope within their critical agenda. Perhaps their most hopeful moments are those in which they look at other Argentinian figures for a way forward against all of these contextual oppressive experiences. Echoing Jauretche's concern over coloniality, and using the band's metaphor of the tree as a place for rest and commonality, Pablo belted out a sequence of poignant lyrics about hope, which rang throughout the concert hall, just as the night was about to end. In it he sings: " 'Where I go I have this illusion', said Jauretche to the child in the corner. 'To walk, pass by, see you smile, and have my song be a little less sad'." These words at that moment in the concert made me think again about the role of *aguante* and its polysemic manifestations, ranging from social support, to politics, and even resistance. *Aguante* was, in its multiple meanings, a manifestation of hope and, therefore, an intervention on a bleak social context deeply embedded in coloniality. It echoed the idea proposed by one interviewee, and mentioned earlier in this chapter, that metal music in Argentina was "not an aesthetic of complaint [...] but rather an aesthetic of intervention." It seemed that metal music, through fostering *aguante*, had become an intervention by encouraging hope for a different decolonial future.

NOTES

1. One notable exception of metal scholarship that has addressed the use of *aguante* in Argentina has been the work of Manuela Belén Calvo (2016a). She has explored the use of the term through an analysis of lyrics from local metal songs and via interviews with scene members. It is interesting to note that her analysis focuses on the use of the word as a form of social support and a way to keep the musical genre alive. The political dimensions of *aguante*, which I describe in this chapter, are mostly absent from this analysis.
2. This phrase is part of the lyrics to the song "Cadenas y Antifaces" by Arraigo (2012).
3. The original phase from Jauretche states, "Si malo es el gringo que nos compra, peor es el criollo que nos vende" ("If the gringo that buys us is bad, the local that sells us is worse").

REFERENCES

Alabarces, Pablo (2006), "Fútbol, violencia y política en la Argentina: Ética, estética y retórica del aguante," *Esporte e Sociedade*, 2, pp. 1–14. doi: 10.1017/CBO9781107415324.004.

Alabarces, Pablo (2015), "Textos populares y prácticas plebeyas: 'Aguante', cumbia y política popular argentina contemporánea," *Alternativas*, 4, http://alternativas.osu.edu. Accessed December 5, 2019.

Alabarces, Pablo and Garriga, José (2008), "El 'Aguante': Una identidad corporal y popular," *Intersecciones en Antropología*, 9, pp. 275–89.

Alabarces, Pablo, Garriga Zucal, José, and Moreira, María Verónica (2008), "El 'aguante' y las hinchadas argentinas: Una relación violenta," *Horizontes Antropológicos*, 14:30, pp. 113–36. doi: 10.1590/S0104-71832008000200005.

Arraigo (2012), "*Fronteras y Horizontes*," CD, Buenos Aires: Mondo Tunes.

Arraigo (2017), "*Nosotrosacayahora*," CD, Buenos Aires: Independent.

Borland, Elizabeth (2006), "Las Madres de Plaza de Mayo en la era neoliberal: Ampliando objetivos para unir el pasado, el presente y el futuro," *Colombia Internacional*, 63, pp. 128–47.

Calvo, Manuela Belén (2016a), "Acerca de la heterogeneidad del rock: El 'aguante' en el heavy metal en Argentina," *El Oído Pensante*, 4:2, pp. 1–19.

Calvo, Manuela Belén (2016b), "Almafuerte: Metal pesado argento and its construction of Argentinian nationalism," *Metal Music Studies*, 2:1, pp. 21–38. doi: 10.1386/mms.2.1.21.

Calvo, Manuela Belén (2017), "Metal extremo y globalización en América Latina: Los casos de Hermética (Argentina), Masacre (Colombia) y Brujería (México)," in M. C. Dalmagro and A. Parfeniuk (eds.), *Reflexiones Comparadas Desplazamientos, Encuentros y Contrastes*, Buenos Aires, Argentina: Universidad Nacional de Córdoba, pp. 170–89.

Calvo, Manuela Belén (2018), "Indigenista perspectives in Argentine metal music," *Metal Music Studies*, 4:1, pp. 155–63. doi: 10.1386/mms.4.1.155.

Cepeda, Agustina (2013), "Narrativas familiares y memoria de la pos-dictadura en Argentina: El caso de hijos de desaparecidos," *Asian Journal of Latin American Studies*, 26:1, pp. 25–45.

Cooney, Paul (2007), "Argentina's quarter century experiment with neoliberalism: From dictatorship to depression," *Revista de Economía Contemporánea*, 11:1, pp. 7–37. doi: 10.1590/s1415-98482007000100001.

Deyoung, Karen (2016), "Newly declassified papers reveal U.S. tensions regarding Argentina's 'Dirty War'," *The Washington Post*, August 8, https://www.washingtonpost.com/world/national-security/newly-declassified-papers-reveal-us-tensions-regarding-argentinas-dirty-war/2016/08/08/4227fbee-5db1-11e6-af8e-54aa2e849447_story.html?noredirect=on&utm_term=.450fde45948c. Accessed November 10, 2019.

Editorial Board (2016), "America's role in Argentina's dirty war," *The New York Times*, March 17, https://www.nytimes.com/2016/03/17/opinion/americas-role-in-argentinas-dirty-war.html. Accessed October 10, 2019.

Egan, Georgia (1984), "Las Madres de la Plaza de Mayo: Prensa, ideología y resistencia," *Spanish in Context*, 3:2, pp. 255–71.

Fanon, Frantz (1965), *The Wretched of the Earth*, New York: Grove Press.

Fanon, Frantz (1967), *Black Skin, White Masks*, New York: Grove Press.

Garriga Zucal, José (2016), "Del 'correctivo' al 'aguante': Análisis comparativo de las acciones violentas de policías y 'barras bravas'," *Runa*, 37:1, pp. 39–52. doi: ISSN-1851–9628.

Hamed, Amir (2003), "Sin novio ni épica: Breve arqueología del aguante (madre de todas las cosas)," *Revista Iberoamericana*, 69:202, pp. 15–29. doi: 10.5195/reviberoamer.2003.5682.

Hill, Rosemary Lucy (2014), "Reconceptualizing hard rock and metal fans as a group: Imaginary community," *International Journal of Community Music*, 7:2, pp. 173–87. doi: 10.1386/ijcm.7.2.173.

McSherry, J. Patrice (2002), "Tracking the origins of a state terror network," *Latin American Perspectives*, 29:122, pp. 38–60. doi: 10.1177/0094582x0202900103.

Memmi, Albert (1965), *The Colonizer and the Colonized*, New York: Orion Press.

Minore, Gito (2010), *Tren Loco: 20 Años – Pogo en el Andén*, Buenos Aires: Yugular Records.

Moreira, María Verónica (2008), "Aguante, generosidad y política en una hinchada de fútbol argentina," *Avá*, 12, pp. 79–94.

Moreira, María Verónica (2010), "Etnografía sobre el honor y la violencia de una hinchada de fútbol en Argentina," *Revista Austral de Ciencias Sociales*, 13, pp. 5–20. doi: 10.4206/rev. austral.cienc.soc.2007.n13-01.

Panzini, Ariel (2018), *Heavy Metal Argentino: La Clase del Pueblo Que No Se Rindió,* Buenos Aires, Argentina: Clara Beter Ediciones.

Pizarro, Angélca and Wittebroodt, Ingrid (2002), "La impunidad: Efectos en la elaboración del duelo en madres de detenidos desaparecidos," *Castalia – Revista de Psicología de la Academia*, pp. 115–35.

Providence, Juan Ignacio (2017), *Rockpolitik: 50 Años de Rock Nacional y Sus Vínculos con el Poder Político Argentino*, Buenos Aires: Eudeba, Universidad de Buenos Aires.

Riches, Gabby and Spracklen, Karl (2014), "Raising the horns : Heavy metal communities and community heavy metal music," *International Journal of Community Music*, 7:2, pp. 149–51. doi: 10.1386/ijcm.7.2.149.

Rivera-Segarra, Eliut, Mendoza, Sigrid, and Varas-Díaz, Nelson (2015), "Between order and chaos: The role of moshing in Puerto Rico's heavy metal community," *Revista de Ciencias Sociales*, 28, pp. 104–20.

Scaricaciottoli, Emiliano (2016), *Se Nos Ve de Negro Vestidos: Siete enfoques sobre el Heavy Metal Argentino*, Buenos Aires: Ediciones La Parte Maldita.

Scaricaciottoli, Emiliano (2018), *Parricidas: Mapa Rabioso del Metal Argentino Contemporaneo*, Buenos Aires: La Parte Maldita.

Scaricaciottoli, Emiliano, Varas-Díaz, Nelson, and Nevárez Araújo, Daniel (2020), *Heavy Metal Music in Argentina: In Black We Are Seen*, London: Intellect.

Snaza, Nathan and Netherton, Jason (2016), "Community at the extremes: The death metal underground as being-in-common," 2:3, pp. 341–56. doi: 10.1386/mms.2.3.341.

Teubal, Miguel (2004), "Rise and collapse of neoliberalism in Argentina: The role of economic groups," *Journal of Developing Societies*, 20:3 & 4, pp. 173–88. doi: 10.1177/0169796X04050957.

Varas-Díaz, Nelson, Rivera-Segarra, Eliut, Medina Rivera, Carmen, Mendoza, Sigrid, and González-Sepúlveda, Osvaldo (2015), "Predictors of communal formation in a small heavy metal scene: Puerto Rico as a case study," *Metal Music Studies*, 1:1, pp. 87–103. doi: 10.1386/mms.1.1.87.

Varas-Díaz, Nelson, Mendoza, Sigrid, Rivera, Eliut, and González, Osvaldo (2016a), "Methodological strategies and challenges in research with small heavy metal scenes: A reflection on entrance, evolution and permanence," *Metal Music Studies*, 2:3, pp. 273–90.

Varas-Díaz, Nelson, Mendoza, Sigrid, and Morales, Eric (2016b), "Porous communities: Critical interactions between metal music and local culture in the Caribbean context," in N. Varas-Díaz and N. Scott (eds.), *Heavy Metal Music and the Communal Experience*, London: Lexington Books, pp. 101–23.

Venkatesh, Vivek, Podoshen, Jeffrey S., Urbaniak, Kathryn, and Wallin, Jason (2014), "Eschewing community: Black metal," *Journal of Community & Applied Social Psychology*, 25:1, pp. 66–81. doi: 10.1002/casp.

Zambaglione, Daniel (2010), "El aguante en el cuerpo: Construcción de Identidad de los hinchas de un club de fútbol argentino," in *VI Jornada de Sociología de la UNLP,* Argentina: Universidad Nacional de la Plata. doi: 10.22579/20114680.80.

Index